STONE
MOTEL

STONE MOTEL

MEMOIRS OF A CAJUN BOY

MORRIS ARDOIN

UNIVERSITY PRESS OF MISSISSIPPI / JACKSON

Willie Morris Books in Memoir and Biography

The University Press of Mississippi is the scholarly publishing agency of
the Mississippi Institutions of Higher Learning: Alcorn State University,
Delta State University, Jackson State University, Mississippi State University,
Mississippi University for Women, Mississippi Valley State University,
University of Mississippi, and University of Southern Mississippi.

www.upress.state.ms.us

The University Press of Mississippi is a member
of the Association of University Presses.

First printing 2020
∞
All illustrations are courtesy of the author.

Library of Congress Cataloging-in-Publication Data

Names: Ardoin, J. Morris, 1959– author.
Title: Stone motel : memoirs of a Cajun boy / Morris Ardoin.
Other titles: Willie Morris books in memoir and biography.
Description: Jackson : University Press of Mississippi, 2020. | Series:
    Willie Morris books in memoir and biography
Identifiers: LCCN 2019044436 (print) | LCCN 2019044437 (ebook) | ISBN
    9781496827722 (hardcover) | ISBN 9781496827739 (epub) | ISBN
    9781496827746 (epub) | ISBN 9781496827753 (pdf) | ISBN
    9781496827760 (pdf)
Subjects: LCSH: Ardoin, J. Morris, 1959– | Families—Louisiana. |
    Gays—Louisiana—Biography. | BISAC: BIOGRAPHY & AUTOBIOGRAPHY /
    Personal Memoirs | LCGFT: Autobiographies.
Classification: LCC CT237 .A73 2020 (print) | LCC CT237 (ebook) | DDC
    976.3092 [B]—dc23
LC record available at https://lccn.loc.gov/2019044436
LC ebook record available at https://lccn.loc.gov/2019044437

British Library Cataloging-in-Publication Data available

CONTENTS

PART II: THE ELDERS DEPART, 1989-1998

STONE
MOTEL

PROLOGUE

Over a span of eighteen years, my parents, Eliza Mae and Zanny Ardoin, brought nine children into the world. Momma was pregnant pretty much every two years, as if on schedule, though none of us were planned. They had incalculable assistance from Momma's mother, Ortense, our grandmother, whom we all called "Mémère," and who was a regular presence in our lives. In addition to these three adults, my memoir focuses on the children at the center of the nine—the twins, Glenda and Gilda, our little brother Dicky, and me, who were constant companions for a period of about seven years, beginning in the late 1960s and lasting through the mid-1970s. I believe that the person I am today began to take shape in earnest during this critical time in my life.

There is another character here, a little roadside motel outside of Eunice, Louisiana. With my parents' purchase of the Stone Motel in 1967, our family upended the typical postwar American family model: a father figure who worked at his job each day and then came home to a wife who managed their kids in that home. We had effectively instead taken on a family structure common *before* the war, in which everyone worked, and often lived, in a family business. "The Stone" became our home, our place of work, and in many respects, our very identity.

The Ardoin Family, Early 1970s

Daddy, aka Zanny Ardoin—mid-fifties, six feet tall, 190 pounds, complexion of a tobacco-shop Indian chief, thinning salt-and-pepper brown hair. He was partial to gray coveralls and heavy, black work shoes. Spoke in a Cajun baritone made deeper by twenty-five years of Kent cigarettes. A "man's man," he did his best thinking walking in the woods with a shotgun in his hands. He had quiet, mumbled conversations with himself; when he couldn't be hunting, he worked out the big issues of his life sitting on the rocker in the front room of the house, which was also the motel office. Mostly, he had it all under control, but gradually the bitter residue of a cruel childhood and the soul-numbing experiences on the European battlefields had finally corroded his core and began to seep through to the surface.

Momma, *née* Eliza Mae "Mae-Mae" Thompson—two years younger than Daddy, she kept herself in great shape; you'd never guess she had nine babies before she was forty-five. Her thick auburn hair was full up front and tapered a little in the back, and always in a bit of disarray, which was funny, because she was responsible for keeping the coifs of dozens of ladies in our little town of Eunice in bountiful bouffants, chic chignons, perky page-boys, and sensual shags. There was always a bit of self-doubt in her voice; she was shy around new people, but warm, funny, and sincere once they sat down in her hydraulic chair. I still picture her sitting in that very chair in her shop, her feet crossed and resting on the foot bar, something she rarely got the chance to do during the long days she put in there. Her shop uniform was a short-sleeved smock with a small floral pattern on it, brown slacks and white nurses shoes. At home she hid her purse, because my little brother Dicky would take her gum.

Mémère—Born Ortense Thompson with no middle name, on December 9, 1904. By the time she reached her late sixties, her frame had shrunken to five feet five inches, and she complained that she couldn't dance or play the accordion with the endurance she once did. Nonetheless, she still made a valiant daily effort to keep up her appearance. She felt best dressed in a crisp new blouse—something with a blue or green floral pattern—black slacks, and simple black shoes. Her once-auburn hair had gone gray; she kept it ink-black with a rinse. With her peers and her children, she spoke French, the first language of Ville Platte, the little town a half-hour drive from Eunice; she used franglais to communicate with anyone born after 1950. After Momma and Daddy, Mémère was the most influential adult in our lives. The first time I recognized unparsed love and absolute security was as a toddler in her arms, in one of the three big rockers in her kitchen. Well into my teens, her little house at 508 East Jackson Street was a refuge.

Cassie—Beautiful, gregarious, mischievous. She once snuck a piece of chewed gum into Momma's cheeseburger, repulsing her and compelling her to return to the Frost Stop to demand a refund. She wouldn't fess up to Momma for years. At eighteen, she casually entered the "Miss Eunice" pageant. Standing in a semicircle on the stage, entranced by an audience staring back at her, she missed her cue to move along with the other girls, holding up the show for a few awkward, humorous moments, before winning the crown. An out-of-focus close-up of her mascara-streaked face ran on the front page of the *Eunice News*. The story by the paper's reliable, beloved town fixture Jerry Hoffpauir described her as a "strawberry blonde beauty." A week after the pageant, she high-tailed it to college in Lake Charles to study music.

Andy—The first-born son and second child, he was bashful, honest, hardworking, humble. Loved the outdoors. Still does. His muscular frame is five feet ten inches; he was the only kid in the family with dark brown hair like Daddy's, not auburn like Momma's, which caused some of us to wonder about his true provenance. For his sixteenth birthday he built a homemade pistol from a plastic pipe he stuffed with Christmas fireworks powder. He lit it and aimed at a bull's-eye he had painted on a cotton-ball tree. Instead of shooting, the pistol exploded in his hand, sending up a mushroom cloud that filled the back yard. When the cloud finally dissipated, he noticed his right index finger was split open. Thirteen stitches.

Gilda—As a young girl, she had attached herself to Cassie, eagerly seeking her elder sister's affection. "I'm are your friend?" she'd whine, needily. "I'm are your friend?!" As a teen she became daring, temperamental, comical, and the artist within her emerged. She designed and built Sears-catalogue-paper witches and drew a series of elaborately detailed caricatures of some of the people she encountered. "The Jaw-jaw Lady," rendered in pencil on four sheets of lined notebook paper Scotch-taped together in the back, depicted one of Momma's beauty-shop regulars who had stopped by the house for an unannounced visit back when we still lived in town. The drawing not only captured the woman's prominent namesake jaws but also made particular note of an apparent bladder-control issue: Gilda had her sitting in Daddy's rocker with pee splashing to the shiny wood floor below. It was a masterpiece.

Glenda—Although she did not enjoy making mischief like Gilda did, she hated the feeling she'd been cheated, and could easily be brought to blows if crossed. Glenda became the peacekeeper of the two energetic, redheaded twins as they burst through their childhoods into their mid-teens. Upstairs in their shared bedroom, the two were known to combust into tussles that got the crystals of the living room chandelier below them jingling. Like her closest sibling, she was sharp, hardworking and athletic. Standing at five feet six inches tall, she would develop the perfect physique for competitive basketball. Or tennis, or kick-boxing, or cheerleading, for that matter. Of the many things the twins had in common, the fact that they each celebrated and worked to emphasize their *differences* was Glenda's favorite.

Yours Truly—Born two years after the twins in the damp and stifling heat of mid-July, my soul resembled an inverted hurricane, tame on the outside, churning on the inside. As a preteen, I would learn to create a barometric calm at my core by blocking out the relentless external chaos of a big, festering family. My head was the largest among the siblings; it invited taunts of "Big Head," "Fat Head," or just "Head" until my skinny body finally grew enough to balance it out. I was comforted by routine; I liked Saturday morning cartoons long after I was supposed to; Sunday nights meant *The Wonderful World of Disney*, followed by *Bonanza*. As I matured into a teen, there was something steeping within me, something I unconsciously deflected with humor and a quick tongue. Daddy recognized this as *sass*, and to his man's-man mind, something ultimately more threatening and sinister, something he would not tolerate "in any boy of mine."

Dicky—Next in line after me, he was skinny and freckle-faced, with thick, curly, yellow-red hair. His favorite thing in the "whole wide world" was his black, stuffed toy monkey. He particularly loathed seafood, which was hard to avoid in a Gulf Coast state like Louisiana and a gumbo-obsessed family like ours. He did, however, like all kinds of other food as long as it was sweet. In fact, he had the nickname "Sugar Lips" bestowed upon him by our former housekeeper, Mildred, and it didn't bother him in the least. He had trouble holding on to information that teachers insisted was important, like the multiplication tables, but could list all the flavors, the precise shelf positioning, and the icing-to-cake ratio of the entire collection of packaged baked goods at Bernard's, the little grocery store down the road from the motel. Soft-spoken, overpolite, and unassuming, he would learn sooner than most of us would about the ugliness in the world.

Thomas—Born with encephalitis on June 27, 1965; lived for two days, then was buried on the last day of that month wearing the pale blue booties Momma crocheted for him while she was pregnant. At the funeral in St. Paul Cemetery on the west side of town, there was talk about one day moving him to be with other family members as they joined him in the hereafter. Though he didn't make it to see the 1970s, we still counted him in at Thanksgiving and Christmas.

Scotty—toddler. All business, straight-laced, no-nonsense. He was curious but did not like surprises. While the twins and Dicky and I played canasta around the dining room table one wet Sunday afternoon, he, wearing only a diaper and rubber pants, busied himself in a corner where earlier I had noticed the upturned carcass of a large dried cockroach. Later, after the game had come to an unusually peaceful close, and Scotty had long waddled away in search of a nap, all that remained of the cockroach were its two brown dorsal wings.

Alisa—newborn. She would grow from a chubby, ruddy-faced "Gerber Baby" into a freckly, lanky, and awkward preteen, and then blossom into a smart, driven teenager, and then fully into another beautiful bearer of the "Miss Eunice" title, eighteen years after Cassie wore the crown. Before heading off to LSU to become a defense attorney, she tried premed at the University of New Orleans, trundling around the Crescent City in Momma's maroon Chrysler Newport, the car she called her "favorite hand-me-down." But all those years ago, all she needed for complete bliss was a bottle of warmed formula and a fresh diaper.

Author's note: I have tried to recreate events, locales, and conversations from my memories of them. Some names and identifying details have been changed to protect the privacy of individuals.

PART I

THE CANASTA SUMMERS 1969-1976

1 | **Blue Barrette in a Puddle of Pee**

The capacity for shame hadn't yet entered Ayla Jane's little seven-year-old spirit. She waltzed into our kitchen on bare feet ringed with several days of dirt; had on a dirty, yellow-and-white cotton dress and dirtier panties. Her hair was a nest of yellow frizz and knots. Nonetheless, her momma or her sister Carlene or maybe she herself had attempted to calm the chaos on her head by fastening a blue butterfly barrette just above her left ear. In its absurdity, it was almost rather fetching.

She was hungry, and the smell of spaghetti made her mouth water.

"That shurrre looks good," she twanged, her eyes shining with anticipation.

Dicky and I looked up at her, shrugged, and continued to eat.

An eleven-year old, I had a well-developed impatience with being disturbed while eating.

"Want some?" I asked through a mouthful of spaghetti.

"Oh, that would be *real* good," she said, unable to control her tongue, which was sliding across her lips.

My little brother Dicky, a freckled, skinny nine-year-old with a head of thick red curls, got up from the breakfast nook and fetched a bowl out of the cupboard, and from Momma's well-worn, broken-handled Magnalite pot on the stove, scooped up some spaghetti with the ground-meat sauce already mixed into it—the way we liked to make it every single Saturday—and pointed her to the empty seat between him and me. "Sit down right there," he said, pinching a fork from the utensil drawer.

She ate hungrily and noisily, growling as she chewed. Her sparkly eyes darted from item to item on the breakfast nook shelf in front of her. A jar of Momma's too-soft pickles, salt-and-pepper shakers in a wire basket, Del Monte ketchup, Tabasco sauce. And a half-gone jar of mayo that somehow had not become fully rancid, even though our custom was to keep it unrefrigerated. It had turned from white to yellow-tinged clear in some places, streaking the jar like swirled wine.

Ayla Jane looked at Dicky and then me and then Dicky again as she chewed.

"Mmmm," she said after swallowing another forkful of spaghetti. "This is real good. I wish my momma made sketty like 'is. She only puts ketchup in hers."

. . .

Ayla Jane's mom, Isobel Sanders, was sitting in her kitchenette apartment in the multicolored stone-clad building to the right of our house. Comprising Room 16, with its double bed and a little kitchen and dining area, and the adjoining, Room 17, which had two double beds, but no kitchen, the apartment would be their home for the summer.

The kitchenette apartments were all clustered together in one building on the east side of the property. Our house separated those from the motel rooms on the west side of the property, lest the apartment tenants be inconvenienced by the comings and goings of the motel customers.

Isobel Sanders spent most of her days in the kitchenette watching TV, or playing solitaire, drinking coffee, and smoking Parliament Lights. Her prematurely graying brown hair was usually knotted up in an untidy bun. Apparently partial to muted colors, she was most often dressed in a beige shift that fell a half-foot below her knees. She preferred not to call too much attention to herself, happy to be in the background, the back row, or better yet, standing off to the side, out of view. Her husband, John, an oilfield roughneck, spent several days at a time, sometimes a full week, on a massive rig a half hour out by helicopter into the Gulf of Mexico, a gig he'd have for the next three months before moving on to another spot along the coast.

Carlene, three years older than Ayla Jane, but not as adventurous as her little sister, was far more comfortable clinging to her momma's side, watching TV or playing cards all day. It would never occur to Carlene to just waltz into our kitchen one fine Saturday noon to sniff around for something to eat.

There were two other Sanders kids, teenagers old enough to stay behind at the family home in Jonesville, Louisiana—"Jones*vull*"—a dead little town 110 miles to the northeast, not far across the river from Mississippi.

"What we doin' today?" Ayla Jane asked, scraping the last bits of spaghetti from her bowl.

"Oh, I don't know," said Dicky. "How about we play *bourré*?"

"What's that?" she asked.

"A card game. We play lots of card games all summer. *Bourré, bataille*, concentration, poker, and old maid, mostly," Dicky said.

"Nawww. I don't like cards," Ayla Jane said. "My momma and Carlene play cards a lot too. But I just don't like it. How 'bout we go outside?"

• • •

In the yard behind the kitchen stood the laundry building, and a few yards beyond that, another building, the first half of which housed Room 21, another kitchenette apartment, with the other half of the building taken up by an area where Daddy kept his tractor and tools. The back yard was also home to a little vegetable garden, stacks of lumber and other building supplies, a couple of wooden tables, a few wooden folding lawn chairs, Daddy's barbeque pit, and a custom-made swing set, constructed of iron pipes welded together and painted silver, its homemade swings made of chain links and wooden plank seats with holes drilled on either side where the chain was threaded through.

A little shack built as a floorless smokehouse for making tasso, *andouille*, and other goodies from *la boucherie* had also once stood in the back yard near the laundry building. Clad in red brick-patterned tarpaper siding, the shack had a pitched, green-asphalt shingled roof, a slatted front door, and little windows on either side. Shortly after buying the motel and discovering that the shack's exclusive purpose by then seemed to be providing shelter for a pretty scary collection of cockroaches that delighted in taking flight if anyone dared to open the door, Daddy fumigated it, tore it down, then heaped its parts into a pile on the big lawn at the edge of the property, and finally set it all ablaze.

It was on that spot, still barren of grass, where the little shack had stood that Ayla Jane insisted Dicky and I help her assemble a makeshift *house* in which to play that afternoon. We carried one of the wooden tables in the yard to the bald spot, propped up walls with pieces of lumber, and laid more pieces of wood for a floor. It wasn't as realistic as the smokehouse that had once been at that address, but at least it didn't have a swarm of flying cockroaches living in it.

• • •

After the table house was all put together, Ayla Jane exclaimed, "I wanna be in the upstairs! Can y'all put me up there?" she pleaded. Dicky and I hoisted her up on top of the table. I decided our little town needed another building, so I got another table that was lying on its side near the swings and moved it into place next door to Ayla Jane's.

"This is gonna be the restaurant," I announced. "I'm gonna serve toast and butter and coffee-milk," I explained as I headed off again to find wood to close in the sides of the table.

Moments later, as I was returning with some lumber, I noticed Dicky tugging at Ayla Jane's leg.

"Come down from there," he said, squinting into the sun shining behind her. "You need to come help me get more stuff for the house."

"Noooo!" she screamed. "I caint right now!"

Dicky ignored her protests and kept tugging at her leg.

"Nooo! I just caint! Let me go! Leave me be!" she screamed again, feverishly struggling to wriggle away from his grasp.

Then all was quiet in the yard.

Without another word, Ayla Jane's little dirty face crinkled up, and pee began falling through the cracks in the table, down onto Dicky's head. Dicky jerked himself away from the table, disgusted, wincing, and shaking his head.

"Ahhh!" he yelled, running off into the house, hands flailing.

Ayla Jane said nothing as she jumped down off the table and ran towards her kitchenette. Pee continued to trickle down from the puddle she made at the top of the table. Her blue butterfly barrette had escaped the frizz on her head and floated in the pee puddle until it too, dripped over the edge.

• • •

The incident thrust me back five years, to the 1965–66 school term at Highland Elementary, where, on my very first day of first grade, my big brother, Andy, a confident eleven-year-old fifth-grader with a buzz cut and wearing new blue jeans and a blue and green plaid flannel shirt, had escorted me to my desk. I was also sporting a fresh buzz cut and wearing new blue jeans and a plaid shirt and was nervously clutching my brand-new blue and red book sack. My desk was situated conspicuously at the front of the room, the very first desk of the first row. On top of it was affixed a strip of Scotch tape where my name had been written in all capital letters with a black marker. It was the first time I had seen my name spelled out in such large letters, and the fact of it startled me. Andy sat me down, and as he bid me goodbye and turned to leave, I positioned my new book sack on top of my desk so I could hide my head behind it, struggling to suppress my petrified tears.

The weeks passed and the calendar emptied into a new year and then a new spring. Easter approached. My teacher, Mrs. Bello, a young woman still in her twenties, wore her rich black hair up in a smooth bun and was kind and always elegantly dressed. Her voice was comforting and reassuring, and I gradually relaxed a little into my role as a first-grader.

We were making Easter baskets with our lunchtime milk cartons and had been instructed on how to properly cut our assigned sheet of brightly colored construction paper, and then how to wrap it around the carton and hold it there with some Elmer's glue. With that part done, the last step was to cut a thin strip of the paper to make a handle for the basket that Mrs. Bello would then staple together for each of us at her desk.

The room was abuzz with excitement. I was the first child to get his basket complete. As my classmates were busy either waiting in line to get their baskets stapled, or were on the way back to their seats, which necessitated them to pass by my desk, I felt compelled to stand on my seat and do a little jig to commemorate my accomplishment. Oblivious with joy, I stopped my jig only upon realizing the whole room had gone silent, a sure sign that something was amiss.

That something amiss was me.

In Mrs. Bello's class, it was a rule that when anyone misbehaved, we were each to stop whatever it was we were doing and thrust a sharp, accusatory index finger at the offender.

All index fingers in the class were pointing at me, including Mrs. Bello's.

I crumpled downward, back into my seat, fully humiliated, and, in my anxiety, a turd the size of a russet potato squashed its way out of me. I said nothing, having no earthly idea what to do. Surely, no one would notice, I thought.

They did.

Soon, as kids walked back to their seats, they were all pinching their noses, saying "Ewww," and pointing at me once again. I sat there as if nothing had happened. When Mrs. Bello realized everyone was pointing at me again, she walked over and, sniffing the evidence, looked at my glowing, buzz-cut head, bent down, and said softly, "Please go to the restroom and let that out." My memory of what happened between that moment and the time I got home that afternoon has been erased, presumably by the merciless weight of complete humiliation.

I do remember, however, that upon arriving at home that day, my big sister Gilda felt it appropriate and necessary to conduct a small but colorful Easter parade that involved pulling our red Radio Flyer wagon filled with her stuffed animals down the sidewalk, singing, "Moy ca-ca in kool. Moy ca-ca in kool," which delighted and triggered laughter from everyone within earshot. The experience, I think, stamped my soul with what would be a lifelong appreciation for Gilda's capacity to inflict indelible and demoralizing shame on those she loves.

• • •

That afternoon out in the back yard as Ayla Jane squirmed to get off that table, having just peed on Dicky's head, no one was laughing. And I felt I knew exactly what she was experiencing, even though she didn't have a class of thirty kids holding their noses and pointing at her.

The Sanders family would leave the motel before school started again in September. While many other families with dads working in the oilfields would take their place in our kitchenette apartments over the years, it was Mrs. Sanders who left us with a legacy considerably more lasting than what other guests had left us, the memory of Ayla Jane peeing on Dicky's head notwithstanding. Isobel Sanders taught my siblings and me how to play canasta, an "old ladies" card game that showed us the value of timing, strategic thinking, patience, and perhaps most important, endurance. For at least the next six years the game would become a powerful, undeniable source of comfort for us, particularly in the months when school was out. These would become our "canasta summers."

2 | Hole in the Road

Glenda melded before everyone else and was already working on two black canastas. She picked a card from the top of the discard pile and shifted it a couple of times in her hand, her thoughts going to where it might be most useful. On the table she was building a black canasta of fives, made black by a Joker, and another black canasta of nines with a two. She discarded a four of spades and cut Gilda a pair of side-eyes like the queen of hearts, defying her to pick it up.

"He tried to blame it on us," she said. "I told him, 'Daddy, I don't even know what you are talking about,' and he looked at me like I was lying."

Gilda had not yet melded. She had a handful of cards, which made everyone a bit anxious—she could win the round all at once if Glenda's discarded four of spades would complete a concealed canasta. She would only need to lay down any sets of three or more cards, and discard to end the round. Or she could lose terribly, with lots of points being subtracted from her total if someone else went out before she had a chance to lay any cards down.

"Yeah, then he looks at me," Gilda said. "'What made you wanna put that hole in my road?! Eh??'" she continued, mimicking his cavernous Cajun voice.

She was holding a jumble of cards and not, in fact, building a concealed canasta. She was holding on to her cards because the only way to meld was to put down her three eights with a couple of twos or a joker, but she didn't have either of those. She picked a fresh card from the overturned pile, a red three, worth a hundred points, and snapped it down on the table, because red threes don't require melding to be played. In fact, if they are not played, they can become a one-hundred-point liability should someone else go out.

"There," she said.

She discarded a five of diamonds. Glenda's eyes seared into the card. If she could pick up that pile, which had built up to a juicy stack of twelve cards, she'd be well on her way to winning the round.

"He did the same thing to me," I said. "He grabbed me and was shaking me so hard my head hurt. I don't know who did it but it wasn't me."

The subject of our assigned guilt was a little depression the diameter of a cantaloupe that had formed a couple yards from the north end of Daddy's new blacktop road. He had been forced to build the road and put up an illuminated sign to point the way to the motel, which had been operating undisturbed along the old highway since the Great Depression. By now he had complained more than a few times that, by cutting off access to the motel, the new highway surely would "bankrupt us all." In fact, the new highway made a rendezvous at the motel all the more private, and therefore more appealing for our customers (they were not referred to as "guests," the highfalutin term that hotels use; Daddy said that if they were guests of ours, they wouldn't be paying), so the business would soon flourish.

Daddy had cornered Gilda and Glenda, and then me, to ask, "What did you use to make that hole in my road?" The question was so unexpected, filled with such anger, such contempt, his confident accusation of guilt so damning, that when he clutched me to assign the guilt to me, I couldn't hold back my tears. My protestations of "What hole?" and "I didn't make any hole in the road" and "Why would I do that?" however feeble, dissolved his conviction that it was me.

"That's what I'd like to know," he said, shaking me violently then thrusting me to the ground before walking away angrily, leaving me stunned and disoriented in the grass. I picked myself up off the ground, scrunched up my eyes tight and shook my head like a dog whisking water off his drenched body. Best to push the incident away from my mind, and the sooner the better. Something Mémère had recommended as a way to keep from completely choking up and becoming paralyzed and even more vulnerable.

"You gotta move you-self away from that kinda thing as soon as you can, *cher*," she advised when we last talked about what she called Daddy's *mean self*. "Don't let him pull you down and then stay down. That would be no good for you. You gotta get up and keep going."

Daddy's tactic was something he had learned in the war. With the right amount of intimidation, you can ferret out a confession among a group of soldiers refusing to rat out one of their own. The problem was that, with the hole-in-the-road situation, no amount of intimidation would work up a confession because no one was guilty. It really was just a small sinkhole, where the sandy earth below had caused the asphalt to collapse. He was incensed at the very arrogance of it lying there like a wart on his brand-new blacktop, especially when the whole notion of having to build a *gotdammed* road in the first place, at his own expense, infuriated him. Now somebody had to be guilty of sabotage, but it was soon clear that it wasn't any of us. If he ever felt any pangs of guilt from falsely accusing his children, we never knew it. In all his years on earth, Zanny Ardoin never learned how to apologize.

• • •

Dicky was in the game mostly to provide a fourth player, since the game works best with an even number of participants. The four of us at the table were close enough in age—the thirteen-year old twins; me, two years behind them at eleven; and Dicky, nine—to have had the same experiences to talk about to fill the hours. But Dicky was always just a little bit behind us, even for his age, so we didn't expect too much out of him. His job was to simply keep the game going. He could be counted on, however, to put down very useful cards because he hadn't yet developed a sense of strategy. All the same, it was Dicky who picked up the juicy pile of cards. After a bit of card-shifting, he put down a black canasta of five fours and two twos, started another with four jacks, and a third with three eights. We all stared in disbelief. He could not go out and get extra points for the concealed canasta, because he still had four cards remaining in his hand. He discarded a ten of hearts.

"Then who made the hole?" he asked casually, chewing on a piece of buttered toast. "If it's none of us, then it musta been Andy. I bet Andy did it."

"He's not that stupid," Glenda said. "Besides, if Andy's going to do anything like that, he'da done a whole lot more than just one hole."

"That road is all he thinks about, since that crop-duster killed those big trees last year," I said. "He's still pissed that they got away with it."

• • •

The crop-duster hired to dust the soybean fields adjacent to the motel property sprayed once a season. Flying low, he released a plume of pesticides over the seven acres, and apparently the cloud wafted right over to the two massive cottonwoods and four mature sycamores that had stood there along the south edge of the motel property for half a century. Forty-eight hours later, the leaves on each of the six big trees went from bright greens to phlegmy yellow-browns.

Daddy was beside himself with anger, and sadness. Calls to the property owner yielded only denials, and an absurd proposition.

"No way did we spray over your trees, Mr. Ardoin," the man on the other end of the phone said. "We only spray over the fields. We can't control what the wind does. The only way you're gonna avoid that entirely is to own the property yourself. Let me know when you decide to buy. I'll give you a good price."

"Dammit to Hell, *non*! That don't make no sense. You think I wanna buy your damned soybean fields?! That's the last thing I need right now." He knew his protestations and heartbreak were in vain. The trees were probably lost, he felt. But he wouldn't know for sure for a year, when the new leaves would typically come back. So for a full year, every time he was out there, he fretted that they would not come back. But, to everyone's immense relief, they did, and in fact those trees are still standing.

3 | Zanny: Kids and Horses

I broke me a few horses in my day. I was just about seventeen, eighteen. Right before that war. Me and my brothers Howard and Cleveland were living at old man Ortego's farm, across that big field, between his property and our daddy's.

I think I was good at horse-breaking because I was just the right weight for that kinda thing. Them horses don't respond as good if you're too skinny or if you're too heavy. Howard was heavier than me and he had a hellofa time on the horses. So after a while of failing at that, Howard starting doing all the cooking for everybody. But no doubt about it. I was the best horse-breaker around, trained by old man Ortego himself. He told me how to do it, and right from the get-go, I just had a natural instinct for that.

• • •

What you *need* is a strong resolve to stay with that horse. That's a wild animal. That horse is only gonna do what you teach it to do. They can be very stubborn. You gotta break 'em, or they just gonna turn out to be no good. They'll be useless.

So you need that strong resolve before you can change that horse.

And—*and*—you need a good *horsewhip*.

If you ain't got one, you can always make yourself one out of a branch. You gotta cut yourself a good long branch. A green branch. From a cottonwood or some other tree like that. I like cottonwood the best because the wood gives when you crack it on that horse's hind. It won't break. Not too brittle.

Once you find you a good branch and cut it off the tree, then you gotta take your time with your pocket knife and clean that branch up. Your branch needs to be a good four or five foot. With your knife, you gotta remove all the little twigs sticking out on it, and all those knots. That thing's gotta be smooth all the way down, or your whip won't crack right on that horse's back.

Whittle that off and clean up that branch so it is about as thick as a twenty-five-cent piece is round at one end so you can grab it good, and then taper it off on the other end.

He-yah!

Yep. A good whip really works to break them horses. Especially if you *also* use some of that psychology on him: stare him down. Let him see you clean up that branch to make that whip. Show it to him. Let him know you got something planned. That horse is gonna know who's boss. You. If you can't do that, you'll never break that horse.

I didn't know it at the time, but that experience breaking them horses taught me a lot about my own life. It taught me that you gotta be tough with people, just like horses. If somebody's not doing what they oughta be doing, then you gotta show them that you mean business. Be firm with them. Works every time.

• • •

It's funny, but in all the years that passed between my horse-breaking days and when my life was finally reaching its stride, I often felt like I *was* that horse, and I was being broken to fit into what everybody expected *me* to do.

• • •

Eh, vieux Glen. Oh, Glen. Glenda!

You feel like cleaning some room? I got three right now. Number 9, 10, and 14.

Towels.

Soap.

Sheet.

Toilet paper.

• • •

This is a twenty-four-hour, three hundred sixty-five-days-a-year business. I got twenty-four rooms. Four kitchenettes. Eight with one bed and six with two beds. I can't afford to put that "No Vacancy" sign up. When they leave in the middle of the night, if it's a weekend, usually busy, we have to clean them and rent them out again. I've rented some of these rooms three times in a night. That's not funny. That's how I feed my family. It might not be the most classy of places, but I can assure you this motel is no different from them big joints all over the world, when it comes to that kinda thing. I don't let myself think about it, really. It's just the way this kinda business works. And anybody who thinks they're too good for this kinda work, well, good luck to them. For me, there is nothing to be ashamed of. This is hard work, and it more than puts food on the table.

• • •

Damned to hell, non. What I'd like to know is who the hell would dig a hole in my blacktop? That thing was paved just a month ago. It's not like I don't have enough to worry about with that highway coming in back there. When I bought this place, traffic passed right in front. Now I gotta pay for that access road or nobody is going to find us, and dammit to hell, somebody got a crowbar or a chisel or something and decided it would be a good idea to dig out a hole right there at the front of my new road, not three yards from the new highway. And now it looks like hell. Now I'm gonna have to get them guys back here and patch that up. It's only gonna get bigger if I don't. Dammit, non.

• • •

My kids all deny it. I got Gilda and Glenda together. They said "No" right away. Of course. Them twins fight like dogs, but they always gonna back each other up in the end.

Andy said, "Daddy. No. I didn't," when I asked him if he did it. I believed him. I let him be. Because it just don't make no sense that he would do a thing like that. He's more grown-up than the rest. But it really don't make no sense that *anybody* would do a thing like that.

I took Morris by the shoulders and tried to shake it outta him. "What you use to dig that hole in my blacktop?" His bottom lip started trembling. "What hole?" he said. He was always the sassy one. I can't stand that. "I didn't dig no hole," he said, and he started to cry. I ought of slapped him down right there. Boy shouldn't be crying. But I just shook him away, disgusted. "Get outta here! And don't you dare touch my blacktop."

• • •

These kids. They don't know how easy they have it. They whine about helping out around here, but they get three squares and a roof over their heads. That's more than what I got. Hell, I had to live in a barn for a few years.

That's true.

My momma had had fifteen kids before she died: Mary Lou, Clarence, Joseph, Arilyn, Adolph, Roy, Anna, Justine, John David—we called him J.D.—Nedry, Florence, Howard, Cleveland, then me, Zanny. And then finally, Earnestine. Some-a them had grown up already and moved on, and pneumonia took a coupla them, but there was still a handful of us around. But that Depression was hitting us hard.

Our daddy was a farmer. Cotton, corn, sugar cane, potatoes, sweet potatoes. He had the last open land on what is now Highway 29 out there, that stretch-a road that goes north from Belle Cove towards Bunkie.

Right behind our house about half a mile was what they called "the flat," a drop of about thirty feet on a ridge that goes from way out west to the town of Washington, Louisiana. We used to go there on horseback, through the woods. All hardwood. Daddy farmed in the bottomland. In the wintertime we'd drive the cattle, horses, hogs, whatever, down through the bottom there. They'd stay butterball tight. We had spring waters coming from off those hills. All through the year, we'd stop and drink. They had seven or eight of them springs that I knew of. That water was always cool. Cool and crisp. And boy, it was the best water I ever tasted.

We didn't have all the highways and roads like we do nowadays. One Sunday—this was back in the nineteen-thirties—Daddy and Momma and a coupla us kids went out to see Uncle Mac in Basile. That was one-a Daddy's brothers. Mac. We were in that old Model-T Ford. We had left early in the morning. It was a slow process. We had-a pass through all them gullies that cut across that wagon trail. That trail is now paved from New Orleans to the Texas border. Highway 190. Cuts across the whole bottom of the state. But back then, if you needed to get to Eunice or Basile or whatnot, you had to go through all them gullies. No bridges, no nothing. We had to get down and push that Model-T through them gullies. If you were in a wagon, the horses or the mules could pull you out through the gully in no time; but with an automobile, you had to get out and push.

So we left real early. There was a powerful north wind, and there was no heater in that Model-T, no heater at all. And them automobiles only had those, uh, *cellophane*-type windows. So it was cold. Cold.

When we finally got over there, we ate and we didn't stay no time. We went right back the same way, and we didn't get home until the early part of the night. Can you imagine, only going that far? Took us all day. Would take you about an hour today on them roads in a modern car.

• • •

Even before that Depression, life was always hard for us. A lotta people were hungry and desperate. A few years after our momma died, Daddy got married again. His new wife, a woman named Earline, said she wasn't going to be able to raise all us kids. She made no bones about it. So me and Howard went to live with old man Ortego on his farm across the field from us. I had just turned fourteen.

Ortego comes to Daddy and says, "I don't have any kids, like you. I need me some help. I got some wild cattle and some-a them Catahoula hounds to drive 'em, and a lotta horses, both wild and tame, and I sure could use me some help. Why don't you let the two biggest boys come stay with me?" He was talking about Howard and Cleveland, but I ended up going with Howard, and Cleveland went to live with Roy instead. We all just wanted a way to get away from that woman.

It took me a while to get used to the idea that we boys were now on our own pretty much. None of our sisters or our other brothers with us—hardly saw them much after that. We had to grow up fast. There was no way around that. That was hard for me and especially poor old Howard. More than once I found him choked up at night in that barn. I had nothing I could tell him to cheer him up. But I guess that experience made us all more tough. I know it did me.

And don't you know, Daddy wouldn't figure it out till a coupla years later that this Earline woman was up to no good from the get-go. She was cutting out on him, messing around with other men right behind his back, and had her hand on his money. When he finally realized what she was up to, he shot her in the head and then himself in the heart with a .22-caliber pistol. I can't tell you how that bothered me for a long time—years after that. I had some really bad, *bad* dreams for a while there.

So that was that. We had no momma, no daddy, and the only thing to do was keep working. Every morning on Ortego's farm we were up before dawn. Howard would cook, and I was taking care of the cattle and horses. Boy, that was some hard work. Then we'd have to walk to school and back. Then work again out there till dark. We stayed there like that for a coupla years till we left for that war.

World War Two.

That war was something else. That war was hell on all of us.

To tell you the truth, I don't really like talking about it.

One thing good I can tell you is that, for the first time in my life, I was proud to be a French speaker, when I was over there in France during that war. Because I was able to speak to the locals. I was able to get us some good food from those farmers, and a safe place to stay on more than one occasion. The other American guys got used to the idea that us coonasses could be useful. That's a big difference from the way we were treated when I was growing up. When I was a boy at school, during my first coupla years before my English was good, we had to keep to ourselves, so we all played together in one area outside. Those other kids from them American families all knew English, and that was what the US government was forcing on us all. They whipped us if we were caught speaking French in the classroom. So for a while there, the only place we could communicate with each other in our own language was outside during recess.

• • •

Yeah, my kids got it easy. Eliza thinks I'm too hard on them but somebody needs to keep them in line. If you don't discipline your kids, who's gonna do it for you? I'll tell you who: nobody. Or worse, that penal system. You gotta break them kids just like you gotta break them horses. That's how I see it, anyway.

We got two businesses to run. This motel is twenty-four hours a day, three hundred and sixty-five days a year. And that beauty shop keeps Eliza standing on her feet for nine, ten hours, five days a week. There's a lot to do around here, and we can't do it by ourselves. She works hard. I work hard. Nobody made it easy for her, or for me.

So anyway, you start off with a wild horse by throwing a rope around its head and neck. And then beginning to show it that you are in charge. Might take all day, might take longer, just to get that horse to calm down enough so you can get that rope around its head, and then begin working with it. If you try to jump on it too soon, it's just gonna throw you right there. Again and again. But if you can stand it, keep at it, then after a while, that animal is gonna let you stay on it. And once you're finally up on that horse, by then, you got a bit on him, got the reins on him. Keep the reins tight; keep control. Make your commands and reinforce them with that whip. He's gonna buck. You better believe. But you gotta stick with it.

All it takes is some patience, some real determination to break that animal. And, like I said, a good horsewhip.

It's best if you look them in the eye while you prepare that whip.

He-yah!

They gotta know you mean business. That's the only way.

4 | New Car, New Home

My family's time at the Stone Motel, which was spread out on three overgrown acres three miles outside of Eunice, Louisiana, began on May 6, 1967, a Saturday. Cassie, fourteen; Andy, twelve; the twins, Gilda and Glenda, ten; Dicky, six; and I, eight, were all piled into the big yellow Cadillac Daddy had driven home on the preceding Thursday afternoon, shocking everyone, including Momma. He explained that we needed a car bigger than the chunky, sunburned black Dodge he'd traded in as part of the purchase deal.

This trip, our first family outing in the Cadillac, was just to be a "joy ride," as Daddy called it, nothing more, although we were soon to learn that there was quite a lot more in store for us.

The Cadillac was already a couple of years old, but no matter. We were all dumbstruck about having a beautiful new car in our lives. The idea of our ragtag selves having a ride in it, to *anywhere*, was a dream. Never mind the destination.

Like many boys my age, I had already developed an intense interest in the way things were put together. To me, the Cadillac was truly, truly *breathtaking*. First for its overall size and shape. Like a spaceship. And then for its sharp lines. And then again for its tailfins.

"This car has fins!" I said the first time I laid eyes on it. "All cars should have fins!"

And that color. Neither harsh nor gaudy, but an elegant, *ethereal* baby yellow, set against sparkling chrome and crisp white details, its spotless black tires crowned with beautiful chrome *wheel-covers* (no simple *hubcaps* for such a masterpiece).

Inside, the car also was a true marvel. Embroidered cloth seats, not those hot sticky vinyl ones like we had in the Dodge. But an *embroidered* paisley—*paisley!*—in the same creamy yellow and white of the exterior.

And everything electric.

"Wow!"

Daddy happily demonstrated the electric windows for us, informing us that that's the way it was to be from then, on: only the driver would adjust the windows, lest one of us destroy their motors with abuse. He warned us not to touch *any* of the buttons in the car, in fact. That this amazing vehicle had buttons for raising and lowering the windows, buttons for moving the seats to and fro, and buttons for operating the windshield wipers at three different settings, including *intermittent*—a brand-new word for me—made my head spin. America was entering a new era, and leave it to the Ardoins to be among the first Eunice families to embrace that reality with this magnificent yellow-finned, automatic-windowed, paisley-embroidered *wonder machine.*

• • •

There was plenty of room for all of us in the massive car, so Daddy's explanation about us needing a bigger vehicle at last made perfect sense. What wasn't so apparent was why we needed something so extremely fancy, compared to our very ordinary, un-fancy lives. After all, Daddy owned and operated an Esso station, and Momma was just out of beauty school. A station wagon might be the choice for most people in those circumstances. None of that mattered from the looks on our faces; bug-eyed, mouths hanging open, we were all quite happy to be part of this surreal experience.

On the road the Cadillac floated like a magic carpet. Smooth, peaceful, *regal.* No sounds intruded from the outside; no potholes jostled us from the street beneath us. It was surely the smoothest riding vehicle any of us had ever experienced. And definitely the fanciest.

After only about ten minutes on the road out of town towards Opelousas, Daddy turned the car into the driveway of the overwhelming, overgrown green lushness of a tucked-in property that nestled a little motel covered in multicolored stone, a gleaming white house in the same stone, and another building on the other side of the house also done in the multicolored stone. He parked right under the motel sign, which was perched above a base of matching multicolored stone that read, surprisingly enough, "Stone Motel," in glowing neon block letters. Smaller letters underneath read "Vacancy" in green neon, with an unlit "No" in front of that. At the side of the road a big, business-sized galvanized metal mailbox sat on a four-by-four square post. On it "ROUTE 3 BOX 55-K," had been hand-painted in black block letters.

"Whadda y'all think if we came here for our vacation this year?" Momma asked, to a round of groans.

"No! Not here!" Glenda protested.

"There's no beach!" Gilda added. "Not even a pool."

"Not here, Momma!" Dicky begged. "It's too close."

I was in disbelief, too, not sure what to say, when Daddy chimed in. "Then how about if we come here to stay forever?"

"What?" asked Andy. "Like we would *live* here?"

Cassie, who, as the eldest, had already been made aware of the news and was bursting to finally say something, said in an annoying sing-song voice, "I already knew. How's that for keeping a secret, Momma?"

"Yep," said Daddy. "We're going to live right here. We just bought the place."

That piece of information converted any horror about the little motel as a vacation spot into sheer delight as it dawned on us that this was to be our new home, *and* that we *also* could go on vacations to the beach.

"Wow!" said Dicky. "This is a *good* place to live."

"Look at all those trees," Andy, a born outdoorsman, said.

"There're two ponds, too," Daddy said.

"Probably can get some fish," Andy said, his voice getting increasingly excited.

"We're going to have an upstairs," said Cassie. "And we get our own rooms. The girls upstairs and the boys downstairs," having already staked her claim when Momma had confided in her the day before.

"Hold on," Momma said. "We have a lot to figure out before anybody gets anything."

• • •

We were there to meet Mr. and Mrs. C. H. Melancon, the sellers, who would show us around. Before getting out of the car, though, Momma issued a stern, "Y'all better behave. Don't touch anything and keep quiet unless they talk to you directly."

Compared to our flat, one-dimensional rectangle of a house in town, the Melancons'—*our new*—house was a palace. The house's adjoining two-car garage was connected to the L-shaped motel building by an archway that had been finished with the matching multicolored stone facade. The garage's high-pitched gabled roof was crowned at its peak with a black cast iron rooster weathervane.

There were two front entrances to the house, one from inside the garage, and the other, more obvious entrance through the motel office door, which was right next to a single-posted, free-standing neon sign that read "OFFICE." The office featured a trio of immense picture windows, under which sat a sofa, a side chair and, adjacent the garage wall, a registration desk with the obligatory hotel-desk bell that issued a crisp "Ding!" when Mr. Melancon tapped it as part of his tour. Behind that room was a dark, private office, where Mr. Melancon had already shown Daddy "the books."

But beyond those two functional rooms, the house, like the Cadillac, was very fancy by our standards. The next room, a "casual" dining room that was fancier than any of the rooms in our old house, featured a built-in china hutch and, overhead, a wagon-wheel chandelier with hurricane-lamp-styled shades, and led to the back of the house, where the kitchen featured another built-in, a green laminated breakfast nook. Adjacent to the kitchen was a TV room.

"They have a room just for watching TV!" Andy whispered loudly.

"Shhhhh!" Momma hissed, as Mrs. Melancon ushered us onward through the rest of the house.

A formal living room was decorated in a way I had only ever seen on TV or in one of Momma's magazines. It had *drapes*, not curtains, and was located at the heart of the house, as was the formal dining room, brightened elegantly by an actual crystal chandelier.

"We bought that chandelier on a trip to Europe," Mrs. Melancon said. "In Vienna. They had to wrap up each crystal piece separately, then the whole thing got all bundled up in a box, and that box was then put into a bigger box—twice its size. Not one piece was broken when I got the delivery."

Separating the two formal rooms was an elaborate, grapevine-themed trellis made of wrought iron that was "forged in the French Quarter," explained Mrs. Melancon.

There were two big bedrooms downstairs, one full bathroom, and one half-bath. Upstairs there were two more bedrooms, three walk-in closets, and another full bathroom with yet another built-in, a vanity table and half-moon stool that were custom-made for the room.

On the outside: the highly-pitched gabled roofs, more ornate cast-iron touches on the living room and master bedroom's multipaned windows, and a matching wrought-iron *balconette*—a term provided to us by Mrs. Melancon—on the second floor. All of this was covered in the same stone as the motel buildings but finished in a bright white, and contrasted on the roofs by Italian slate shingles the blue-gray color of bayou egrets. When all of the elements were taken collectively, the visual effect was that of a fairy-tale house, from another time and definitely another place.

5 | **A Motor Hotel**

fter the house tour, we were led outside by the Melancons to have a walk around the property. It was during this walk that we learned that the C. H. in Mr. Melancon's name stood for "Charles Horace."

"I have lived here on this land for decades," explained Mr. C. H., sweeping an open-palmed hand around to emphasize the expanse of the property. It was as if he were demonstrating a new appliance or, better yet, a brand-new car, like the women on TV game shows did.

"Before this was a motel we had a cotton gin, a lumberyard, a housemoving business, and before all that, a grocery store, which is that building right there that is now the kitchenettes. We had that store and the lumberyard right over there at the edge of the property," he said, pointing east.

"My daddy told me, 'You ought to build a hotel right here,'" Mr. Melancon continued. "'They're doing it out there in California. Call 'em *motor hotels* in fact. Customers can park their cars right in front of their rooms.' The whole concept just about made me dizzy. Right then and there I could see my future."

And so, just as a new decade was dawning, and the remnants of the Great Depression were still being felt in places far away from the Louisiana plains and bayous, Mr. Melancon hired a team of carpenters and, using connections in the lumber industry to save money, began building the L-shaped motel adjacent to the family home on the west end of the property.

In six months' time, the motel's foundation was built on concrete pyramid blocks, the outer building was framed and divided into fourteen rooms, each having its own bathroom; and the building's pitched roof was sealed with leprechaun-green asphalt shingling. The only structural feature that remained to be completed at that point was the outside finish of the new building. Mr. Melancon had his heart set on Formstone, a stone facade he had seen in a magazine, and had arranged for an outfit out of Baltimore to come to Louisiana and cover the new building in their signature seamless multicolored stone-mimicking siding.

All of this work happened uninterrupted over the course of half a year, except for a day or two of severe rain and wind brought in by the occasional tropical storm pushing up through Louisiana from the Gulf of Mexico.

The Great Depression didn't severely alter the lives of rural Louisianans, Mr. C. H. explained, "since there wasn't much commerce here to begin with. People were already quite good at making do with what they could grow or raise for slaughter. They bartered services for goods and vise-a-versa, and that had been pretty much the norm long before anybody in New York City decided to jump out of a window."

While the recent collapse of the national economy did make everyone understandably nervous, C. H. Melancon was not deterred. By the end of the 1940s, he felt enough time had passed to build a new business. The Baltimore outfit was happy to have the work. They arrived in Eunice by train.

The crew set about installing the Formstone on their first day. The first step involved applying metal lath directly onto the building. Then they applied the plaster, using molds to shape the stones.

"It looked to me very much like applying stucco," he said. "Right before that plaster had a chance to fully dry, they sanded and colored the 'stones' to make them look as real as possible."

The job took two months, during which time Mrs. Melancon had made arrangements to furnish the rooms, each with its own unique decor. Beds, nightstands, desks, chairs, linens, rugs, wall hangings, all arrived in batches day by day until the place was ready to open later that year.

• • •

As I listened to Mr. Melancon give us the history lesson of the motel, I kept an eye on Daddy's face. All through the house, room by room, and then outside, around the property, as Mr. Melancon talked, Daddy's face was wide with pride. What earlier seemed to be an out-of-the-blue purchase of the Cadillac now made even more sense to me. When he drove up to introduce the Melancons to his family, Zanny Ardoin wanted to impress these people, upstanding members of the First Baptist Church, that we weren't in fact, a bunch of hillbillies. He needed them to see a driven *businessman* who had the brains and determination to transform one successful little filling station into a thriving motel business that could attract locals as well as vacationers from far and wide, and he wanted the rest of the world to see it, too. He was finally coming into his own, from his roots as a boy pushed out of his home to fend for himself at fourteen, who would go on to witness firsthand unspeakable atrocities of war in Europe, to a man returning to America as a worldly *entrepreneur* ready to start a new life, have a family, and provide a good living for us all.

6 | **Are We Crazy?**

By the time my parents and the six of us children who were born by then rolled into the motel driveway in that big yellow Cadillac in 1967, the Melancons had been in business there for decades.

The three acres of property had changed into an overgrown jungle of pine trees, magnolias, cottonwoods, cypress, oaks, and sycamores; as well as a variety of fruit trees. Ignored peaches and plums, tangerines and figs—all left to rot or be picked apart by birds. A grape arbor the length of a school bus stood abandoned. The white paint on its latticework had been washed away by the summer rains; its vines, choked dry by climbing weeds, had fully atrophied years before.

The Melancons' grocery store building had been gutted and became the kitchenette apartments; and the lumber business was long gone, sold to a man who had lived his whole life in the area, a Mr. Bernard, who moved the remaining stock about a mile down the road.

The family house was the only part of the property still in decent shape, having had a recent coat of white over its stone facing. But the motel rooms were another story. All were in serious need of updating. The once unique and beautiful carpets were threadbare; mattresses lumpy from age gave off the stale odor of mold and cigarette smoke; chipped and scratched veneers of the 1950s-era nightstands and rounded-edged dressers and side tables; torn, thinning upholstery on the side chairs, also from the era of black-and-white movies instead of reflecting the optimism, excitement, and color of the approaching 1970s. In most of the rooms, these furnishings all would have to be replaced.

The timing of this sale could not have been more perfect. C. H. Melancon and his wife, Millie, were both in their late sixties by then and eager to let the place go.

• • •

Standing in the driveway, as they watched the moving truck drive off the property, Daddy said to Momma, "There's so much that needs to be done," with a tone in his voice revealing more anxiety and doubt in him than she wanted to hear. "I hope we can do it all. Are we crazy?"

"Well, we have lots of helpers," Momma responded, not sure herself if the adventure they'd just begun was going to work out, but she had already made up her mind that she would damned-well do whatever it took for it to do so.

"It's definitely going to be, um, interesting," she said as calmly as she could muster.

• • •

"Hello!" came a voice from over by the motel sign next to the road. Momma and Daddy looked over to see the voice belonged to a short man who looked to be in his late sixties, at least. The wide bottom half of his body gave him the gait of a buoy as he walked. He was accompanied by a petite woman around his age.

"How y'all do?" asked the man as he approached Momma and Daddy. "We come to say hello and welcome y'all to the area. That's our house right there," he said pointing to the property obscured by a five-foot wall of honeysuckle. "I'm Percy Oakley and this is my wife, Therese."

"How y'all do?" Daddy replied, shaking Mr. Oakley's hand.

"And I'm Eliza," Momma said, shaking Mrs. Oakley's hand. "Y'all want some coffee?"

"No, that's okay. We don't want to be no trouble. Y'all are just moving in," said Mrs. Oakley.

"Not at all," Momma replied. "Come on in for a little while. It's a mess in there, but we have the office put together, so we can sit in there."

Inside, the Oakleys sat on the office couch, Momma sat at the front desk chair, Daddy in his oak rocker, the first piece of furniture he put into place, followed by the free-standing ashtray he would soon fill with cigarette butts.

"Looks like y'all gonna have a lot of work to do," Mr. Oakley said. "The Melancons had a good run here, but over the years they let a lot of things go."

"Yeah," said Daddy. "It's gonna be a big job to get this place in shape, but that's what attracted me to it in the first place. I'm looking forward to getting right in and getting to work."

They wouldn't stay more than twenty minutes. The difference in age between the Oakleys and Momma and Daddy was at least twenty years. There wasn't going to be a strong social connection, but the meeting was appreciated, it seemed, by them all.

Once they were gone, Momma said, "That was nice of them to come by. It's good to know your neighbors." Whether or not that would pan out to be in any real sense, true, would have to be determined over time.

• • •

In the first year at the motel, Daddy, with Andy, thirteen—and sometimes me, nine, by their side—made it his goal to rid the property of all of its neglect and overgrowth. The trees, bushes and shrubs growing in the "wrong" places were exactly what made the place so enchanting to the rest of us, as were all the random bits and pieces of Mr. Melancon's legacy: the abandoned, roach-infested smokehouse, that arched arbor where grapevines once braided, an unused water cistern perched atop a rickety wooden base, taking up space behind the motel building, and just beyond that, an algae-choked pond, on the edge of which the Melancons had burned their weekly trash.

"We're gonna need to fill in that pond," Daddy said to Andy. "And that water tower will have to come down."

Of course none of this "improvement" stuff made any sense to us kids. Andy was just as confused by Daddy's thinking, but ever the dutiful son, he couldn't imagine questioning his daddy.

But Gilda could, and did.

"If y'all take all that stuff away and tear out all those trees and flowers and stuff, it's going to look naked," she pleaded. "That grapevine thing is great. Please don't take that down, Daddy."

"T-Gil, you're too young to understand," he said in his deep Cajun patois. "This is a business, and people don't want to come to a place that looks overgrown and abandoned. I promise not to get rid of everything. I got a plan for all that," he said, convincing himself more than convincing anyone else.

His plan apparently involved taking out any feature on the property that called too much attention to itself, rendering anything curvy or wild or whimsical into straight, predictable lines, nothing contorted by nature; no junky buildings; no mess, no mystery. So down came the grape arbor and the *boucherie* smokehouse. A sidewalk designed in the shape of an S to accommodate a massive mulberry tree was destroyed with a sledge hammer and pickaxe. The big tree itself was also destroyed. And other beautiful mature trees on the property received the same fate: a thirty-foot Ponderosa pine in the back yard between the garage and the laundry building was "in the wrong place," so of course it had to be destroyed and hauled away.

"NO!" Glenda pleaded the morning the big pine was to come down. "Why do you say that tree is in the wrong place?" she asked.

"Them big tree roots are gonna destroy all them drainpipes running under that ground. It shoulda come down a long time ago" was Daddy's firm reply. "Y'all just don't understand these kinda things. Now y'all get outta the way."

We refused, the twins and Dicky and me, standing just out of the immediate work area, but still close enough to watch the proceedings.

"I said y'all get!" Daddy yelled. "It's too dangerous for y'all to stand around. Get!"

Even Andy, who usually did whatever Daddy instructed without question, sensed this tree was one too many, but any reluctance he may have had was quickly dismissed.

"Don't you start, too," Daddy snapped, sensing Andy's disappointment. "Let's get to it."

The transformation of the property from the magical to the mundane would take every bit of the first year and continue well into the next. We never stopped objecting but gradually accepted that what Daddy had in his mind simply would not change. And it was heartbreaking for us to watch.

7 | Where the World Begins

There was something unspoken about Gilda, Glenda, Dicky, and me playing canasta around the dining room table that I somehow inherently knew: in our house that table was a *refuge*, not only from the pressing ninety-degree heat that bore down on us daily during the relentless Louisiana summers, but even more so from Daddy's unpredictable wrath. This refuge at home was second only to the safe haven I had found, starting in infancy, in Ville Platte, where for me the world truly began at Mémère and Pépère's house.

Pépère's massive blacksmith hands hover gingerly in circles over my little stomach, where the crippling pain undulates. The pressure is so immense it startles me. I am silent. My eyes dart around the room. My legs thrash.

"Try to be still, *cher*," Pépère says softly before returning to his prayer, mumbled almost inaudibly in a blend of French and some other language, something my five-year-old brain isn't meant to comprehend: The ancient, intimate tongue of the Louisiana *traiteur*.

After only a minute or so, the intense warmth coming from my grandfather's fingertips and his strange but not entirely foreign mutterings begin to do their work to still the electric bolts that moments before had been violently jabbing my gut, as if trying to break through to the outside, and causing me to crumple over onto the kitchen floor.

When Mémère figures I have more than just a touch of indigestion, since the peppermint and Coca-Cola—her remedy for most everyday ailments—she'd given me haven't helped, she calls Pépère in from his shop outside, where he was repairing a wheelbarrow handle for Madame Soileau, who lives just next door in her pristine white house, always the tidiest on the block.

"Take a big, slow, deep breath and let that out, *cher petit* Morris," he now says clearly, in the lyrical patois of all our Cajun ancestors.

I take in a half-breath of air and timidly breathe out.

"*Non, cher.* More big than that. *Comme-ça,*" he continues, sucking in his own big breath of air to demonstrate, as he pulls Mémère's old patched quilt over me. Standing stiffly and silent behind her husband, Mémère's face has gone white; her eyes watered with worry.

I do as instructed—suck in a big, deep breath and then let it out.

"That's good, *cher.* Now you gotta say this next prayer with me: *Notre Père qui es aux cieux, que ton nom soit sanctifié . . .*"

I recognize the Lord's Prayer right away. "*Notre Père qui es aux cieux, que ton nom soit sanctifié . . .*" I repeat, then say the rest along with him: " *. . . Donne-nous aujourd'hui notre pain quotidian . . .*" Give us this day our daily bread.

Pulled fully inside the prayer, I finally begin to relax. The sharp jabs in my stomach have now completely disappeared. My legs stop moving. I breathe normally again, relieved, but not surprised. It is not the first time my grandfather has healed me or Momma or one of my siblings.

There are many *traiteurs*, faith healers, in the little bayou towns all over south Louisiana, but Pépère's gift is particularly powerful, and his skill has become known widely. People come from as far away as Baton Rouge for him to treat a variety of ailments. Severe headaches and persistent stomachaches mostly, but also many complaints wrapped up under the catch-all of "nerves."

Lying there now in that recuperative state on the smooth mustard-brown sofa in the living room in my grandparents' little house on East Jackson Street, all of my senses are fully alive again, instead of uniformly trained on the upheaval going on in my belly.

Aside from the faint scent of the sofa's aged Naugahyde, there is a sweet, musty, more *human* mix of smells that have collected in the house over the years. They assemble in the delicately crocheted doilies Mémère has placed on the side tables, under lamps, and over the back and arms of the bloated green recliner. The scents also gather in the oblong rag-weave rug that lies atop the worn varnished planks of the hardwood floor. Each of these items holds decades of soothing smells that have collected in the room or wafted in from the kitchen. Of chicken and sausage gumbos past, of sweet fig cakes, roasted *ponce chaudin*, and countless links of Saturday morning *boudin*. All this of course also intermingles with remnants of the White Shoulders perfume, the Aqua Velva after shave, and the subtle perspiration of neighbors and relatives, who, when the weather is too cool for a visit on the porch, have coffee or, on nights in December, a shot of bourbon in a cup of eggnog with my grandparents.

A dark, elaborately carved mahogany cuckoo clock on the wall above my head tick tick ticks away the minutes. Tick tick tick. And a wisp of air pulled in from the attic fan in the house's center hall is just cool enough to compel me to tuck my exposed foot in under the blanket.

In this state I observe my grandparents' faces, as if for the first time. Pépère, sixty-two, has wide eyes with irises the bright green of a summer *mirliton* just plucked from the garden. Those *mirliton* eyes say he is at complete peace with the world, and that notion is reinforced by the quiet, reassuring tone of his buttery voice. The cheeks of his oval face are shaved only on Sunday mornings and other occasions involving church. All other times, an eighth of an inch of blue-gray stubble that matches the quarter-inch of spread-out twigs of hair poking up from a mostly bald skull is the norm for him. Today, like most days, even church days, when he makes an effort to remove it with his pocketknife, there is black under his fingernails. I figure that has something to do with why they came to call people like him blacksmiths, although to him and Mémère and most of the people in their little Cajun town, he is a *forgeron*. And, on top of that, a *traiteur*. This combination makes perfect sense to me, because both jobs involve repairing or putting things right for people.

Standing five feet five inches, Mémère is sixty but looks closer to forty. People often say that she and Momma could be sisters, and they mean it. Like Momma's, Mémère's thick head of hair is still the lush auburn of a fricassee roux, her eyes the color of pecans, and her pale skin virtually wrinkle-free. She smiles with those brown eyes more than with her mouth, which she keeps reserved for rapid-fire chatter, a trait she has passed down to several of us grandchildren. It is also in those eyes, however, that the melancholy of an otherwise full life strung with subtle deprivations reveals itself in full relief, a trait Momma has inherited from her. On most days, like today, her clothes are simple, humble. She is partial to housedresses in patterns with pin dots or small botanical elements that don't call too much attention to themselves, and to practical, comfortable slippers. For Sunday mass and special occasions like weddings and christenings, however, she allows her true tastes to emerge; those clothes are bolder, more assertive, evident in the big floral prints and bright yellows, greens, and blues, and the patent leather shoes she prizes for their shine.

"Now take another big breath, *cher*," Mémère says, sensing that her husband's work with me is done. She is most often by his side when he treats family or neighbors or people who've made a special trip to town for his help. "Let all that *misère* pass right out of you, *cher*."

I do as instructed: another big breath in, a big breath out. And finally all of my *misère*, the internal misery that my mémère has just pinpointed, flutters up and out of the room, like a chatter of released teetee birds.

Pépère bends down and kisses my forehead. His stubbly face lightly brushes my skin, the familiar feeling a unique comfort to us both. The violence in my stomach gone, I feel not only immense bodily relief, but a sensation my little brain isn't yet sure how to process—I'll learn later as I grow to experience more of the world that what I am feeling that day in my grandparents' house is *safe*. I feel safe. Completely safe. For me it is a sensation peculiar to this place, and to the times I've spent in the company of these two fine people.

• • •

For years as I grew up, even after Pépère had passed away, Mémère and that simple four-room home on East Jackson Street hugged me with a sense of comfort I was not able to feel from my siblings and parents and the fourteen-room house that was our home thirty minutes away in Eunice. For me Mémère's world was a shimmering magnetic bubble, where love and security were delivered generously and wonderfully accompanied by a cool, consistent breeze sucked through the house's screen doors and windows by that humming attic fan above.

• • •

A green screen door at the front of the house kept the mosquitoes and other bugs out of the kitchen, where a long green-and-white linoleum floor, done in a windowpane pattern, and the three unmatched rocking chairs on top of it, welcomed you. If your timing was just right, you might also be greeted by the smells of a thick, meaty gumbo bubbling on top of the stove, or a buttery rich *gâteau aux figues* made with figs picked in the back yard, wafting from the oven.

On the right wall above and below the sink hung simple pine cabinets painted white and green. They were handmade by Pépère. The scalloped molding that crowned them was hand-cut with a coping saw from a pattern he drew in pencil, freehand. The eight little propellers that kept the cabinet doors closed with a spin were whittled with a pocketknife. The only store-bought extravagance, the cut-glass knobs, each the size of a big toe, came from the hardware department at G. Ardoin and Company's on Main Street.

The kitchen sink had two spigots, one for hot and one for cold. Out of the cold spigot came "Mémère water." It was unlike water from anywhere else; it was always cool, even in the most sweltering of Augusts, with a taste that made me think of a fresh, rushing woodland stream, and a delicate dash of minerals to tickle each side of my tongue. My siblings and I considered Mémère water, chilled further in a tin pitcher, or mixed with cane sugar and lemon juice, the best in all the world.

At the kitchen's left wall, right behind the front door, hung a little darkly varnished oak shelf with ornately carved sides. On it sat a bulky black phone with a clacking rotary dial. Scribbled with a nubby pencil in Mémère's unsteady hand directly onto the wall all around the phone shelf were the numbers of everyone she could possibly call. (Many of her friends and relatives would not have a phone of their own in their lifetimes.) With the exception of her and Pépère's names, she had never learned how to read anything composed of letters.

Up on the left, built into a dormer notch so it sat vertically into the ceiling at the back of the kitchen, was the large attic fan. When its motor was ignited with the flip of a switch poking out of a protruding little black box affixed to the wall, the fan jumped to life and quickly began to suck outside air through the house's window and door screens and pushed it out again through the louvered vents of the mysterious attic. For a child, the ignition of the fan was startling but exciting; the goings-on up there behind its blades were excellent material for dark imaginings: Andy had convinced me that a creature he called the "devil horse" lived up there, where he had been patiently waiting for a delicious little boy to come along and satisfy his hunger.

Down in the opposite corner below the attic fan stood a curvy chrome table topped by green speckled Formica; we would play PoKeNo, *bourré*, and *bataille* there. It was during one jolly game of *bataille* that Mémère laughed so hard her dentures popped out of her mouth, prompting even more laughter around the table.

Under a window dressed in a curtain of happily dancing cherries, pears, grapes, and bananas, a wrought-iron foot-pedal Singer sewing machine was positioned near the table. On it Mémère had made those curtains, and all the others in the house, as well as Mardi Gras costumes and school clothes for her three children, and most of her own clothing.

• • •

The other rooms of the house included the living room to the left of the kitchen, which featured two facing sofas, one in a rust-colored Naugahyde, and the other covered in a rough green fabric that reminded me of burlap. The colorful bird in a still-functioning cuckoo clock issued reliable cuckoos from above. A little white coffee table and a fat, black upholstered recliner completed that room.

The two small bedrooms at the back of the house were each furnished with a bulky bed, and there was just enough room for a dresser stuffed with clothes and linens that spanned the decades. A dresser drawer pulled open released an enchanting bouquet of lavender, crumbling paper, and starched fabric.

The bottom drawer in Mémère's dresser held a box of tintypes and old photos; while the hanging clothes in her closet concealed a large, ancient, dark oak-framed, color-tinted photo of her mother, Eliza. Eliza wore a dour, buttoned-up-to-the-chin, brown dress; her hair was pulled up in a tight chignon. Her expression stern, her eyes hollow. Coming face-to-face with her stare in that dark closet during a game of hide-and-seek could give a child a heart attack.

• • •

Mémère's world, fully knowable in any direction on foot, included her house at its center, and no more than half of a town block on all sides. On the left side of Mémère's was the tidy white house of Madame Soileau; her perfect front porch with its teal metal gliders and gleaming white swan planters flanking the front steps was the envy of the neighborhood. On the right side, the oldest house on the block, belonging to the Hadleys, *Madame* and *Monsieur*, was clad in gray weathered asphalt shingles. All three of these houses, like most of the ones throughout the town, had corrugated tin roofs onto which the afternoon rain pattered, lulling those inside to beautiful duo-toned dreams.

Just across from the Hadleys, at the corner of East Jackson and LaTour Streets, was Lake Young's Grocery (in Mémère's tongue, he was simply "Mister Lick"). The store was a leaning shack of a building with torn and peeling brown fake-brick asphalt siding. Inside this dark, virtually windowless building (except for three small rectangles of glass cut into the uppermost part of the street-facing wall), Mister Lick sold nothing fresh. On his crooked shelves, there were no vegetables outside of cans, and there was no meat except for the andouille sausages and *tasso*, the "ham" made from cured pork shoulder that Mister Lick smoked himself in the back of the store.

The andouille and *tasso* were more than respectable, but better versions could be had at Aubry's, a bigger and brighter store just down LaTour Street in the block after Tante Versie and Oncle Florence's house. Most often, the reason any of us kids stopped in at Mister Lick's was for the Jack's cookies, hard round ginger snaps with pink or white icing, or the "stage planks," the larger, wavy-edged cookies coated with red icing. There was another attraction to be had at Mister Lick's. Just inside the entrance to the little store, through a screen door that advertised "Evangeline Maid Bread: Stays Fresh Longer," standing on top of the meat counter on the right, Mister Lick's offered a row of penny candy machines that held Boston Baked Beans, little jawbreakers, Red Hots, and gumballs. Each machine dispensed a real hand*full* for a nickel.

A stroll to Mister Lick's for Jack's cookies or some candy, then back across the street to pop in at the Hadleys to say a quick hello, and then back to Mémère's again, could take anywhere from ten minutes to a full hour or more, depending on the conversation to be had on either of the stops along the way.

• • •

The menacing sun would be down soon. As in so many of the summer nights of my childhood, I was lured through to the back of the house and out through the screen door, by the cooler air of the long, blue, wooden-planked porch, where, after the sun had fully disappeared and the crickets and frogs had begun their evening symphony, I was collected in the eager arms of a grandparent, usually Mémère's (but often Pépère's) and lulled to sleep on a sliding metal glider or the swinging slatted porch bench suspended from a rafter above.

But first there was a lesson in my grandparents' first language, the French, undisturbed by modernity, that had been passed down from ancestors driven out of Canada and into Louisiana in the 1750s.

"*Que fais-tu venu tard comme ça ce soir?*" she whispered to me in that night's porch lesson. I was to ask this of Momma the next time she came home late from her shop.

"*As-tu besoin d'aide pour dîner ce soir, maman?*"

"*Laisse-moi porter ça pour toi.*"

• • •

As the years passed, even after she remarried, Mémère's world remained magical. In her world there was a peace; there was a calm. There was no threat, no loud, unfounded accusations, no fear of always imminent, often random violence delivered from the back of a big flat hand. It was the only place in my small world where I experienced full, unconditional love and honest, reliable security that would not disappear tomorrow. Here, I didn't have to feel guilty when I was not working, when I was instead playing in the yard, eating a big red-icing-covered cookie, or dancing with my mémère to the *chank-a-chank* Cajun music coming through the radio.

8 | Mémère: *Pauvre Bête*

et's see. You know, I don't read, me. I don't write, neither. Except my name. I can write *Ortense:* O. R. T. E. N. S. E. *Or-tonce.* And I can write Pépère's name, DeJean: D. E. J. E. A. N. *Day-shon.* Oh, and I can write my numbers, me. One, two, three, four, five, six, seven, eight, nine, ten, zero.

When I'm a *petite fille*, a little girl, I'm only make the fourth grade. After that, I had to work, *cher.*

But I'm not stupid, me. I can make it. That's why I got all them numbers I write on the wall over there all around that telephone. Somebody give me they phone number, if I write it down on the wall like that, I always remember who it's for. Don't need no name to write out. Just they numbers and I got it, me.

I take my English off the TV. That's the best I can do.

It's not perfect English, but people understand me, *que même.*

• • •

I had three babies, me. I had Andrew first. We call him Paillasse. That means "clown." Them boys at the school say he look like a clown, him, with all that red hair and freckles. So everybody start to call him Paillasse. And all the kids in the family call him Uncle Pai. Paillasse was born, *huit d'avril*, um, eight of April. After Paillasse I had Florence. Florence was born twenty-first of *mai*. So I have me two boys. And then one *petite fille*. *Ma petite fille*, Eliza Mae. She was born sixteen of *septembre*. Mae-Mae was my *bébé*.

Paillasse and Florence each gave me one grandkid. But my Mae-Mae, she gave me nine! Can you imagine Eliza Mae have nine kids? Let's see:

She had Cassie, Andy, then the twins, Gilda and Glenda. Then little Morris, then Dicky, Thomas, who die, him, *pauvre bête*, and then Scotty and Alisa. Nine babies. *Talk about!*

• • •

You know, I'm lonesome like hell, me.

Paillasse tell me I'm not more lonesome than anybody else. I said I don't say I'm *more* lonesome. I said I'm lonesome. I say, "Why y'all so mean with me?" *Que même.* I said, "What I do so wrong?" I tell him I worked all my life, and I'm poor, me too. And I don't know . . . Florence is come mean, too, not just Pai. Florence, he's go to the store for me. If I ask him. Other than that, he don't offer.

Mae-Mae tell me she want me to go stay there with all of them at that motel, when I'm come *old* old. On the little *apartment* on the back. When I'm old and I can't cook no more, Mae-Mae gonna bring me a plate. *Peut-être.* But I'm not sure I'm gonna go there, me. I *like* my little house right here in Ville Platte.

• • •

When my husband, DeJean, died, I have sixty-three years, me. When I'm marry him, it was *janvier*, January. I have just sixteen. Sixteen. Year. Old. Can you imagine?

We had all those years together. I miss him, bad, *cher*.

He was just sixty-five, him, *pauvre bête*. He holler at me, "Ortense! Ortense! *Je suis malade! Je suis malade!*" and he grab his heart tight. I'm take him some Coke and some peppermint. That's good when you have the *mal au ventre*. Helps make you burp. But his face is all white. All white. I'm scare, me. I'm run outside to Florence and Versie's *la bas*.

"Y'all come! Y'all come help me! *Il a eu mal au coeur! Il a eu mal au coeur! Il a eu mal au coeur!*"

• • •

When I'm first married with DeJean, I take a job at the big canning factory, me. All day long I cut *des patates* and stand on front that big, um . . . In French you say *tapis roulant*. You know what that is? All those *patates* I cut pass *comme ça* to go on the next place where they get wash. It's um, let's see. Um. Assembly line! No, no no. It's not that. It's uh . . . a con-vey-or belt. Con-vey-or belt! That's what that is. Conveyor belt.

But that's my work. I stand there and cut *patates* all day.

And I like that work, me.

Except my feet hurt so bad at the end of the day, but that's okay. I get a dollar-fifty an hour. And I like to work, me. I work hard. It's a good place over there. I get to see some people and talk while we work. That's much better than stay home. To me anyway. Some people don't like to go, but I like to go.

I stand on my feet all day peeling them *patates* and then come home and wash my dress, so it can dry and I can put it on again the next day. Like I said, I'm happy to have that work. Not everybody can work.

Poor old Miss Fournerat. She live over there by that gully. She can't work, her. She got bad legs. She try to come to the canning factory for a job she can do sitting down, but they didn't want her. They can tell that she not make enough work like the rest of us. *Pauvre bête.*

Now DeJean work hard, him too. DeJean make a little *forgeron* shop where he fix things for people. *Forgeron.* On English, that means "blacksmith." I know that word. He melt that metal and fix those horseshoe. There was a lot of horses all around Ville Platte in those days. So there was plenty of work for him to do. He fix all kinds of things for the people. Them horseshoes, mostly, but he fix them iron fences, wheels for them horse buggies, tools for work, broke *bicyclettes* even, and one man brought a lamp that broke. So he fix it, just like new. He had a good business there. Everybody like him.

I like DeJean's work too, because that *forgeron* shop was right there outside behind where we used to put the car. So he was there all day, and I was at the canning factory. At night I come home, and he was all black in the face from that fire. It was hot for him in the summertime, but he didn't care. He worked hard. We both worked hard, *cher.*

My DeJean had another job, him. He was a *traiteur.* On English, they call that a healer. A faith healer. He put his hands on people and said his prayers over them. If everything was just right—the prayers, the way he moved his hands, the strong force from the sick person, then it would work. They would leave already feeling better or would get better soon. There are a lot of *traiteurs* here around Ville Platte. For this job, though, he didn't get no money. People would bring him a chicken or a used coat, or some *patates* from their garden. We got a pretty *gâteau au chocolat* from a lady that come all the way from Baton Rouge. She had that rheumatism—something I got myself. DeJean told her that he wouldn't be able to make it all go away, but that if she had a strong belief, that she would feel better *que même*. When she was leaving, she tried to pay him with money, but I had to explain to her that that is not necessary. That *des traiteurs* don't take no money because that's a gift they got from God. And God never asks for money for His help. Anyway, that woman went all the way back to Baton Rouge, and don't you know she came back two days later with that *gâteau au chocolat!*

• • •

Pauvre bête. When DeJean died there was no one around to help him. He had a heart attack right there on my living room floor. I tried my best to help him, *cher*, but he didn't make it. It's sad, though, that all his life he helped heal people, and when it was his time to be healed, there was no one around who could help him quick enough. Everybody asked about who would get his gift when he died, but he didn't tell nobody. He was probably going to pass that down to one of Eliza's girls, but he didn't get to do that, so all that *traiteur* tradition in our family is probably *finis. C'est vraiment triste.* It's very sad, *cher.*

And I miss him. He's gone. It's *all* gone now. I don't have no work no more. After that job I didn't work for a long time, but then I got me a job making *boudin.* I used to cook the meat and chop *des oignons* and then work with that machine that put the *boudin* in the skin. I like that job too, because I like me some good *boudin, cher.* I used to bring some home for me and Pépère before he died.

But now I don't work no more at all. And I'm all by myself here in this little house. That *Lonesome* hurts so bad sometimes I can't hardly stand it.

• • •

So after DeJean die, Paillasse tell me to take the car and go to Snook's. If I go to the dance, they gonna say, 'She's *amoureuse.*' But Pai say, "You like everybody else. You don't have to stay on the house and cry all the time."

He tell me, "He's dead. It's not your fault. It's not your fault. You not kill him. The best thing you can do is fix yourself and go to Snook's. And you drive good. You know how to drive."

So I start to go to Snook's.

And don't you know, God do just what he want. Make you do what you need, even if you don't know it. At Snook's there was some good man who start to talk with me. And that's where I met Billy Joe. When I first see Billy Joe, he look nice enough. He had a happy face. He looked clean. He had some good hair, he was tall, him. And he was a good dancer. I start to dance with him. But there's three ladies: me and two other ones. I say to Billy Joe, "Take the younger one. There's more young than me. It's better you take the young one."

But any time the music start, he come get *me*. And you know I like to dance, me. And after a li'l while, the other men don't come to dance with me no more because they see I'm with Billy Joe.

At first, I didn't really like Billy Joe that much. I was still with DeJean in my head. That's hard for me. Hard to think that he was gone and buried. But Paillasse was right. It was time for me to let that go. But what made me start to like Billy Joe, *que même*, was that he was *good* to me. He didn't try to kiss on me. He never go wrong with me.

"I don't want to do any of *that*," I tell him. "I want to dance and have me a good time." Not *that* kind of a good time. So, he respect me. That made me start to love him, *peut-être*. He was good for me. He never let me go to see Mae-Mae and the kids and not give me one or two or three or five dollars to have me some money with me. He's call me "Tee" and "Hon" and whatever. He's more flattering than DeJean was with me. DeJean talk like Florence and Versie sometimes. But that's okay. DeJean was a good man, too.

Boy, but that Billy Joe.

He drank. Yes, but I decided it was okay because it was not just him who drank. Most of the time he was not a problem for me, but then sometimes he made some *tracas* for me. I figured out how to put my money, so he wouldn't get to it to buy him some liquor. I know he look on my purse and my drawers in the bedroom, so I hide my money in my curtains, *cher*. He never thought to look in the curtain, so that way I hold on to my money. I don't have too much, so I have to find a way to keep what I got.

One day he got mad because he couldn't find no money on the house, and he holler at me, "Tee! Why you so mean to me? Why you don't trust me? You know I'm a good man!" He holler and holler but he never hit me or push me. When he get too *couillon*, I go to Madame Hadley next door. Marie Hadley always knows my troubles, all my life. I don't like to go to Florence and Versie's house when that happen, because they don't like Billy Joe, and they judge me. Madame Hadley don't judge me. She help me. I stay on her house on her sofa sometimes when Billy Joe get too *couillon* for me, *cher*. You know "*couillon?*" *Couillon*—that means "crazy." Billy Joe was a big *couillon* sometime.

No matter what, I was glad to have somebody on my house with me. I'm scare to be by myself at night. Them niggs—*um*, them niggas, they bang on the door and try to get in at Mémère Soileau's house *la bas*.

I know Morris tell me, "Don't say 'nigga,' Mémère," and I know he's right. But that's all we know, us old people. That's how they call themselves, so I don't know what else to say. I say 'negress,' too, so you know when it's a woman I'm talking about. Because that's the word, *peut-être*.

Anyhow, Mémère Soileau have a dog like me, but no man on the house. They know if you got somebody with you. They watch you. And they know. Mémère Soileau's dog bark and bark at the nigg . . . niggas, when they bang on her door. And she call the police. They come, but them niggas run. I'm scare, me. I wouldn't like to be Mémère Soileau all by myself like that. *Pauvre bête.*

9 | That Christmas Glow

By early December, Daddy turned his attention to readying the front of the property for Christmas, and particularly to the fir trees that stood, one each, directly in front of every motel room, purposefully planted there by Mr. C. H. to provide a discreet veil over the comings and goings of the guests. There were twenty in all.

One by one, using two brand-new pruning loppers he had purchased from Harry Smith's Hardware in town especially for this job, he and Andy brutally hacked back the once-bountiful bottoms of each fir. It was my job to pull the felled branches away from the trees and pile them up for burning later. My hands quickly became coated with the sticky sap that I would find frustratingly impossible to wash off with just soap and water.

"Go outside and use some turpentine," Daddy said later when he saw me trying to scrub away the sap at the kitchen sink.

After lopping all the bottoms of the firs, the next step in the decimation party involved using the significantly less violent hedge clippers, with which Daddy "sculpted" the remaining treetops into smooth orbs, a job he preferred to do himself, lest Andy or I somehow manage to further destroy what was left of the tree. The resulting effect of stripped trunks and rounded tops looked like green drumsticks poking out of the ground. But the freshly cut firs did emit a soothing, and somewhat dizzying, pine bouquet that put the smell of Christmas, quite literally, in the air.

"You didn't have to chop them up so much," Momma complained when she saw them. "I liked them full. They looked like actual Christmas trees before. Now they look terrible."

It all was particularly ironic because Daddy's hacking project was in preparation for anointing the trees with cords of the multicolored pointy Christmas light bulbs that were still in vogue at the time. He had envisioned that, along with the neon tube lights that already illuminated the perimeter of the motel and apartment buildings, the Christmas lights would be a nighttime sight to behold. The combination of neon tubing and Christmas bulbs did in fact prove to be rather striking and Christmassy, but by daylight, unlit, the poor trees just looked naked and sad. Momma was beside herself with disappointment in the result.

"Well, they'll fill out again by next year," Daddy replied, ceding that he'd overdone it on the fir trees. They didn't. The decimated firs were to live out their remaining days on earth as green drumsticks.

To accompany the lighted trees, Momma also ordered lights for hanging around the picture windows on the house and the bushes in front of the apartments on the other side of the property, all selected from the Montgomery Ward catalog. When it was all plugged in and lit up, the spectacle attracted a nightly parade of gawkers who drove the three miles from town for the show.

• • •

Improvements to the property continued another full year. Daddy led the removal and pruning of most of the property's overgrowth. He and Andy dismantled and hauled off the abandoned water cistern, and despite protests from Gilda and Glenda and Dicky and me, they also took down the grape arbor, after it was found to be infested with termites.

By the next December, Momma, having gotten over Daddy's green drumstick catastrophe, was inspired by the success of the previous year. She returned to the Montgomery Ward catalog, from which she ordered a "life-sized" plastic Santa and reindeer set for the lawn in front of the office, and a snowman, again "life-sized," to be flanked by two yardstick-high red candles with white wax drips and yellow flames, all standing guard in front of the never-used formal entryway at the center of the house.

It was a full tableau. The twenty fir trees and the house's big picture windows all aglow in colored bulbs, Santa Claus sitting in his red sleigh, a sack of toys slung over his shoulder, and issuing a virtually perceptible "Ho Ho Ho!" as his reindeer, perched in mid-air, were about to take flight, and all presided over by a happy Mr. Snowman standing sentry in the glow of two magnificent Christmas candles. Surely, it was one of the most elaborate Christmas displays the town of Eunice had ever seen, rivaled only by St. Landry Bank's picture window display featuring a fully realized mechanical Santa whose sizable body oscillated this way and that; a gloved white hand slowly waved to people in their cars below as they drove down Second Street. Though he was standing next to an eight-foot-high shiny aluminum Christmas tree illuminated by a rotating color wheel that cast red, then gold, then green hues onto its sparkly foil branches, the bank display paled in comparison to the multilayered light show at the Stone Motel. And once again, the nightly parade of gawkers drove the three miles to see the spectacle.

• • •

A light sleeper, Gilda was awakened by the sunlight beginning to overtake and wash out the Christmas lights wrapped around the fir trees in front of the motel rooms below. The glow had filtered easily through the window sheers in her and Glenda's bedroom upstairs. It was a cool December morning, exactly a week before Christmas, a Thursday. She really didn't much feel like getting out from under the covers, but she needed to pee, so she sat up, stretched a bit, got out of bed and walked over to the bathroom. As she returned to her bed, she noticed the light through the window was moving. Unbelievable at first, it hit her bluntly that it wasn't sunlight at all. It was *fire*.

"FIRE! FIRE! FIRE! FIRE!" she screamed, gasping for breath.

Glenda shot up in her bed. "What? Fire? What?" she said in a stupor. Her Big Ben alarm clock said 2:10 a.m.

Cassie, in her room just down the hall from theirs, jumped out of bed and looked through the curtains over her window to see the ominous orange glow from over the pitched roof of the garage.

"There's a fire!" Gilda screamed again, running in her nightgown barefoot through Cassie's room and bounding down the stairs, with Glenda flailing right behind her. Cassie wrapped herself in her bedspread, and ran right behind them down the stairs.

A jumble of all three panicked voices, screaming:

"Fire, everybody!"

"Get up!"

"We're on fire!"

"Hurry!"

Momma and Daddy, and Andy, Dicky, and I all emerged startled from our beds. An immense wave of collective, magnetic adrenaline pushed everyone through the house right behind the girls and out the front door to see stunning orange-red flames shooting into the sky from the center of the first section of the motel, in the area of Room 5. Surreally, all the Christmas lights were still *on*, even in front of that room, though flames licked up at the night sky from its roof.

"Oh my God!" Cassie screamed. Gilda and Glenda held onto each other, and the rest of us stood barefoot on the cold grass in front of the office paralyzed for a moment, then suddenly everyone seemed to be screaming or crying, or both.

"No! No! No! No!" Daddy said in a drone, his normally dark red face now milk-white in the horror.

"Call somebody! Call the fire department!" he yelled out to Momma, but she was already inside on the phone doing exactly that and doing her level best to hold back the panic striking through her soul. As she tried to talk calmly to the person on the other end of the line, she had unknowingly made a fist so tight her fingernails were cutting through the flesh of her right palm.

After the call, she gathered herself and ran back to her bedroom to collect Scotty, still asleep in his crib, and wrapped him up in a bundle. She gathered his baby things and headed back out, to find Cassie standing there with outreached arms.

"I'll take him," she offered, and did so.

"Get your shoes and coats, everybody!" Daddy was yelling outside.

The flames over Room 5 were now reaching over towards Rooms 4 and 6 as well.

"We gotta move the car out of the garage," Daddy said. "Let's move!"

Moments later we were all in our coats and shoes, and then outside again waiting for the fire trucks and still stunned, but fully awake. Our minds were racing. Daddy got in his truck and backed it out away from the buildings; Momma did the same with her car.

Andy and the twins were banging on the doors of all the rooms to make sure people got out. Only four rooms were occupied that night. Customers in Rooms 10 and 7 got in their cars and drove away, but one man, who'd been in Room 12, pulled his car over to an empty spot across the road, and went back to sleep. The car belonging to the only other customer that night, the man who'd occupied Room 5, was no longer in front of that room.

As two fire trucks, sirens blaring, pulled onto the property, a section of the roof right over Room 5 collapsed with a crunch that sent more flames, a burst of embers, and smoke in all directions. And as if choreographed for maximum horror, the overheated power transformer at the top of a pole at the edge of the driveway exploded, sending its own embers and metallic smoke billowing outward, and cutting the power to the entire property. In a flash, the bright, multicolored lights on the twenty fir trees and picture windows, the Santa-and-reindeer set, Mr. Snowman and the two Christmas candles, the neon tubes of the motel sign and those that illuminated the perimeter of the motel and apartment buildings—all went out.

"Y'all need to stay with Momma in the car," Daddy called out to us kids. "Except Andy. You need to be with me," he said as the two of them ran over to meet with the firemen, who were scrambling to connect their hoses.

The fire chief could be heard on his radio calling for more trucks. "See if y'all can get the Opelousas guys over here," he said. "We won't be able to handle this one by ourselves." Then to Daddy, "Is there a pond on the property?"

"Yes. We got one behind the building and another one down at the edge of the property over there," he said, pointing east.

"We're going to have to pump that one when we run out of the water in our trucks," said the fire chief.

"Do whatever you need. Go! Go! Go!" Daddy said. "Go!"

In the car, Momma and Cassie, who was still holding Scotty, sat in the front seat, with Gilda, Glenda, and Dicky and me in the back. It was impossible to stop shaking.

Suddenly a tap at the car window. It was Daddy. "That fire chief said for us to get any small valuables we can carry out of the house, but y'all gonna have to hurry. He ain't sure they will be able to save the house."

At this, Momma, who had been biting her lip and clinching her bloody fist to maintain her composure, could not hold it in anymore. She gasped and began sobbing, a howling of grief from deep within her. Cassie grabbed her and hugged her. All of us were sobbing now.

"Y'all need to hurry," Daddy said, trying to keep his own voice calm. His hands were shaking. "Go!"

Moments later I was in my bedroom, getting my schoolbooks and my favorite shirt and a pair of pants from the closet. I was dumbfounded about what else, if anything, I should grab. *I can't think. I can't think. I can't think.*

I found myself walking through the dark house carrying my stuff, looking at the new living room sofa and behind it, the fancy drapes the Melancons left, the matching side chair and curlicue coffee table with the marble top, the wrought iron French Quarter trellis, Mrs. Melancon's Viennese crystal chandelier. Through the door, to the long, oval brown dining room table where we celebrated holidays and played cards and board games, the built-in china hutch that held bric-a-brac and Momma's crochet stuff instead of any fine china; then into the kitchen, with its green laminate breakfast nook, the little shelf of condiments; and then finally, into what was the Melancons' TV room, where now sat Momma's big boxy deep freezer, which held venison, squirrel meat, and those TV dinners Momma bought for us for those nights when Daddy was eating at one of his Lions Club or Kiwanis Club meetings. Then out through the back door, facing the laundry building, Room 21, and the tractor shed. *Are they all going to burn too?* And finally around the side of the house and back over to the car.

Glenda and Dicky were standing at the open trunk. Gilda was still in the house gathering her favorite things: her guitar, her Monopoly game, an oversized sketchpad, a fishing-tackle box that held her art pencils, and a pillowcase filled with her best clothes.

Glenda had attempted to load everything she owned into a bed sheet that she could grab up and haul outside, but that proved too heavy and ungainly to move, so she narrowed her selection to just the essentials: a box of long brass hair clips she used nightly to keep her bangs straight, some underwear, a good pair of jeans, and her hair dryer in its blue and white case; its flexible hose attachment dangled below it.

Cassie emerged with her guitar, a box of photos, some of her favorite record albums, her Mayfair Vanity Mirror (the settings on which delighted me because they allowed her to see herself in daylight, evening, or office light), a pillowcase stuffed with clothes, and the big floppy, pink stuffed dog she kept on her bed.

Dicky brought out Mr. Hadley, a furry, black, stuffed-animal monkey with a rubber face, feet and hands, one of which held a rubber banana. Mr. Hadley was named after the husband of Marie Hadley, Mémère's best friend and neighbor in Ville Platte. He salvaged nothing else.

I put my stuff inside the trunk, and the three of us stood there silently. Another truck had arrived. I counted eleven firemen in all. Three spouts of water trained on the burning building; fire hoses crisscrossed all over the yard and driveway; the red lights of the trucks still looping. The fire had taken over Rooms 3, 4, 5, 6, and 7.

A few yards from us, just behind all the firemen, with his back to us, his tall frame haloed by the eerie, horrifying glow of the growling fire, stood Daddy, motionless.

We would not know until he turned around after a long while that he had been standing there on the gravel, paralyzed. And crying. It was the first time any of us had seen him cry. He had made many of us cry over the years, but the man had never shed a tear that we knew about, until that moment. When he finally came over to us, we could see his strong hard face had softened in defeat, his eyes were beaten downward, his mind, like ours, now apparently erased by the shock of it all. We could not know what our dad was thinking through all this, but it was not difficult to imagine that as he stood there watching his motel burn, he was seeing his big gamble at making something more of himself than a mere gas station owner, go up, literally, in flames.

• • •

When the fire trucks were all gone but one, a little after seven that morning, the longest half of the L-shaped building, the entire line of rooms from Room 1 to Room 8, had been reduced to a black pile. A putrid odor, a mix of all things burnable, hung in the air. Burnt wood, burnt stone Baltimore siding, burnt roof shingles, burnt glass, burnt rugs, burnt numbered doors, burnt windows, burnt beds that vibrated for a quarter, burnt toilets and bathtubs, burnt TV sets, burnt air conditioners, burnt nightstands, burnt side chairs, burnt wall hangings, burnt "Do Not Disturb" doorknob signs, burnt Cashmere Bouquet motel soaps, burnt towels and sheets and bedspreads, burnt stone columns that supported the building's portico, burnt drumstick fir trees, burnt Christmas lights and extension cords.

Burnt.

Among the rooms lost was Room 2, where Mémère liked to sleep and keep her stuff when she came to visit us to escape her loneliness for a week or so. She would bring her electric percolator with her, so before bed she could brew herself a pot of coffee. Room 2, like all the others, was different from each other room, and exactly the way Mrs. Melancon had decorated it all those years ago. It had two single beds facing east and between them, a little brown oak one-drawer nightstand with ornate spindle legs. Lamps in the room were standard mid-1930s-issue hotel supply company lamps. Pale wooden round bases and stems, with greenish-yellow shades. The bedspreads were gold, green and white popcorn stitch still intact from the previous decade. As she drank her coffee, we watched *The Monkees* on Channel 5 (she loved watching TV; it was how she learned to speak English), then went to bed.

Also lost was Room 8, which had been used as a storage room for extra mattresses and box springs, desks, chairs, nightstands, and odds and ends for the rooms, and where Momma had secretly stashed all of our Christmas presents. It would not dawn on her until the next day that the presents, like all the contents of that room, had been destroyed.

Not burnt: most of Room 9, and all of Rooms 10, 11, 12, 14, and 15 (in the time-honored tradition, there was no Room 13). There was water and smoke damage that would render them unrentable for a while, but in the end, the short part of the motel's L was still standing.

As was our house. The little Formstone arch that connected the motel building to the house was credited by the fire chief with keeping Room 1 from completely collapsing onto the garage, which suffered only a scorched outer wall, and a few scorched slate shingles on its roof.

We still had a house.

• • •

By sunrise Thursday morning, the fire had been fully tamped down, and the trucks had gone. We were all still in a state of shock and disbelief. Each of our faces had been washed over with a blank gaze: eyes bloodshot, cheeks and mouths pulled downward by the weight of our new reality; and an eerie pall had taken over where just twenty-four hours before, the house was filled with the chatter and hum of a big family fully awake and readying for another day. But we got right back to work. There would be a lot to do.

Momma suggested that those of us who wanted to should get dressed and go to school. Cassie and Andy and Gilda and Dicky wanted to stay and start with the cleanup. I felt I needed to be away from it all for a while, so I thought that going to school would be a good way to clear my head. Glenda agreed and joined me at the road when the bus came. The bus, usually filled with the sounds of children talking, was tomb silent.

"Everybody okay?" asked Mr. Chester the bus driver, in a tone more somber than his usual dour drawl.

"Yes, we're all okay, Mr. Chester," Glenda said. She sat on the girls' side facing the untouched rice field across the road, and I sat on the boys' side, facing the still-smoldering motel.

As the bus pulled away I could see that in the yard Daddy and Andy were already busy at work. I immediately regretted my decision to go to school. I felt a tear roll down my cheek and hit my shirt pocket.

The school day would be short. Within a half hour of the first bell, after the news had begun to spread through town, the principal, Mr. Thibodeaux, tapped on Mrs. Wyble's door and after a few words with him in the hall, she approached me and said she had just learned about the fire. At that, I could not control the tears I'd been suppressing all morning. She ushered me out to Mr. Thibodeaux's office, where I sat silently until Cassie came to pick me up and take me, and then Glenda, at a school across town, home.

. . .

Back at the motel, anything that looked hazardous was being heaped onto the burnt pile. Daddy had already arranged for bulldozers and dump trucks to start clearing away the ruins. The workmen would bulldoze, hoist and haul for the next four days, including Sunday.

Cassie and the twins and I attacked the surviving Rooms 10 through 15. We removed all the bedding and rugs, hauled the mattresses and furniture outside to air out, and tossed out anything not salvageable. We scrubbed the floors, the walls and ceilings, and the smoke-stained tubs and toilets and lavatories.

At her beauty shop in town, running on sheer adrenaline, Momma kept every one of her appointments from Friday onward. She had to be there. The money she made standing on her feet ten hours a day before returning home to join in the cleanup, would keep us all fed and intact while the motel was gradually put back together.

. . .

The L would not be rebuilt as such. The insurance company said it wouldn't provide coverage unless the new building was not connected to anything else. So instead, a year later, after the work was all done, the motel became an "11" instead of an "L": two rows of rooms facing each other, with a parking lot separating them. For the new row of rooms, the Formstone siding was no longer available, so Daddy settled on plain beige bricks for the outer walls. Our world, and the little motel at the heart of it, was never going to be quite the same.

10 | Our Father

His thick black work boot clamps me to the ground so I can't escape. He pulls out a piece of electrical cord from a big pocket of his coveralls and forces me to watch him.

"Look at me! Look at me, gotdammit!"

He flicks open his pocket knife and starts to skin some of the rubber coating off the wire. "Look at me! Look at me!" He peels the wire carefully, stroking it with his knife.

He is making a whip.

Of all the beatings before, I can sense that this one coming is going to be really bad. He wants me to know this.

I squint to watch him skin the wire.

"Open your damned eyes!"

I need to prepare myself. My throat is dry, and I feel myself trembling.

I suppose I am guilty. I did chisel a piece of stone off that motel column. Just a little piece. No bigger than a biscuit. A piece where the blue color on it was still intact, with no black burn marks on it. I thought the whole thing was going to be hauled away with the rest of the ashes and pieces of the building. All I wanted was a souvenir. I didn't know he had plans to reuse that column. I didn't know.

But in that moment, I can't speak to tell him any of this. He whittles the bottom third of the electrical cord down to the copper wires inside, which soon splay out, like a whisk.

One-two-three.

He tears down at me with his electrical wire whip.

Please, God, let me wake from this dream.

Our Father, who art in Heaven, hallowed be thy name . . .

The hot-cold stings hit my arms and open hands first, then my back, and my face, and my legs.

. . . forgive us our trespasses . . .

The more I scream and flail, the angrier and angrier he gets, and the wire whip comes down faster and faster and harder and harder.

. . . as we forgive those who trespass against us.

I begin to see this bizarre scenario as if floating above it or looking into it from a telescope. It unfolds in silence. Sometimes in surreal slow motion; other times it speeds up like film out of control before it flaps loose in the projector. Light filters out everything but the two characters, a towering man with a deep red complexion branded into his skin by years in the sun, and a skinny, pale, ten-year-old boy, screaming and flailing on the grass.

Spit, sweat, and blood droplets hang in mid-air.

I see the boy clamped down to the ground under giant, weathered work boots. His body writhes. His arms dart about and his legs kick wildly as he tries in vain to stop the blows. Above, a massive right arm swings down onto the child again, and again, and again.

. . . deliver us from evil.

"Where is everybody? Somebody please stop this! Is everyone hiding?" None of that enters my mind as I observe from above. There is no room for that.

Abruptly, the "dream" is burst by an urgent, anguished, beastly howl that fills the yard. The howl wakes me into full consciousness again. Now it is the real me on the ground, fully in my body. I am not dreaming. I am convulsing. For a moment, I can no longer feel the pain bearing down on me, not because of Pépère's prayer, but because of this distracting *sound* that continues and absorbs everything. What *is* this sound? Everything is drenched with this bellowing howl. It bounces off the buildings, bursts up from the grass, and is hurled loudly by the trees in the yard. And it resonates, like the low, second note of a foghorn, "Oohhhhhhnnnnn," with the lung-scraping pain of a whooping cough. An ancient, coarse, guttural cry that rises up from deep down within a beast clutched by the teeth of a trap gnashing into its flesh.

Through squinted eyes blurred with tears, I again see the electrical wire-whip tearing down on me, again feel the repeated hot-cold slashes of copper and rubber, and the grinding claw of the heavy work boot crushing into my leg, and then realize that the sound—horrible, impossible, *inhuman*—has been coming from me.

11 | Billy Joe

illy Joe Olberg showed up one Saturday night at Snook's, a low-ceilinged, cavernous Cajun honky-tonk just west of Ville Platte, and the best night out in all of Evangeline Parish. At Snook's you could order a "setup," which included a fifth of Old Charter, six Cokes, and a bucket of ice, though Billy Joe was partial to MD 20/20 or a quart of malt liquor.

"Yep. I could see just by lookin' at 'er that she was a good woman," he said, explaining how he and Mémère met when she first introduced him to our family that Easter Sunday in her house on East Jackson Street. Seeing how he was to be Momma's stepfather and step-grandfather to us kids, this meeting was important to everyone, most especially Billy Joe.

"And let me tell you, she was quite the dancer," he continued. "Quite the dancer. She had no competition amongst all those ladies there," he drawled in his sticky Alabama twang. "Tee-heee."

Six feet two inches tall and skinny, with enough stringy, graying yellow-brown hair left at the sides and back to convincingly cover his otherwise balding head, Billy Joe Olberg looked and sounded like he belonged elsewhere. Mémère had at least a decade on him, but his lax posture, the dark semicircles under his eyes, and the red blotches on his face made it hard to believe there was any difference in their ages.

He had arrived in Ville Platte on a Continental Trailways bus two months before, from Daphne, Alabama, following a tip from a brother-in-law who had heard about construction jobs in Louisiana. The timing couldn't have been more opportune. He had been warned by more than a few denizens of Daphne that he should think about making a new start. *Someplace else*.

In Daphne, Billy Joe had amassed a string of complaints against him. Fueled most often by his overfamiliar relationship with MD 20/20, his rap sheet included urinating in public, vagrancy, rent evasion, disorderly conduct, and default on personal loans.

"Pee-po don't lack it iffin you stiff 'em," his brother-in-law Johnny Jack said to him as he boarded the bus. "You attract trouble lack shit attracts flies, and it don't help that you got that glass eye and that hole in your head."

Billy Joe couldn't argue with that. He was fully aware that his two distinct deformities, each acquired from a different mishap that he refused to explain whilst sober, made people uncomfortable when he pointed them out, something he only did after the MD 20/20 loosened his tongue. If he could stay sober, no one would ever be the wiser. And that was a big If. The glass eye looked pretty real, and you'd have to be standing over him or be pretty tall to notice the divot in his skull at all.

The story was, he had lost his eye rolling around in the dirt in a schoolyard fight with Raymond McInish, his best friend, who had grabbed his head like a bowling ball, plunging his thumb clean through Billy Joe's right eye socket. Not ten years later Billy Joe acquired that notch in his head one afternoon, drunk out of his mind, when he tripped and fell headfirst into a set of swinging doors. He suffered a concussion but pulled through well enough. He'd be plagued by headaches for the next three years, but beyond that had no other symptoms.

• • •

At Snook's that Saturday night Billy Joe met Mémère for the first time, he danced with her and only her, even though she urged him to dance with the other ladies.

"I promised her I'd be up yonder the next Sirr'dy night and the next after that if she's gonna be there too," he said, putting his arm around Mémère as she rolled lemons for the Easter lemonade. "And sure enough, she showed up."

Mémère explained that she had indeed looked forward to their second and subsequent meetings at Snook's. It had been nearly three years since DeJean fell over on the living room floor with a heart attack, his third, and the one that would kill him. There was something still very young about her at sixty. She was in great physical shape, loved to dance, and had lots of stamina. And she had finally had enough of staying home on weekends.

"He flatters me," she said. "Nobody else is doing that. So I dance with him, me. He was a good dancer. We pass us a good time." She looked happy.

That was enough to cast away any doubts that may have danced in our minds about this seemingly odd coupling.

• • •

In May, after they married at the Ville Platte courthouse, Momma urged Daddy to help the newlyweds get a start by hiring Billy Joe to help him and Andy with carpentry work around the motel. He and Mémère would set up house in Apartment 18–19.

"You got any experience putting up siding?" Daddy asked Billy Joe on his first day of work.

"Well, not exactly, but I have done quite a bit of carpentry work, so I reckon I can figure it out pretty quick," said Billy Joe.

"I got these two buildings and the back-a that one there we gotta do," Daddy said, pointing to the laundry, the Apartment 21 building, and the backside of apartments 16–17 and 18–19.

"That's gotta be our first job," Daddy explained. "After that, we'll get up there on that roof of 21 and pull up all that old tin and put down some new shingles. You think you can handle that?"

"Oh yessir!" said Billy Joe. "That shouldn't be too complicated."

For the first few weeks the work progressed smoothly. Turned out Billy Joe was indeed a capable carpenter and took direction eagerly. What was not apparent at first, at least not until about a month into the work, was that he was not as capable of staying sober. Apparently, at night, back in the apartment with Mémère, he had been sneaking more than a few chugs of MD 20/20. When he didn't show up for work one morning, Daddy rang their apartment.

"*Allo*?" Mémère answered.

"*Allo*, Ortense," Daddy said. They spoke briefly in French. He told her he was wondering where Billy Joe was. When she reported that he had a *mal au ventre*, a stomachache, last night, but was on his way, Daddy asked her to let him know he should join him and Andy behind the old motel building, where they were working that day.

"Okay, *bien*," she said and hung up.

Behind the building, Daddy and Andy had already hauled out a pickup-load of siding that would go over the old, peeling clapboard. It was the last building on the property that would get the "faux stone" tar-based siding treatment Daddy thought would tie in well with the Formstone that covered the front side of all the old buildings and the beige brick on the new one.

An hour passed before Daddy decided to check on Billy Joe again. Again, Mémère answered the phone. This time, however, she informed Daddy that Billy Joe couldn't work that day because of his stomachache.

"Okay, well . . .," Daddy started to tell her before she interrupted him.

"*Demain*," she said. "Tomorrow."

The siding and roofing work continued with or without Billy Joe for a couple more weeks. In that time there were at least two more occasions where Billy Joe showed himself to be too unreliable to count on for real help, so Daddy finally had to break the news to Momma that Billy Joe would have to go back to Ville Platte.

"That's not what I had wanted," Daddy told Momma. "Your momma can stay as long as she likes, but this is just not working out. That man is not paying attention, and I have to babysit him more than I have time for. I got too much to do to have to keep up with that kinda thing."

"Let me tell her," Momma said. "She'll understand."

Mémère did understand. She'd been getting her own education about the fact that Billy Joe had a serious drinking problem and that it didn't look like it would be going away any time soon. Plus, while she liked to be near all of us, deep down she missed her house in Ville Platte.

"Y'all still gonna come visit, okay?" she asked as Dicky and I hugged her goodbye.

"Definitely," I replied. "Soon as we can."

Their time with us at the motel had a little bit of a numbing effect on Dicky and me. Later, when we did spend some time at their house in Ville Platte, the atmosphere there was noticeably changed, but not so much that we felt the need to stay away completely. But with Billy Joe around, we weren't ourselves as much, couldn't relax and be as unselfconscious as before he came into her life. He made an effort, but we just couldn't warm up to him.

"I don't like it when he's there," Dicky said. "I wish we could go back to when it was just her."

"Me too," I told him. "But I still love being there with her."

"Me too," he said.

It was a situation Mémère clearly recognized, but she didn't know what to do about it.

"Y'all miss Pépère?" she asked me one afternoon on her back porch when we were alone. I nodded my head. "I know y'all do. I miss him, me too, *cher*," she said, looking up into the clouds.

12 | Apache

On this morning Daddy's dark, lined face was deep red-brown, a deeper dark than normal, like he had been holding his breath for a while, and, although he was technically breathing, the veins at his temples looked like they could burst at any moment. Sweat dripped from the corners of his forehead, even though it was twenty-six degrees outside; the little rattling heater attached to the underside of the dashboard was well outmatched by the rain and sleet that pelted the Apache. For anyone with swampy bayou blood in his veins, forty degrees was pretty damned cold, let alone twenty-six, and especially under this kind of relentless rain. No one said anything as he struggled. Big, calloused left hand on the steering wheel, left boot on and off the clutch, right boot on the gas, right fist gripping the rubber-knobbed stick shift, doing his best to keep the truck upright on its four tires, from sliding back down the steep, saturated slope of the Bayou Rouge levee.

Andy, fourteen, bloated in all his layers: tee-shirt underneath sweatshirt, underneath flannel shirt, underneath all-weather coat, and topped off with an ear-flapped hat. His legs were covered with long johns; two pairs of thick socks over those; then a pair of good jeans and, finally, rubber wading boots from Harry Smith's Hardware over all that.

Arms crossed, hands tucked into his armpits, he bounced in his seat, the squeaking springs making the only sound not coming from the rain, the scraping dry-rotted wipers, the racing engine, or the spinning tires beneath us.

I had on very similar clothes: layers on the legs and torso, but my coat wasn't as nice as Andy's; in fact, it was one of his hand-me-downs. A green corduroy Montgomery Ward's special he'd outgrown a couple of winters ago. My one pair of white athletic socks wasn't ample for this cold wet air. I couldn't feel my toes.

Somewhere in a pocket of our respective gear we each had a shiny new eight-dollar compass that Daddy had ordered through *Conservationist* magazine. When they arrived by parcel post, he handed one each to Andy and me, said he figured that we'd pay him back. A ten-year-old, I couldn't imagine where I'd get eight dollars, or, if I had that much money, that I'd use it to buy a compass. I told him I felt bad about accepting it, but he said I could take my time paying him back. I never did.

• • •

The 1959 Chevrolet Stepside Apache. On the outside, all rounded corners, except for the tailgate, which was secured on either side by a short chain link once encased in black rubber that had long since fallen off somewhere on the road. Fenders around the back tires like two big blue Twinkies. When it left that assembly line in Pontiac, Michigan, it was freshly painted a beautiful deep enameled twilight. Fifteen years in the merciless Louisiana summers, and the outer layer had been baked away and now came off powdery on your fingers. The Stepside feature, that little step on each side of the truck, right behind the doors, just big enough for two sets of little feet or one set of big feet, let you know its designers had thought about you. When we needed to haul something around the property, the step was the prized place to hitch a quick ride without having to sit inside or in the back, especially if the bed was already loaded down.

Inside the cab, a hard steel dashboard, also deep blue; a black, enamel-coated steel steering wheel; and one long gray vinyl seat with curved edges. The speedometer, which sat behind a chrome-framed horizontal rhombus-shaped glass, had long stopped working, so we never really knew how fast we were going. The windows were hand-operated, up and down, with a smaller triangle-shaped window, the vent window, that you pushed open with a little chrome latch to get some cross-ventilation. Gun rack on the rear window. The cab forever smelled like cold steel, vinyl, work boots, Kent cigarettes, and squirrel musk.

The little square heater was bracketed to the bottom of the dashboard. To turn it on you had to twist together the two gray wires that dangled below it, then flip a chrome toggle switch. It seemed to me to have been an afterthought to the designers of the truck, who had so thoughtfully included the steps on each side. I learned later, however, that the Apache did not come with a heater at all. That was an extra Daddy added himself in 1962, hence the *custom* ignition process.

Nonetheless, when the wire-twisting and toggling were done in sequence, the little heater immediately began sputtering just hard enough to break the chill in the cab. It relied a lot on the body heat of the passengers to do its job well. After a while, when the sun, the bodies, and the little heater had pooled their energies sufficiently, it would be necessary to turn off the heater by disconnecting the two gray wires; the toggle switch worked only to turn it on in either the up or down position; it was not required to turn it off.

Under the hood, the Apache's big V-8 engine gave it reliable power on the road, but against the slippery rise of the levee, the engine alone couldn't cut it without good tires to get some traction.

• • •

"Damned to hell, *non!*" Daddy yelled out to the world, his nose practically touching the windshield, struggling to see through the black, driving rain and sleet. The only illumination he had was coming from the headlights and the little red glow at the tip of his Kent. None of the interior electrics in that old Apache worked, so it was nearly a blackout in the cab.

"That's some serious rain," he said, a bit more resigned now. He had clearly decided it a bad idea to add to the fear and panic already apparent in us with more yelling. But he was so obviously struggling; a fierce, violent struggle against Mother Nature and the steep, slick levee. The tires whirred against the slick grass. Just as he was able to get enough traction to advance the truck a couple of yards up the side of the levee, the beast the situation had become at that point pulled us back down again, jerking all of our heads back, sliding us backward into the pitch-black below us until Daddy managed finally to get enough brake traction to stop the slide. The sleet came down faster and faster. Pack! Pack! Pack! against the old windshield and the steel roof above us. Pack! Pack! Pack!

And so upward, then downward again, then upward again, we went. Again, and again, and again.

And Daddy again jerked the steering wheel this way and that, but this time he approached the levee at an angle instead of perpendicular to the road above. My eyes puckered shut, I envisioned the slipping and twisting Apache suddenly flipping on its side and hurtling us all over and over and over again, down the levee and into Bayou Rouge below.

Once more, after advancing us only a few yards, the levee shoved us back down again, backward, and down further into the blackness pierced only by the red glow of the brake lights, which cast an eerie haze onto what had been our campsite. The idea that we'd ever actually make it up to the road at the top of the levee seemed so distant, so fearfully remote, such a fantasy.

• • •

Only a few short minutes before (it seemed hours had passed), around a quarter after one, Daddy had roused Andy and me from our sleeping bags, though none of us had really gotten any sleep; the old sour canvas of the big army tent had so many holes in it that as the rain and sleet pelted down, we had to contort ourselves to stay dry.

"Get up! We're going!" he yelled. "This weather don't look like it's going to let up. Y'all hurry before that levee gets too slick, or we'll be stuck down here!"

The musty old tent, which he'd acquired in World War II, was lashed by the rain and sleet as we scrambled, disoriented but somehow focused at the same time. We had slept fully dressed, a common practice in the woods in this cold, so it was only a matter of getting our boots and coats on quickly and hustling to get everything packed up and back into the Apache. For trips like this, the bed of the truck was fitted with a small white fiberglass camper shell that bolted into place. Hand-cranked louvered windows on either side, with a flip-up windowed door that latched closed against the tailgate. Because of the camper shell, once thrown inside, our camping gear was secure enough to get home. No need to pack it all in neatly under the circumstances.

We rolled up our sleeping bags and then scrambled to collect everything else: four folding chairs, a Coleman lantern, a galvanized five-gallon water jug with a spout, a cast iron Dutch oven, a smaller pot for frying, a little covered pot for making rice, and a paper grocery bag holding a few plastic plates, two plastic bowls, a pack of forks and drinking glasses, and some paper towels. All went right into the bed of the truck. The red ice chest that held lunchmeat, sliced yellow cheese, a few cokes and some beer went in next. And then the big tent itself. Had the circumstances been different, the folding and retying of it would have been somewhat more elaborate, but not today. We pulled up all the stakes around the tent, and the big thing collapsed on itself. We each grabbed a piece and all came together to bundle it as tightly as possible, then shoved the big, bulky wet thing into the truck. The whole process, from the time Daddy had yelled,

"Get up!" to the point where we were all finally sitting, wet, in the truck, had taken us sixteen minutes.

• • •

Daddy had lots to worry about, and it pissed him off that this camping trip was being screwed up by this stressful evacuation up the levee in the middle of the night. As much as he liked to tell a good story—and he knew this trip would one day make a good story if he could get us out in one piece to tell it—he was in no mood for this. For him the camping and hunting trips were his best escape from the daily reality back home. The motel he'd bought three years before still wasn't up to full speed since the cruel, soul-twisting fire the previous December took away half of it. The insurance money covered only 80 percent of the rebuilding costs; the ugly truth was that until it was up and running at full capacity, he wouldn't be able to pull in enough to pay for the rebuilding. Ultimately, he would have to settle for a motel that was one-quarter smaller than the one he'd just begun to pay for. With the arrival of Alisa in February, he now had ten mouths to feed including his own, and that reality seldom left his mind. Even with Momma working ten-hour days in her beauty shop to help put food on the table, it was a fact that our big family could easily find itself at the very edge of survival with just one serious illness or even one more setback of any kind.

Daddy was a hard man, shaped as much by his past as so many of his generation who'd lived through World War II, and the Great Depression before that. He rarely talked about his war memories, but we all knew he kept a small collection of photos from those years in a little cardboard box on the top shelf in his closet. He had taken the photos with a Kodak 35-millimeter camera he bought when he enlisted: a few images of him and his war buddies facing the camera with their arms around each other's necks, but more than not, the photos showed the bodies of Holocaust victims piled in trenches. That he didn't dispose of the pictures showing the piles of bodies, or that he'd brush us away if we asked about them, betrayed a deeply embedded wound about that awful part of his young life. Surely he left the war a changed, considerably older-spirited man. How could he not have?

He had entered the war already hardened by the lousy hand life had dealt him and his fourteen siblings. Several of them wouldn't live to see their twentieth birthday; pneumonia was the most common cause for that.

It killed his mother a few weeks after she'd had her last baby, Earnestine. His father managed to find ways to keep everyone housed and fed by separating them, sending most of them to stay with relatives or neighbors, which was the case with Daddy and his brother Howard. The teenagers were handed over to the owner of a neighboring horse farm, where they slept each night in the barn and worked each morning before walking to school; then they did farm chores well after sundown each night, seven days a week. The call to war for them was a relief, an opportunity, an adventure, an escape. Howard joined up right away because at seventeen he was of age, or close enough, to get in. Daddy would work breaking horses on the farm another year before he could enlist.

• • •

Lately, it seemed that all these years later it was only in those deep woods on these camping and hunting trips where Daddy could find a few hours, maybe even a full day, of relief from the worries tugging at him from his current life or the occasional escape of one of the jarring memories of his past.

Even more so than Daddy, Andy was only ever in his element in the woods, camping and hunting. It was the one situation in the world where he was truly comfortable in his skin, where all his doubts disappeared. He was a quiet, easily intimidated teenager who worried more about his awkwardness around people, especially girls, and that was all made more complicated by a really bad complexion he felt had cursed him for no good reason.

"No matter what I do," he told Momma one Sunday morning in the kitchen, "it don't go away," his voice nearly cracking with frustration. Her advice, rooted in beauty school training, was to avoid foods that were believed to cause acne, like chocolate or anything fried, and to wash his face with the Phisoderm cleanser she gave him from her beauty shop. "And after you wash your face, you have to keep your hands away from it. You can't pick at it," she said. I felt awful for him. Cassie, the twins, and I all got pimples, but nothing like what Andy was suffering. It seemed he had been condemned to have bad skin, and it haunted him most every day.

Andy cleaved to Daddy even though he was the first of us to be on the receiving end of one of Daddy's powerful backhand slaps to the head or punches to the gut, or to wither from the berating rants about his inadequacies, such as his poor performance in school. Yet it was obvious that he wanted to become a man very much in the same vein as his daddy: forceful, strong, steely, powerful, feared, and that if he could just endure the violence long enough, he would grow up to be exactly that man.

In the woods Andy was fully in charge of his life. He loved nothing more than the leaves crunching and rustling at his feet, or on rainy days, the wet swamp, fecund logs, earthy odors of the bayous and sloughs, among the pine, oak, and the local favorite, cypress trees, with their knees poking out through the water. The squirrels and birds made him feel welcome and comfortable. If he was lucky, a deer might cross his path. He had bagged plenty of squirrels, but at fifteen, he had not yet had his first deer, and that made him anxious and excited with anticipation for each hunting trip.

• • •

On this trip I was not old enough to have my own hunting license but could hunt as long as I was with a licensed adult. Daddy's rule was that we had to be at least thirteen before we got our first rifle, and that was a couple years away for me. The camping trips were a way to build enthusiasm for the sport and the life that goes with it: getting up early enough to be in the woods, positioned and ready to shoot before daybreak; taking a two-hour drive in the Apache to get there; pitching a tent; cooking outdoors; swimming naked in the bayou. The only part of all that that enthused me was the cooking.

• • •

The night before the sleet storm Daddy had cooked squirrel *sauce piquant* in a cast-iron Dutch oven, a pot of rice, and a pile of French fries, each cooked in smaller cast-iron pots, and all done over an open fire. The sauce piquant involved chopped onions, bell peppers, garlic—it was my job to peel and chop those—and canned tomato paste and mushroom gravy, and of course, squirrel parts. A few weeks before, during squirrel hunting season, Daddy and Andy skinned, gutted, cut up, and had frozen several batches of squirrels they'd killed. If the fact that squirrels were rodents didn't put you off eating them, then witnessing the skinning and gutting, or their eyeless heads bobbing up and down in the pot usually did the trick. The best I could do when Daddy insisted I eat squirrel meat was to eat a leg, being careful not to bite down hard on a BB and concentrating instead on the sauce over rice, which was edible if I didn't think about it too much.

To this day, that night's French fries, however, dumped into a big paper grocery bag with salt and pepper, then shaken together to season them and remove the excess oil, are the best I've ever had. Something to do with the paper bag, which had infused a bit of its own wood-pulp flavor. I was thinking about those fries in the Apache that wet morning as we attempted to climb the levee, how they smelled coming out of the hot grease, and then after a good shake in the grocery bag. As the truck slipped this way and that, thoughts of those fries helped keep me from panicking.

I sat there in the Apache, wincing, hardly breathing, and working hard to push back the idea that if Daddy could not get the truck up the slick slope of the levee soon, the focus of his rage might well turn from the truck and the levee to one of us. In recent years his personality had changed considerably. The once loving, joyful, funny dad had at times become a threatening, violent stranger to us all. He had attacked Andy, as well as our eldest sister, Cassie, with punches, slaps, and shoves, with threats and insults, and seemed to be developing a new, particular focus on me lately. As he struggled in the truck to get us up the levee, cornered by circumstances, I expected him to lash out at any moment. In this state of mind, he could create any number of reasons why Andy or I, for no reason other than our mere presence, would be worthy of his wrath. It would not have been the first time.

• • •

I tried to imagine being in the truck under less troublesome circumstances. In the immediate couple of years after Daddy bought the motel, the Apache was called into service for quite a lot of heavy duty as he set out to clean the place up a bit. It was used to yank unwanted trees out of the ground with steel chains attached to its back bumper; as well as to haul supplies from town to remodel several buildings on the property. The laundry room, a storage building, the tractor shed were each refaced with what took several truckloads of asphalt siding that had to be special-ordered from New Orleans. The truck was used to move mounds of dirt and gravel, fence posts, lumber, air conditioners, and kitchen appliances.

Its most dramatic haul, however, was the massive black water cistern that had stood on a wooden tower behind the motel and was put out of commission in 1966, when an adequate well was finally dug to supply the whole place with water. If you dared climb the eighteen feet to the top of the tower to peer into the cistern, you'd see it was empty except for a few dozen silver-dollar-sized banana spiders that made zigzag designs in their webs.

Outside of that pretty impressive little thrill, Daddy insisted the cistern was useless, and it had to come down. So inside of a day, he and Andy dismantled the tower and slowly brought the big black tank down to the ground, where they rolled it into position beside the Apache. It was more ungainly than heavy, so with the help of a few of our extra hands, it was lifted up and laid on its side to rest on top of the bed of the truck. Once it was secured to the back with thick ropes, Andy climbed on top of the cistern, and, holding on to one of the ropes like he was riding a rodeo bull, he waved and yelled "Yee-haw!" as Daddy slowly pulled onto the road and drove the three miles into town, where he had arranged to sell the cistern for scrap metal.

• • •

In its later years the truck continued to have all kinds of utility as a beast of burden as well as providing an occasional escape for some recreation. Besides the hunting trips or dump duty, excursions to town for groceries and whatnot, there were other trips made for amusement. On summer weekends, if Daddy approved, Andy drove Gilda, Glenda, and me (sometimes Momma and Cassie as well) to a creek way back in the woods down a dirt road about two miles from the motel. Officially it was called Crystal Creek, but everyone knew it better as "Queer's Creek," a term that struck my curiosity and put me on guard at the same time. Already, to my young ears, the very term *queer* had a titillating quality about it, but I was also very aware that connecting myself to anything queer would get me more negative attention than I wanted. I had heard the term on the playground at school, and it was never said in anything but a hostile way.

Apparently, the creek had earned its nickname because it was rumored to attract skinny-dipping and probably some illicit activity in the surrounding woods, but disappointingly, to my curious young self, we never actually witnessed any of that. It was also rumored to be sixty feet deep, but that was never verified either. What had been verified, however, was that it wasn't really a creek, but a large pond and had existed long enough to become home to various fishes, eels, and mussels in its shallower areas.

At the far west end of the creek were "the cliffs," which rose about eight feet above the water. Diving off of those could work if you cared to swim out that far, but when we had the truck with us and backed it up to the edge of the water, the open tailgate proved a much more accessible launching pad for some great diving. Cassie and Andy were particularly good divers; the best I could do was pinch my nose and take a running jump into the water. The most surprising thing about the creek was that, while it was fraught with danger—the legendary sixty feet, the jagged cliffs, poison ivy here and there, and the whole swim-at-your-own-risk intrigue of the place—we experienced no drama to report, no catastrophes, no casualties, except for a busted toe or cut from a random piece of glass every now and then.

• • •

I kept looking at my Timex.

Twenty-eight of the longest minutes of my life, slipping and then climbing, then slipping and climbing, had passed already. Rain and sleet pelted the Apache – Pack! Pack! Pack! against the windshield and the roof of the cab; wipers going full steam; the little box heater rattling; Daddy's face fierce with determination and cold sweat; Andy shivering and bouncing in place; me in between them, bug-eyed and wishing I were anywhere else in the world, and glad the anger and frustration on Daddy's purple-red face was not aimed at me. There was no one to blame for this predicament, and this morning Daddy wasn't focusing on blame. He was clearly determined that he'd get that Apache, and us all, off that slick slope and onto the road at the top of the levee, even if it took all day.

But it didn't. Thank the universe, it didn't!

In the twenty-ninth minute in the Apache that morning, everything that needed to happen to get us off the slope happened, and finally, like it was a lovely dry afternoon in the sun, the tires of the Apache gripped whatever bit of earth and grass they needed to grip to bring us closer and closer and closer, and then *on* to the top of the levee, onto the road, onto solid ground.

On this morning, Daddy, in fact, wasn't the man who could turn on you at any moment; knock you to the ground, then deliver a vicious kick to the ribs; ridicule you in public or in front of company; maniacally punch the breath out of you. On this morning he was nothing like that man.

This morning, as he finally, triumphantly maneuvered the mud-splattered Apache to the top of the levee—in its back, our dirty, jumbled, wet gear tossed this way and that—he was instead a man we had known only in fleeting moments in recent years; moments like this, when circumstances compelled him to fiercely defend us instead of savagely berate us; to cherish us, the "cargo" in his truck, instead of resenting the burden we represented; a man anyone would be happy to be around; be proud to call *Daddy*; a man who inspired genuine love, sincere respect, and deeply felt gratitude. Behind the wheel of his beloved Apache, he was a hero.

13 | The Doe

By the time I turned thirteen I had been squirrel hunting and camping off-season a handful of times but had not been deer hunting. On my first deer-hunting trip, Daddy walked with me for half an hour into the Thistlethwaite woods and positioned me in what he thought was a good spot, right near a slough. I was to stay there all morning, have my baloney sandwich and grape soda around noon, then head back to the truck by two. I sat down against a cypress, making sure there were no snakes or bugs or anything else that might crawl on me, and waited with my shotgun pointed outward.

I was never comfortable with that shotgun, a 16-gauge Daddy had handed down to me, and that Andy, despite having two of his own, coveted because it was worn and rugged and, in its worn ruggedness, beautiful. As far as I was concerned, he could have it, but I had to at least show I was making an effort. This awkward weight on me to be a man, to hold and shoot the gun properly, to clean the barrel, to bag a squirrel or two, and ultimately, to get my first deer, all really overwhelmed me. I had no idea how to be like that. I felt trapped and decided the best thing to do was to go through the motions and, when hounded for not shooting anything, I'd just be prepared to shrug and say, "Maybe next time," and pretend to be as disappointed in me as they were.

At the tree my mind wandered far from the woods surrounding me. I wanted to be home, to be warm, dry and doing anything but this. I didn't hate Daddy and Andy for wanting me to be part of this aspect of their lives, but the pressure to fit in and evolve into someone just like them was powerful, and tiresome.

I leaned the shotgun against the tree, careful to angle it away from me should it fall, and with a stick scratched away at the leaves around me to make sure there was nothing in them that I didn't want that close to me. An earthworm, some roly-polies, and other tiny insects, but not much else, turned up, so I felt a bit more at ease sitting there, for what might have been four or five hours, bored, cold, and damp. Often on these trips what I did instead of sitting there in the swamp all that time was wait an hour and then go back to the truck to read until Daddy and Andy came out of the woods.

The woods were very much alive. The trees had their own language, their crowns rustled against one another, swishing and swaying in a strong wind, or their leaves quietly fluttered in a mild breeze. The calls of birds provided most of the sound: egrets, ibises, a variety of ducks, geese, hawks, wild turkeys, and occasionally the very rare and special sighting, especially this far from the Gulf, of a white pelican. The birds' singing and chirping and squawking got progressively louder as the sun rose and the morning wore into midday. Now and then, in the distance there was a gunshot or two, but otherwise it was all about the birds, the gossip amongst the trees, and an occasional bullfrog belching somewhere in a nearby slough. In the early fall, when temperatures were still in the 80s, the sound of mosquitoes and other buzzing insects added to the cacophony, but this late in the season, the cold had already forced away everything that could fly to warmer spots or to hibernate in the earth. Mercifully, the insects were largely gone.

• • •

Shotgun blasts in the distance.

One, then two blasts, then others, and the sounds were moving closer to me and my tree. I picked up my shotgun and reviewed all the little details I'd been taught: *make sure the safety is on until you are ready to shoot, position yourself so you are standing firmly so you don't fall back after shooting at something. Be ready.*

As the sounds of other hunters got closer, the remaining birds took flight. An audible energy replaced the quiet. That was all the warning I got before I heard the thumping of hooves coming closer.

Then there she was. Stopped abruptly in her tracks. Staring straight at me. Face-to-face with a beautiful young doe; white fur under her jaws and down her neck, golden everywhere else except for a bit of white at the tip of her tail, punctuating her body like an exclamation point. Enormous gray eyes stared right at me, no more than five yards away. I had my shotgun ready and was poised to make the perfect shot, a shot that from that close, would surely do the job. In that instant, however, I was frozen and staring, stunned and possibly as startled as she. I couldn't pull the trigger, no matter how much I'd been taught to do precisely that. Instead she and I had a moment of silent conversation, a moment when we both knew that I was not going to be the one to kill her. Someone else surely would do that today. But not me.

She leapt off and I stood horrified and repulsed that I even thought that my killing such a thing was actually possible, for me, or for anyone. Really, who could do such a thing? How could I do that and ever live with visions of that beautiful doe's petrified eyes penetrating my own?

I sat down, trembling, sweaty and cold at once. I wanted to completely disappear. Be away from this place, not have to ever think about it again. And not have to explain, either. The hunters soon were out of hearing range. I could not think. Could not feel. I wanted to sleep and awake with this having been but a dream. I put my gun back on safety, picked up my hunting bag, collected myself, and started the walk back to the truck. I would tell no one of this, especially not Andy. I was relieved that I didn't have what it took to have killed the doe, and I couldn't imagine what Andy would have felt were he to learn that his little brother had gotten one before he did.

14 | Wonderland

While the Apache had a full, year-round job that varied from season to season, its most consistent chore, performed about once a month, was the trip to the dump to haul the barrels that held the garbage from our house and the motel.

The barrels were actually six, fifty-five-gallon oil drums that had been cut open at one end with a machete and mallet, resulting in a matching set of jagged tops, not unlike the lids of green beans opened with a dull can opener. We kept the lids around to keep trash from flying on the road en route to the dump.

The six open barrels, as well as two that remained sealed until they were needed later, were lined against the back fence behind the garage in a row of four, two deep, and collectively held about a month's worth of dry trash. When they were full, one of us had to climb on top and jump up and down to mash the trash as far down as it would go. The wet stuff, mostly food scraps, went into a separate small, galvanized *slop can*, a trash can with a lid that sealed properly. It was always the nastiest of the cans, since the food rotted and attracted flies and their maggots.

Daddy had paid a Mr. Guillory thirty dollars for the eight drums. Mr. Guillory was the man who bought the Esso station Daddy had run for twelve years before we moved from town to the motel. He wasn't as successful as Daddy had been with the station and had to sell it a couple years later. It was rumored that he had become a heavy drinker, driven so after his baby daughter drowned in a foot of water in their plastic swimming pool two summers before.

As trash cans, the barrels had a lifespan of several years because of the oil coating inside and the thick paint on the outside. Gradually, though, they rusted and rusted some more until they began crumbling and had to be tossed, along with the trash they held, on their one final trip to the dump.

Loading the barrels into the back of the Apache was hard work. When compacted and full, each barrel weighed about a hundred pounds. It took two of us to load a barrel. Daddy saw it as a man-making exercise, but we saw it for what it was: free heavy labor. It was also work that should have required gloves, because the rust would cut into your skin. Daddy didn't see much point in gloves. He wanted us to develop rough, calloused hands like his.

The Apache held six of the barrels and the slop can. Six full barrels, lids covering each barrel, or weighed down with a cinder block if the lid had disappeared (most likely a casualty of a wind gust on a past trip). Anything too big to fit in a barrel, like an air conditioner, a cracked toilet, or rusted drainpipes, was hoisted on top of the load. The bulging blue truck quite often resembled the Beverly Hillbillies' truck, tires smashed under the weight. Finally, for the ride to the dump, we crammed into the cab of the truck, or squeezed in between the barrels. The dump was about three miles on the highway going east, then about a half-mile down a gravel road that took us past a plain, one-story clapboard building with a pink neon sign that read "Lounge" in its only window (Glenda was convinced the building was a whorehouse and swore she once saw a naked man through that window) before ending at the massive dumpsite, right around a sharp curve.

When Daddy or Andy couldn't do it, Glenda or Gilda did the driving. We preferred to go without Daddy, because without him we could take our time and go *splorin'* for junk.

And the dump was a wonderland.

Acres of mounded trash, and treasure. Mixed in with the piles of fly-infested raw garbage curdling in the sun were plastic milk jugs, typing paper, and a Styrofoam head like the ones momma had mounted on the counter in her beauty shop to comb out the wigs and wiglets. This one had its blank eye spaces colored in, in blue ink, by a girl I envisioned had used it years ago in the beauty school she never finished. Or else *why throw out a good Styrofoam head?* Rusted box springs for a twin bed; a gray, dented Bundt-cake pan; a bunch of faded plastic funeral flowers with a glitter sash that read "In Loving Memory." *Who died?* A basketball hoop with chips in the enameled orange paint; tires that would fit an eighteen-wheeler; two Ann Page pineapple juice cans; a stack of clean, undelivered telephone directories; pieces of a large picture frame; a lone, beautiful, verdigris-covered brass hinge that I imagined went on a fanciful chicken coop. *I want that, but there's only one. Maybe its companion is somewhere near here, if I look hard enough? One day I'll find a use for it.* Kicking stuff around. No hinges but some blackened banana peels, a green strapless flip-flop, broken dishes. Nearby were kitchen table chairs, two water-bloated couches, a trio of doorless refrigerators. *How did three refrigerators get here at the same time?* A child's little green bunny rabbit, bicycle tires with the inner chrome rim rusted, some eight-track tapes with their tangled tape spilling out, parts of a pink play kitchen set. *What happened to the little girl who used to play with that?* A hairbrush, cracked window glass, a bag of old clothes and shoes, crushed lightbulbs, millions of cigarette butts, chewed-up beef bones, a busted, hollowed-out watermelon, a rusted car muffler bent in half, pine branches, a blue-green kiddy pool with whales hand-painted on the side. Somebody had some artistic talent, but sadly the pool had been split open. *Did a large kid jump in and break it?* A footstool missing a leg, terra-cotta pieces, a little Mexican guitar minus its neck and strings. *Looks like one of the giveaways you could get with a fill-up at the Canal gas station in Lafayette.*

Having climbed and kicked through mounds of trash for an hour or so, we each reeked of sweat and sour garbage. And, after hauling its bulging, putrid load to the dump, then making the trip back home with the empty, but stinky barrels, the truck also stank like hell. The final act in a trip to the dump involved a good hosing for the truck and each of the barrels, with whoever was operating the hose pressurizing it with a bent thumb over the nozzle to create more power in the spray. Then the hose, no matter who was doing the hosing, was finally turned onto ourselves to rinse off all that sweat and stink.

15 | **A Perfect Day**

Four-thirty a.m., Tuesday, July 1. "Everybody up!" Daddy barked. "Gotta get on that road. Now!"

Gilda, Glenda, Dicky, and I had been psyched for this crabbing trip for two impossibly long, *whole* days now, so we were up and ready in what seemed like only seconds. Daddy knew better than to ever give us much notice for these kind of things. More of a notice would only have given us more time to hyperventilate from the anticipation of a day trip in the truck. Like hunting and fishing, crabbing *necessarily* began in the twilight blue-black hours of the morning. And, at this cool hour of the day—*cool* being relative of course, because it meant it wouldn't be ninety-five degrees till at least nine—the road would be mostly empty, so the sixty-minute ride would be pretty easy.

We were headed for the marshy terrain of Cameron Parish, which has a southern border with the Gulf of Mexico. It was going to be hot. We were dressed in beach clothes. Shorts, tee-shirts, flip-flops.

"Y'all got everything? Come on, let's get going!" Glenda, who seemed just a bit more awake at this hour than the rest of us, said. Apparently, she had already thought through a list of what she meant by *everything*.

"Let's see. We've got nets? Check. Some smelt? Check. Safety pens, a bolt of string? Check."

Glenda was fond of making and repeating lists. It was my belief that this trait of hers stemmed from having Daddy repeatedly tick off the list of things she'd need when cleaning a motel room. His favorite, "Towels. Soap. Sheet (he always left off the last 's' in *sheets*). Toilet paper," became a mantra, a running joke for all of us.

She then took us through the rest of the gear we'd bring, which included the blue ice chest for the smelt, the red ice chest for the lunchmeat, bread, mayo, ketchup, mustard, and drinks. Four ice-filled dollar-store Styrofoam chests for the crabs we were going to catch; six in all once we used up the smelt and ate lunch. We would go through at least two rounds of this list-ticking before she was satisfied that we were ready for the road.

"I call the front seat," she proclaimed, probably because she felt her list-making-and-checking duty entitled her to this right.

"Me too," Dicky said.

That left the bed of the pickup for the gear and Gilda and me, an arrangement that suited me just fine. I loved being able to lie back and look up at the stars. Gilda and I would huddle up together covered by an open, unzipped sleeping bag, shielding us from the wind gusting in around us as Daddy drove through the darkness towards the Gulf.

I guess I had envisioned an organized, prearranged specific crabbing destination, but in truth, the whole of Cameron Parish *was* the destination. Or rather its side roads, where salt water encroached from the Gulf onto the land, and where crabs thrived. In these ditches, with a piece of smelt tied at one end, and a short stick tied to the other, a crabber needed only toss out his or her line and wait for a mere minute or two, to lure in a couple of crabs or even three. This proved to be a very successful technique, one that Daddy had demonstrated for us at our very first stop that morning.

He also demonstrated how to employ the bamboo poles we'd brought to extend and place several triangular crawfish nets in strategic spots in the water.

"You gotta hold your pole tight and steady to pull them crabs up," he explained.

It seemed he was more at ease than he'd been in quite a long while. His tone on this trip was friendly, and he was generous with his patience; the vibe he'd been giving off carried with it not even the slightest sense of threat. It would be hard to imagine under these circumstances that he'd be anything other than a happy, helpful dad. A nice, very welcome change for us all.

"It don't take too long. If y'all are real quiet, you can pick up a few of them crabs each time you check your net."

The crawfish nets held five or six crabs at once so, like the individual line-and-smelt technique, the net procedure was quite successful. Unless you were Dicky, who couldn't get the knack of pulling in the crabs once they'd bitten the smelt. He was also not fond of the slimy organ meat or of the crabs themselves. He had long established his revulsion at anything to do with seafood. Still, he made himself useful with the crawfish nets, easily pulling them up and out of the green-brown water and dumping the twitching crabs into an ice chest.

The sun was high and hot, but there was a good breeze coming in off the Gulf of Mexico. Gulls that typically clung to the shoreline ventured farther inland here, their squawks the only consistent sound outside of our voices. There was a very soothing smell in the air as the salt-water scents of the Gulf collided with the freshwater scents of the marsh and mixed in with the sweet, heat-softened creosote coming from the telephone poles that lined the road.

In the breeze, dressed in beach clothes, without any toilets to scrub or grass to cut, we very quickly turned the *work* of crabbing into more of a long game to see who could get the most points. One point per crab.

"I've already gotten at least twice what y'all got," Glenda bragged not long into the day.

"Huh? That's bull," Gilda said. "I got way more than you."

"Doubt it," Glenda replied.

By two we'd filled up the four Styrofoam chests, as well as the blue one and the red one. So, as we headed back to Eunice, there were six full chests in the bed of the Apache, along with Gilda and me, hunched and sunburned and pretty miserably tired, and Daddy, Dicky, and Glenda in the front again, all quite happy with our haul.

When we arrived home, Momma, who'd had her own full day already, glanced wearily at the six filled ice chests, then at us, dirty, sunburned, stinky, and exhausted.

"Oh, ya-yie," she said. "Y'all go get in the tub right this minute! I don't want all y'all's stink all over my clean house." She realized it would be her who'd have to handle the cleaning and freezing of all those crabs. She thought she was prepared for an ice-chest or two, at most, but six?

• • •

To process crabs for the freezer, you have to first blanch them in boiling water for a couple of minutes, then let them cool down a bit. Then, one by one, remove the "apron" on the belly side. After that's done, the outer shell on top of the crab is pulled away to reveal the lungs and other inedible parts, which are scraped out with a spoon. Then the crab gets a rinse under the tap in the sink, and finally, it is put in a plastic, twisty-tie bag for the freezer. There were hundreds of crabs to process this way.

Momma's resigned expression melted my heart for her. That, plus the thought of the seafood gumbo she'd make, with those crabs bubbling away in a big stockpot, had me volunteering to help her get a start on them. Like the paper bag fries Daddy made on the banks of Bayou Rouge, Momma's perfect seafood gumbo left an indelible mark on my taste buds.

The twins had already headed upstairs to take their baths, and Dicky was in the tub downstairs. I figured I might as well wait to take a bath after spending some time in the kitchen with Momma and all those crabs.

"If I didn't love crabs so much, this would make me crazy," Momma said. "I'm gonna have to make a gumbo this weekend."

"Oh, God, my mouth's already watering," I said. "I want to watch you when you do that so I can make it just like yours."

"I can't imagine being out there in that sun catching these crabs all day long like y'all did, but when it comes right down to it, I love that y'all were able to get so many."

Daddy, who was relaxing on his rocker in the front office, popped open a Schlitz and lit a Kent.

"Well, that was a perfect day for it," he said. "You coulda come with us and watched, Eliza."

"I woulda done more than watched," she said. "Don't you believe for one minute that I woulda not gotten right in there with y'all and got a bunch of those crabs myself."

Momma and I sat together and cleaned through a couple of ice chests, then covered the rest of the haul with new ice for the next morning, when Gilda and Glenda would join us to get them all blanched, cleaned, and bagged for the freezer.

It *was* a perfect day.

16 | *Prends Courage*

Over the years we each developed a keen awareness of when Daddy was upset about something, times when it was best to stay clear of him. Whether or not any of us had anything to do with whatever set him off was not important, Mémère said. Pretty much every one of his violent reactions stemmed from something one of us had done to offend him, like make a remark he thought was disrespectful, or clumsily drop a lightbulb that then shattered and flew everywhere, or spill a little bit of hot okra gumbo on the way to the table, or let our minds wander when he was lecturing us about how good we had it. But there were other instances where it was simply a matter of being in the wrong place at the wrong time after something unrelated to any of us had sparked a reaction in him.

If we were not careful during one of his internal disturbances, we could expect to be on the receiving end of the blunt force of the back of his massive right hand, which would involuntarily go flying outward. This phenomenon started with a trigger in an incensed brain, where a reflex shot a jolt of electricity down into his face, forged his jaw into steel, traveled southward to form a woody knot in his throat, then move farther down his body, to constrict his heaving chest, where it suddenly darted to the right, through his tensing shoulder, and then finally, violently propelled his right arm taut, and splayed his hand into rigid spokes at its terminus. It was a formation ideal for maximum impact.

Even with ample experience, there was no way to fully predict when Daddy would tear into a rage. Like the relentless sting of the Louisiana summer sun, this uncertainty was an always-present, and therefore *accepted*, characteristic of our childhood. It was our *normal*.

• • •

After such an attack, it always took me a while to shake away the violence. Typically, in the moments right after a beating, my stomach would retch. I'd take three quick sucks of air to interrupt the full-body spasms. Holding myself in a ball on my bed, this cycle continued, even a full twenty minutes after. After the repeated slaps to my head, and kicks to my side. After a fistful of hair, yanked from its roots, left behind freckles of dried blood on my scalp.

After about twenty-five minutes had passed, my whole body still shuddered, in waves. My head throbbed; it felt like my brain was pushing to escape the skull that held it in against its will. My lungs were sore and my side ached, terribly. I could sense my heart, my liver, my stomach, and the bones that formed my ribs. Like I could touch them directly, with my fingertips.

My eyes were raw; they still burned like embers. My nose leaked.

At thirty-five minutes, one more lingering body spasm. Two more sucks of air, smaller than before. And then finally, one long, deep inhale. The intake of air provoked another cough. Then an equally long and deep exhale that finally faded and brought another beating to a full close.

• • •

What I called my bed was actually just a twin-sized, foam, motel room mattress on the floor of the unused vestibule in the living room, at the front of the house. In place of a headboard, I incorporated a desk with two small built-in drawers and a shelf where I kept the few possessions a typical twelve-year-old might have: a handful of books I'd bought at school through the paperback club, and a black RCA transistor pocket radio, on which I caught signals from Mexican stations at night. I had no understanding of Spanish, but the fact of it coming through that little hard plastic device powered by a nine-volt battery gave me a sense that there was a real world out there for me if I could make it out of that place and go find it.

• • •

The living room was the fanciest room in our house. From the day Mrs. Melancon revealed it to us when we toured the motel for the first time,

I'd held that room in high regard. The wrought-iron trellis separating it from the formal dining area, the custom drapes, the crystal chandelier she acquired on a trip to Europe, and the ornate French Provincial furniture. I respected this formality, this sense of decorum. And I didn't want to be the one messing all that up. Also, I liked being as inconspicuous as possible. So each morning I made sure to roll up the mattress and tuck it under the desk, so, to the casual observer, the vestibule by day remained an empty, unused entryway from outside the house to that special room. I made sure that none of what I experienced there on my foam mattress intruded into the grandeur of the larger room.

I had migrated to the vestibule from the double bed I had shared with Dicky in the room he and I shared with Andy, who had his own double bed. Dicky had a recurring habit of wetting the bed, which made the notion of sleeping through the night an uncertainty. That fleeting warmth of new urine was always followed by a shock of cold wet sheets. Sharing a bed with Andy didn't work for me either; he was a sensitive sleeper. I'd get a punch to the head if I moved too much, and with my habit of uncontrollably waving my feet back and forth, like windshield wipers, that was not a realistic option for me.

• • •

When Momma came to check on me in the vestibule, she sat down on the mattress on the floor with me and put a hand on my shoulder. I couldn't control my reaction: I abruptly recoiled, reigniting the trembling.

"Please don't touch me," I said. "I can't talk right now." I knew she wanted to comfort me, but the last thing I wanted to do right then was be comforted. I wanted, I *needed*, to be alone. I wanted to escape into my thoughts. Any time I got a beating, the first stage of healing was physical, but the next phase was just as hard. I found myself disappearing into my thoughts to get through it. I felt helpless sometimes when Dicky needed encouragement, or Andy needed help with some chore, and I just couldn't get up the energy to help him out. He never asked unless he really needed it, and I felt awful when I couldn't make myself get up and go.

I tried to imagine a future where Daddy wasn't around. As soon as I could grow up enough to get out of that house, find my own place where I didn't have to worry about being attacked, where my actions were not judged, and I was not punished for being something I had no control over. I imagined my own home, my own kitchen, my living room with a new TV and stereo, and my bedroom where I would fall sleep without being anxious.

I thought of the food I could make for myself using the lessons I'd learned from Mémère and Momma; the trips I could take; how the people in my life would be the types who didn't threaten me, who didn't cause me pain, who didn't judge me, and who, instead of looking at me with hate in their eyes, genuinely liked being with me. People like Mémère.

• • •

Later, when I was finally calm, I asked Momma if I could go stay a little while with Mémère.

"Yes," she said, knowing that Mémère had a way with me no one else had. "That's a good idea. Let me call her. I'm sure she'll be glad to have you for a couple of days."

When Momma and I arrived at Mémère's an hour later, she'd made a fricassee with ham hocks, chicken thighs, and potatoes, and thankfully, no turnips. I don't like cooked turnips. Momma ate with us and, after about thirty minutes, headed back to Eunice. "I'll come pick you up on Sunday. Okay?"

"Yep," I said. "Thank you, Momma. Bye."

When she was gone, Mémère and I went to the back porch.

"Tell me what's happen, *cher*," she said. "You momma tell me you daddy hit you again. *Pauvre bête.*"

I didn't really want to talk about it, but I knew she wanted to talk, and that it made her feel good to be able to help me if she could. She was aware that she was the only person in my life I felt comfortable enough with to completely confide in.

"He told me I was not going to amount to anything. That I would turn out to be some kind of a parasite. We're learning about parasites in biology, and that doesn't make sense to me, so I said, 'That doesn't make any sense,' and he slapped me and was yelling, 'Shut that damned sassy mouth! That's another one of your big problems. You're too damned sassy. You need to learn.' Then he started slapping me again. And I kinda blanked out after that."

"*Prends courage, cher,*" Mémère said softly. "You have to try to hold yourself tight, to keep you mind together. Don't let him mess you up, *cher. Prends courage.*"

Take courage. I wished it were that simple.

"I'm doing my best," I told her. "I don't know when he's gonna find something to hit me for. I never know when it's gonna come."

"*Prends courage, cher*," she repeated. "You can make it through this. I know you can. Do you best to keep away from him. I know it's not always possible, but you gotta try to outsmart him. When he's somewhere, you go somewhere else. Stay away from him."

"Okay. That's what I've been trying to do, Mémère. But he's been hitting me more and more now that I'm getting older, and I don't really know why he's picked me out."

"You momma tell me he wants you to be more like Andy. More like them other boys who like to go hunt and fish and this and that. He want you to not be with you sisters, so you grow up to be more like a man. I know that's probably hard for you, *cher*. But maybe try that. And try you best not to say too much. You momma said she gonna talk to him again. Tell him he need to stop that beating you all the time, all the time."

"I hope she can. He's not easy to talk to without him getting mad."

• • •

We sat for a couple of hours on that porch, listening to the symphony coming from the chorus of crickets, frogs, and cicadas all around us in the yard. The summer heat made them sing, Mémère said.

"Time for bed, *cher*," she said after a while. "It's getting late."

I slept on the sofa under the cuckoo clock in the living room. The windows were open just enough to let the whirring attic fan above the bathroom doorway suck the evening breezes right through the full length of the house. The hum of the big fan, the cool breeze blowing all around me, and the songs of the outdoor creatures put me right to sleep. I had not fallen asleep that easily since the last time I visited her.

• • •

So back home I would go on Sunday feeling somewhat healed.

At home the sense of safety created when my sisters and Dicky and I sat and played canasta was not as reliable as the one created by the embrace and welcome at Mémère's; the silent, invisible cool from the central air conditioning in our house not quite as soothing as the tingling breeze created by her humming attic fan overhead, but it was a safe place for us all the same. Even though he'd prefer that I was spending time with Andy instead of the twins, Daddy saw us playing cards instead of watching TV all day—which he said was what "them no-good lazy niggers and fat housewives do"—as somehow a more respectable and therefore permissible pastime.

Sunday might indeed bring the four of us time to play before getting back to our work. The thick St. Augustine grass that thrived in the moist heat probably needed cutting; we might need to load the trash barrels into the truck to make the month's run to the dump; surely there were sheets and towels to wash, dry, and fold, and motel rooms to clean; and we could never know for sure what lay in store for us with the short-timers, customers there for an hour or two of relief, or with those in the apartments, with us for longer stays, for more complex reasons.

17 | The Boy from Apartment 18

He had the face of a kewpie doll. Chubby cheeks, each a burst of cherry over a French vanilla complexion. Luxurious blue-black curls. Benjamin Landrineau was no more than six years old, the only child of young parents who, for a couple of weeks, had taken the spacious Apartment 18 at the farthest end of the motel property while they waited for their new home to be finished in Opelousas, fifteen miles east on the highway.

"Can I play here?" he asked shyly the first time I encountered him in the back yard behind their apartment. "My mommy said to ask if it's okay."

"Oh, um, it's okay," I told him, wondering how he got around into the back yard. There was a fence and a gate we kept closed to separate us from the customers, but he looked harmless enough.

"Want some candy?" he asked.

"Um, that's okay," I said, wondering how to extract my nearly thirteen-year-old self from this child, but sensing that I should not just leave him there in the back yard alone. "Shouldn't you be inside? Maybe your mommy is looking for you."

At this, he emitted a small, lingering "Noooooo" that trailed away to a hush. In the moment, his eyes dropped downward, off of mine. He continued, "She knows I'm here. She said I should come out here to play. M-mommy is sad to-day. Daddy socked her again last night."

"Oh. That's not good," I told him, gulping back my own personal awareness of what that was like.

"Do you have any toys to play with?" he asked, changing the subject.

"Um, well, no, not really. I'm too old for toys. Maybe my little brother has some. He's close to your age. But he's sick today. He can't come outside."

As the words came out of my mouth I remembered that Dicky really didn't have anything suitable for a six-year-old either, except maybe Mr. Hadley, his stuffed monkey, but he'd not want me to let a strange child play with Mr. Hadley.

"Hmm. How about I push you on the swing for a little while?"

"Okay," he replied, perking up.

I lifted the little boy up onto the swing and gave him a couple of soft pushes. He seemed to like it enough but didn't say anything, so I grabbed the ropes and stopped the swing.

"Was that too fast?" I asked.

"Can we go faster?" he asked with a lilt.

"Sure." I gave him a few faster, but cautious-enough pushes, still wondering how I was going to remove myself from this unpaid babysitting job.

"Look, I have to go," I told him after a couple more pushes. "You shouldn't be out here by yourself. Maybe your mommy is okay now?"

"Yeah, okay. Can I come swing again tomorrow?"

"Um, maybe. I'm not sure I will be around, but maybe," I told him, still trying to work out a way to get out of this predicament. I walked him back to the door of Apartment 18 and left him there standing in front of it.

The encounter troubled me for a couple of reasons. I couldn't help but wonder what he was going through at home. His mom was being hit by his dad, and she was clearly affected by this. So much so that she encouraged her six-year-old to go out and play in a strange back yard alone. I assumed this was so she could deal with her emotions without his little face looking up at hers.

That night I tossed and turned with Benjamin Landrineau, this little cherub, on my mind. All six-year-olds are needy, but this situation with his parents has got to have made Benjamin's need more urgent. It was in his obvious neediness that something in me emerged: I realized I wanted to protect him, to take care of him. But I thought I should fight this urge. It didn't make any sense. Also, I knew I had no business meddling in the life of one of the customers, even one so young and obviously vulnerable. Besides, I had no time for this; I wanted to be able to go outside in my own back yard without having to encounter some lonely child.

I decided I just needed to brush him off, to let him know I was not the right age to play with him. He needed to play with someone his own age, even if that someone wasn't around, wasn't available. It was not my fault he was alone in the world outside his apartment. Yup. That's exactly what I intended to do if I saw him again: I'd let him know plainly that he had to find other ways to amuse himself. The motel bill didn't cover babysitting services. I'd be polite, but firm.

The next day I managed to avoid the back yard altogether.

On the third day, just as I was beginning to relax about the whole thing, thinking he'd worked out other ways to amuse himself, I walked outside to find him standing there, waiting by the swings. An impossible, confectionery smile separated his bubble cheeks when he saw me.

"Hi!" he said loudly in a voice full of anticipation. "Can you swing me?"

How long has he been waiting? I wondered. I had hoped the situation had resolved itself: maybe his mom hired a babysitter, or maybe they decided to move to a different motel and packed up in the night, or maybe he had figured out how to play on the swing without me.

"Um, okay," I said flatly. "But only a little while. I have stuff I have to do."

On the fourth day, I stepped carefully around the back of the house, craning my neck to see if he was out there. No sign of him, so I moved on towards the laundry room. As I was about to step up onto the laundry porch, I caught a glimpse of him, standing just outside the fence by his apartment. The sight startled me. *How long has he been out here? Is he waiting for me again? Why won't he leave me alone?*

My heart was racing. He saw me seeing him, so I had to approach him. As I walked towards the fence, he squeezed through the crack between the fencepost and the apartment building.

"Hi, Benjamin," I said, feeling myself being sucked into his cherubic spell again. *I don't have time for this! I have to do something. Something to make him stop bothering me.*

"Come with me over here," I instructed him firmly, pointing to the row of hedges that abutted the drainage ditch on the property line. He followed me obediently around the hedges and into the grassy ditch behind them, where we were hidden from anyone who might be looking in that direction at that moment.

I was in a bit of a panic. My heart was still racing. I had no idea what I was going to do. I needed to let him know he couldn't play with me. Right then, as he looked up at me, about to say something, I grabbed him by his little shoulders and shook him violently.

"Go away!" I yelled behind clenched teeth. "Go back to your house! I can't take care of you!"

I shook him again. His little head of blue-black curls snapped back and forth. I pushed him away from me with such force he fell onto the grass and gasped. His cherubic cheeks puffed out, his lower lip trembled. And he was crying. *Silently.* And looking up at me in disbelief and desperation. I was dumbfounded by this. He should have been screaming. The silent tears streaming from his puffed face confused me. Most kids his age would be wailing wildly at this violent treatment, but he simply sat there, tears falling, obviously startled, but somehow controlling himself. I was suddenly struck with the realization that he had experienced this before. He had been trained to mute his pain, to keep it all inside. To himself.

I squatted down and grabbed him up into my arms and then stood him upright with me. I hugged him; I had no control over what I was doing. Something propelled me to hug him again, and pat his curls and brush them out of his face, then wipe away his tears and tell him not to worry. That I didn't mean to shake him. That I was sorry.

Then I gathered myself.

The need to be out of there was urgent in me.

"You just need to go home," I said softly, but forcefully. I brushed the grass off his clothes and wiped away the remaining moisture on his fat little cheeks. We walked back around the hedges, and I gave him a soft push in the direction of his apartment. "You need to find a way to play without me," I told him. At this, he gave me a little nod in silence, then walked back to Apartment 18.

The rest of the day I was tormented. I carried a knot in my chest, and again that night I had trouble falling asleep. I tilled my thoughts, over, over, and over again: Benjamin Landrineau and his mom and dad would leave soon, and it was none of my business what would happen to them. To the mom who was being hit by her husband, and the husband who hit her, and to their little boy who didn't have anyone to play with, and who wasn't allowed to cry aloud when he was hurt.

I resolved that night in my bed that I would never hurt this little boy, or anyone, ever again. This simply could not happen. Ever. I would never again put my hands on anyone, especially a child half my age and size.

But the very next day, the scenario played out, very much the same way, *again.*

It was during this second time, when I was shaking little Benjamin again, that I then had more awareness of what was happening. And when, as it happened, I was *not* caught off guard like I was before. I should have been able to see it coming, and to ward it off before it went too far. Then I realized *I couldn't.*

I got him back behind the hedge again, and although he hesitated at first to follow me, his open heart *trusted* me. He trusted that I was someone who cared for him. Someone who wouldn't hurt him. So he followed me. But in just moments I was shaking him once more. Violently.

His little face crumpled again. Then he turned away from me. His little torso trembled like a wounded animal fearing for its life beneath a much stronger beast. This was not supposed to be happening. Not again.

For me, however, as it happened, it felt kinda normal. *Normal.* In the moment as my heart raced and I was shaking him, I felt powerful, in control. And *thrilled.*

And then it all stopped. My thrill turned into disgust. I didn't recognize this person who could grab someone so small, so clearly innocent, so helpless and trusting, and confused. I didn't recognize this person I'd become at all. This monster. Myself.

• • •

After the second shaking incident, after I apologized and reassured Benjamin it wouldn't ever happen again, after I nudged him back home where he would be safe, where his mommy and daddy, people who surely must have loved him, would take care of him, I was sickened by the awareness that this, in fact, may not have been the case for him. That I would never know what he would endure long after his family checked out of the motel and moved into their new home. And I was even more sickened with myself: it would have been so simple for me to just be his friend, if only for a little while.

18 | At the Table

Although the dining room table got far more use as a game table, it was very much a table for dining. With seating for eight, it was the centerpiece of the wood-paneled, gold- and brown-flecked-carpeted room and was lit from above by a brown chandelier designed to look like a wagon wheel. A built-in china hutch provided space for Momma's never-used wedding china, some family photos, her crocheting supplies, and knickknacks.

When called into food service duty, the table held bounties from the adjacent kitchen. On weekday mornings, French toast cooked in the cast iron frying pan; hush puppies and fried fish and shrimp on Friday nights; chicken and andouille gumbo, jambalaya, Daddy's *sauce piquant* every now and then, and of course, spaghetti on Saturdays. And on Sundays, barbequed pork chops, sausage, and chicken on Daddy's oil-barrel pit out back. For dessert, Momma's syrup pie or fig Bundt cake, or one of any number of in-vogue treats whose recipes could be found in *Redbook*, *Woman's Day*, or *McCall's*: Mississippi Mud Cake, 7-Up Cake, and Sock-It-To-Me Cake were making the rounds in America's kitchens.

A four-by-six-foot cutout in the wall separating the kitchen and dining room made it easy to move food from the stove to the table and allowed conversations to flow between the two rooms.

On a shelf above the diner-inspired built-in breakfast nook in the yellow and brown, vinyl-coated, lattice-wallpapered kitchen, amid the collection of dining accessories stood the green Bakelite General Electric radio Momma acquired with ten books of S&H Green Stamps. The little radio provided a soundtrack for our game playing. Although Cajun music was plentiful on our local radio stations, none of us kids were particularly fond of it. A source of amusement at weddings, barbeques, and *boucheries*, perhaps, but not for everyday enjoyment like it was for

Mémère and our older relatives. Instead the radio was tuned to the one local pop music station broadcasting from Lafayette. Songs that wafted into the dining room from the kitchen one canasta-perfect September Saturday afternoon: "Dreams of the Everyday Housewife," "Tie a Yellow Ribbon," "Too Late to Turn Back Now," "Delta Dawn," "Bad, Bad Leroy Brown," "Half-Breed," "The Night the Lights Went Out in Georgia," and "When Will I See You Again?"

As our canasta game inched onward, KVOL's Bobby Jagneaux's Cajun-tinged but nonetheless reliable radio voice announced, "And here's Carl Douglas," as the one-hit-wonder strains of "Kung Fu Fighting" chopped their way out of the little radio. *"Huh!"*

He'd play three more songs—"My Love," "Will It Go Round in Circles?" and "Shambhala"—before cueing up the Butcher Air Conditioning jingle: *"Be safe, be sure, with Butcher Air Conditioning . . ."* And we had dutifully learned the lyrics to each of these songs he played as well as most of the jingles, so it was only natural that we sang along, with Gilda and Glenda singing on top of each other.

• • •

Momma said she thought Gilda and Glenda's competitiveness started in the womb, where apparently Gilda had gotten most of the food for herself, because she came out almost a half pound heavier than Glenda. Though Glenda did indeed catch up in a matter of weeks, the competitive life mold for them both had already been cast.

In a few years Gilda would make good grades and discover a knack for drawing in grammar school, be pretty convincing at the oboe in junior high, sail through high school as a basketball jock, excel at the respiratory therapy courses in trade school, start what was supposed to be a one-job career at the hospital, and marry the man she'd stay with for the rest of her life.

Glenda, meanwhile, quietly also made good grades in grammar school. And by junior high she discovered she was pretty good at the clarinet but was more seriously bitten by the tennis bug, an affliction that bloomed into a trophy-winning avocation later in life. It was in high school where her expanding tennis prowess joined a newfound set of skills on the basketball court that mirrored Gilda's and propelled her into full-on jock status. Though the spectacle of redheaded twin sisters on the basketball court naturally made people forge an association of them and the sport, Glenda broke out as the more jocklike of the two.

So it was this competitiveness that informed much of the way each girl approached playing cards. Glenda was prone to taking a steady, conservative approach, being careful with her decisions, melding as soon as possible for a sense of security. Gilda, on the other hand, more the gambler, liked surprises, liked keeping us in suspense, liked holding back her cards for a concealed canasta whenever possible. In Monopoly, she was fond of the high-end properties, the big risks, the bigger rewards.

Dicky and I, meanwhile, were happy to approach playing the games the same way: we just tried to enjoy them, happy to be included, as if we were wide-eyed dogs riding along in the car, tongues out, with our heads out the window. At least until the twins had a go at each other again and we had to duck and cover.

• • •

At the end of a day of playing, the cards were left in place on the dining room table, where everyone could keep an eye on them, lest one of the twins get the notion to make some "creative" adjustments. This particular game would last three days. It ended when Gilda, who had gotten over three thousand points but was pickled with jealousy over Glenda's forty-five hundred points, could not bear her sister's imminent victory. After very carefully and dramatically shuffling the two decks, instead of dealing everyone their eleven cards for a new round, she tossed the stack right at Glenda's head with such force that at least one of the cards broke the skin on her face, leaving an instant, if small, red scratch right above her nose.

"PIG! You coulda blinded me!" Glenda screamed as she leapt out of her chair and lunged towards Gilda. Dicky and I had the good sense to pull away from the table, find a safe corner in the room, and watch as the two thirteen-year-olds clawed, punched, scratched, bit, and kicked each other until they wore themselves out. With no adults around—Daddy was, as always, outside doing stuff, and Momma was at her beauty shop in town—this was the usual way these rounds of canasta ended.

"I'm tired of this," Dicky said. "Let's go to Bed-nah's."

"Not me," Glenda said, brushing her frazzled hair back into place, and rubbing the scratch above her nose. "Maybe later."

The next day, if we could locate two full decks of cards from the mess in the dining room, a new game would be started like nothing happened. There was a certain reliability, a certain consistency in the cards that inspired resilience in each of us.

19 | I Bet I Know What Y'all Want

No matter what we actually had come for, milk or bread or eggs or sugar, Mr. Bernard's greeting, "I bet I know what y'all want. Y'all want some can-dih," charmed and tickled us. We all called him Mr. *Bednah*, because that's how he called himself, and that's how his long-dead daddy, Yves, his brother Zeke, who worked with him in the store, and their Uncle Jacques, who had run the lumberyard down the road till he dropped dead from a heart attack in 1955, all pronounced his name.

He had plenty of reasons to presume we wanted candy. His small grocery store had limited offerings, but his candy selection was bountiful and a favorite destination whenever we had finally saved up a quarter or a few nickels. He had tubes of Necco Wafers, convincingly designed boxes of candy cigarettes, Hershey bars, Lemonheads, candy necklaces, Zero bars, PayDays, yellow bags of Sugar Babies, boxes of Red Hots and Boston Baked Beans, Butterfingers, Three Musketeers, Now & Laters, and lots of gum: Chiclets, Dentine, Wrigley's Spearmint, Juicy Fruit, and Wintergreen. He also had a tempting selection of prepackaged baked goods, to which Dicky was partial: Honey Buns, Ho-Ho's, Twinkies, pink and white Sno-Balls, and an array of Lance products. Despite all that, we mostly stuck to the penny candies he had in glass jars behind the counter: Tootsie Rolls, Mary Janes, Banana Splits, Jolly Ranchers, and, for a nickel each, beautiful, jewel-colored striped candy canes in a variety of flavors. The green- and red-striped watermelon ones were my favorite.

"Momma said 'No candy,' today, Mr. Bed-nah," I replied. "Just a milk, a pound of baloney, and a bread."

"No candy? Humph!" he said, reaching into the glass-paneled cooler for the big red-skinned log of baloney. He handled mostly everything with his left hand. His right arm ended about three inches above where his hand had once been, and was now only an exposed, rounded stump covered over with skin that still sprouted hair. According to Daddy's tales about the Bernards, the stump was the sad result of a single split second of mind-wandering one bright Thursday morning forty years ago when Mr. Bernard should have been paying more attention to the strip of white oak he was pushing through the spinning blade of Uncle Jacques's big table saw.

He tore a piece of brown butcher's paper from a roll on the counter and placed it on the enameled white scale. Using his stump to guide the log of baloney back and forth along the meat slicer, he said nothing. No more mind-wandering for him. The slicer made a smooth whir as he sliced, and no matter how many times I had witnessed him doing this, I couldn't help but wonder what he was thinking as he pushed the log of baloney back and forth over that spinning blade.

After slicing the pound of baloney, each slice having been layered in a stack atop the brown butcher's paper, he carefully picked it all up off the scale and moved it on the counter, then tore off a piece of butcher's tape from a big dispenser next to the register, wrapped it all up, using his one hand and the stump, to make a *perfect* package. It was quite a show. He then put the tidy brown package, the half-gallon of milk I had fetched from the cooler in the back, and the loaf of Evangeline Maid bread I had picked up off the shelf by the front window, all in one paper grocery bag.

"Thank you, Mr. Bed-nah!"

Once outside the little store, I picked up the bike I had used to ride there, Glenda's big, ugly, chipped, white-and-silver boy's Schwinn, which she bought from Andy with twenty-five dollars she had earned cleaning rooms, after Andy had saved up enough to buy himself a barely running used Yamaha motorcycle the year before. This transaction was made possible by their many hours of hard work: Glenda cleaning the motel's rusty-water-stained toilets, lavatories, and bathtubs, changing its bedsheets, and sweeping out its carpets, before school and after, holidays, and weekends, and Andy serving as Daddy's mule from sunup to sundown when he wasn't in school.

I mounted the big bike, crunching the grocery bag closed against the right side of the handlebar. Down the road twenty or so yards in the opposite direction of home stood the little yellow and white Catholic church, built in the footprint of a large cross. On Sundays, the white parishioners sat in the long nave; the black parishioners sat in the two little sections that straddled the altar and made up the crosspiece.

Parked in the grass near the church parking area was a beat-up green pickup truck. I recognized one of the parishioners, a middle-aged black man in baggy khakis, a white shirt, and a floppy straw hat. He was propping up a big hand-painted sign that read "Sugartown Watermelons 4 for $1."

"Four for a dollar. Hmmm," I said to myself, pedaling down the blacktop towards home. It was another hot July day, and I was lost in a daydream of all those watermelons chilled and sliced open to expose their beautiful, sweet red flesh. I pedaled onward, still clutching the paper bag against the handlebar, and building up a sweat in the heat that at once radiated from above and bounced back up to me from the blacktop. Just a little more than halfway home, totally unaware that the condensing half-gallon of milk was saturating the fibers of the paper bag, I stumbled in disbelief when the wet carton finally tore through the bag and fell, bursting onto the hot asphalt, sending milk all over the road, the bike, and my legs. The Evangeline Maid bread had been mashed on one side, but the unfazed loaf was already expanding itself back into recognizable form, and Mr. Bed-nah's carefully wrapped baloney parcel was still immaculate.

"Dammit!" I screamed out to the universe. I gathered myself, hammocked the baloney and bread into my tee-shirt, then picked up the busted milk carton and what was left of the paper bag. The milk spreading over the road was already steaming as it seeped into the blistering asphalt. With all that going on—the sun beating down, the baloney and bread scooped up into my shirt held in place with one arm pressed against my belly, and the busted carton and obliterated grocery bag clutched in that same hand—I managed to right the bike.

Still in a state of disbelief, I walked the bike and myself the rest of the way home.

An hour later, after I had gotten home and rinsed myself and the bike off with the garden hose under the big pine tree in the front yard, I was on the bike again, but this time Glenda was pedaling and I was riding double on the handlebar. We were accompanied by Gilda and Dicky, doing the same on Gilda's bike, all of us heading back down the road towards Mr. Bed-nah's and the church to get ourselves four watermelons and another half-gallon of milk.

20 | Scorched Sheets

Eula Belle Dupré, a holdover from the Melancon days, quit her housekeeping job in a huff one day after she finally had had enough of Daddy's insulting and oppressive bossing.

"Mr. C. H. never talked to me like that, Mr. Ardoin!" Eula Belle said through tears the day she quit. "I can't take it no more!"

What Eula Belle couldn't take anymore mostly was Daddy's need for control, his need to explain, to lecture on how things were supposed to be properly done, even to people like Eula Belle, who had done the job virtually every day for more than a decade.

"Towels. Soap. Sheet. Toilet paper," he said each morning as she arrived to do the rooms, not, "Good morning, Eula Belle," or "How're you doing, Eula Belle?" but "Towels. Soap. Sheet. Toilet paper."

"I got it, Mr. Ardoin," she replied, trying to smile. "I have it all in my cart." Surely she was thinking, "Who the hell is he to tell me what I need to clean a damned motel room?!"

After Eula Belle left, Cassie took over the job for a while before she, too, escaped Daddy's hammering, to college in Lake Charles. And so, three years after we moved there in 1967, the housekeeping duties for the motel became the responsibility of the twins.

Gilda took the laundry, which was situated in its own building behind our house. What with its size, built to accommodate the industrial equipment, a pitched roof, windows all around, and a little front porch, the laundry building resembled a free-standing house. In it each day, seven days a week, Gilda's job was to wash, dry, and fold all the sheets and towels as well as do the family clothes. For that she got a dollar a day, and she preferred that job by far to Glenda's, which was cleaning the motel rooms as they were vacated, and which paid more than double because its hours were unpredictable and absorbed more of her time.

The laundry was connected to the back door of our house by an embedded path of concrete chunks and odd pieces of ceramic tile. The ground between the two buildings was shaded completely by a sprawling magnolia tree that perfumed the back yard with the cloying scent of its enormous white blooms and kept grass from growing there. The bare "floor" that resulted had solidified into a hard dirt crust over the years. Eula Belle had taken to sweeping it with an old broom she kept behind the laundry door for just that purpose.

A community of twenty tame, and another ten or so feral, cats had settled on the property. A good number of them made their homes under the house and the laundry, so they were a constant presence, the tame ones weaving themselves around our calves as we walked, and the feral ones running and hissing when approached. They all waited for their once-a-day feeding of dry cat food scooped from a fifty-pound bag stored in the laundry. Daddy conceded to us this generosity despite his belief that the cats could all amply feed themselves with mice from the rice and soybean fields that surrounded the motel, and the scraps we threw them from the kitchen door.

The industrial laundry room fascinated me. To the right upon entering were wide shelves that held the towels, arranged by size. Washcloths, medium towels, bath towels, and bath mats, as well as the sheets, bedspreads, and mattress pads for the motel bathrooms. At the left as you entered was a long and wide handmade wooden table covered in oilcloth that was used for folding the laundry. Above the table were shelves that held cleaning products: Vani-Sol, a highly toxic acid-based product that ate toilet stains, canisters of ZUD powdered cleanser for removing rust from the lavatories, as well as a box of Cashmere Bouquet motel soaps, and a section for the motel drinking glasses, which were enclosed in white tissue paper that read *Sanitized for Your Protection.*

Two shiny, rounded steel machines and one big green boxy one stood in a row at the back of the room. Riveted to each shiny machine was a thick, red, steel rhomboid-shaped plate with simple white letters spelling out MILNER, the L and N joining to form a corner. The three big official-looking machines and the tidy stacks of precisely folded bright white linens they produced all stood in stark contrast to the rustic, unfinished walls of the wooden building that housed them.

Gilda said the washing machine could handle sixty pounds of sheets and towels at once. She kept an eye on the fifty-pound bags of washing powder and dry bleach that stood on the floor to the left of the washer, so she could alert Daddy when it was time to order more. For every load of whites, she inserted one scoop each of washing powder and bleach into a hatch on the top of the shiny machine.

After the washing and rinsing cycles were finished, Gilda transferred the machine's heavy wet contents by hand to an equally shiny steel "extractor" next to it. We called that machine simply "the spinner," because it spun the wet laundry at such a force that most of the water was removed. She closed the spinner's steel lid and pushed its big ignition arm into the *On* position, an action that simultaneously locked the lid in place and starting the machine's gradual spin. It reached eighteen hundred revolutions per minute and, once whirring smoothly at full speed, could be heard all the way in the back bedrooms of our house. If the heavy contents weren't evenly balanced, the inner barrel would scrape against the outer chassis as the machine got to full speed and create a dreadful, loud banging noise that signaled to anyone within earshot to drop what they were doing, run into the laundry room, and quickly pull back the ignition arm to turn the whole thing off, then rearrange the laundry inside it, and start over.

Next to the spinner, with just enough space for an adult to squeeze through to get to the back of the machines, stood the big, six-feet-high boxy green UniMac gas dryer. Its pilot light had developed a habit of blowing out with the slightest breeze. To relight the pilot, Gilda stood back there behind the dryer, held down the pilot button with the thumb of one hand, somehow struck a match with her other hand, and then made sure to hold down that button for at least a full minute. If she wasn't patient enough to count to sixty, the pilot would not stay lit, and she'd have to start over.

Upon ignition, two things happened: the dryer's pulley-operated barrel jolted into rotation, and a blowtorch swoosh of flame shot through the inner workings of the big machine to dry its contents. In its heyday a built-in timer shut the whole thing down according to the operator's estimation of drying time, but that had long since stopped working, so it was necessary to keep an eye on the machine. One Friday morning in July, not long before she left us, Eula Belle had learned that the hard way when the big machine was left on too long and its contents ignited. The resulting immense heat shattered the glass door and sent smoke billowing out and filling the room.

"Mister Ardoin! Mister Ardoin," Eula Belle screamed from the laundry porch. "Come quick! The dryer's blown up!"

Though Daddy was quickly able to choke the flames back with a couple blasts from a fire extinguisher and contain it all within the drum of the machine, the smoke had already infused a nostril-piercing stench of char into all the clean sheets and towels on the shelves at the opposite end of the room.

Eula Mae got Gilda to help her gather and take everything into town to rewash it all at the public laundry on Laurel Avenue. To keep up with the daily load of sheets and towels, Daddy had to put back into service a little Maytag home dryer that had not been used since its days at the old house in town before the move to the motel. Though it was considerably smaller in capacity, all the drying was done in that little machine for the next three weeks until a repairman could install a new heat-tempered glass and gasket for the door, and a new timer for the machine.

• • •

On the side of the laundry room opposite the big folding table, practically the entire length of that wall, stood a gas-heated mangle iron where in the olden days all of the motel's cotton sheets and pillowcases were fed though a large rotating cylinder that brushed up against a smooth metal press. As the sheet emerged again from the back of the press, the operator grabbed its opposite corners, glided it up and out, then folded it, and put it aside, before feeding another sheet through. The sheet that came out was beautiful and crisp, unless, of course, it had lingered too long against the hot press in the back, which, in those cases, scorched it and made it useless in the rooms. Those marked sheets ended up on our beds in the house.

"These burnt sheets are so ugly, Momma," Dicky complained one night. "How come we can't have the good sheets like the customers get?"

"Well, ain't that just a slice of pie," Momma said to him, cocking her head for emphasis. "They're not burnt, they're just scorched a little. Be quiet and count your blessings."

21 | **Sparrrkling!**

Glenda was eleven when she began cleaning motel rooms. On school days she rose at six a.m. and was able to clean four or five rooms before getting herself ready and out to the road to wait for the school bus. Moments after her black Big Ben rattled her awake, she bounded down the stairs to the front office to grab the master keyring, scan the rooms rented that night, then head out the back door to the laundry, where she grabbed enough clean sheets and towels for at least two rooms, and her cleaning bucket, which had in it a toilet-cleaning brush, a plastic drink cup filled with Cashmere Bouquet motel soaps, a can of Zud powdered cleanser, and a bottle of that rust-eating Vani-Sol.

She had been warned by Daddy that no matter how rusted they'd become from a faucet left dripping hard water overnight, she was to use only the Zud on the lavatories and tubs.

"That Vani-Sol is too damned strong for anything other than a toilet," Daddy said. This was definitely true. The Vani-Sol bottle was stamped with an ominous black skull and crossbones. Its fumes, released in a white cloud when poured, were so strong that if breathed in for more than a second, they could knock you out cold, and its corrosive acid could eventually eat through metal pipes. Imagine what it would do to your lungs. No matter, when she was in a hurry, and a big orange rust stain was staring back at her from the lavatory, she covered her nose and mouth with a cloth, poured a little Vani-Sol on it and, *Voila*! it disappeared in seconds. Scrubbing that thing down with Zud would have taken way more time than she was prepared to give it.

As she headed through the garage with a stack of linens and her bucket, she also grabbed a broom to sweep out any loose bits on the carpets.

· · ·

Each of the motel's twenty rooms had a personality. Unique furniture, wall decorations and light fixtures, bedspreads, color schemes. Glenda's favorite room, Room 9, looked the most contemporary, among the old rooms anyway. It had furniture and accents from the current decade and wood paneling instead of plaster walls. Another favorite was Room 14, which gave off a certain vibe. Its furniture from the 1940s and '50s was all still quite beautiful, and the fact that it should have been Room 13 was intriguing. According to industry lore, hotels never have a Room 13. People don't want to stay in a Room 13, so the hotel planners skip over that number or start numbering at 100 to avoid that bit of superstition altogether.

For most rooms, cleaning was a quick job. After the bathroom was cleaned and restocked with towels, the bed linens were stripped and bundled, and the bed was remade with clean sheets. The bedspreads were not changed after each customer; only when they were obviously soiled, or were beginning to smell stale, were they changed. After the bed was done, a quick wipe-down of the other furniture in the room: a vanity, side chairs, and nightstands. The final touch was a quick sweeping out of the carpet. It was Glenda's habit to then have a quick run around each aspect of the room, and declare, "Sparrrkling," in the bathroom, then "Sparrrkling," in the bedroom, and then once more, as she was ready to declare it ready for re-renting, a final "Sparrrkling!" cast over the whole room with an imaginary scepter before she closed the door behind her. That whole process, from entrance to exit, took her about ten minutes.

Every now and then, however, a room was in such bad shape it would be considerably more than a ten-minute job. Trash strewn about the room to be picked up; bloody sheets, mattress covers, and bedspreads happened quite a bit, and always meant a trip back to the laundry.

"That was so gross!" Glenda announced as she entered the office having just finished cleaning Room 12. "Those pigs threw their greasy chicken bones under the bed. I had to push the whole bed aside to get them out. Last week it was even more disgusting in Room 10—the guy just tossed his used rubber, and it stuck to the TV! I had to use toilet paper to pick it up and then had to Windex the whole TV! Gross!"

In the bathrooms she had encountered even grosser situations that stopped her cold: vomit splatters, shit on the floor, bloody towels, all of which had to be cleaned up and, in cases like that, the whole room aired out a few hours before she could cast her magical wand and declare the room "Sparrrkling!"

Glenda was the motel's primary housekeeper from age eleven until she transferred from the LSU branch in Eunice to the main campus in Baton Rouge eight years later. And she would clean them on and off after college when called upon by Daddy to help out. In her estimation, she cleaned at least ten thousand rooms over the three decades our family owned the motel.

22 | The Regulars

"Bob Hope was just on the phone," Daddy called out to Glenda, who was passing through the office on her way to clean some rooms. "He wants number 9. Can you clean that one first?"

"Yeah, sure," she groused between clenched teeth. She hated nothing more than having to rush to get a room cleaned. "There's plenty of other rooms already ready to rent," she said to herself. She'd been cleaning the rooms for two years at that point, and just as he had done with Cassie and Eula Belle before her, Daddy could not fathom the idea that Glenda had yet figured out the things she needed to clean a room.

"Towels. Soap. Sheet. Toilet paper," he said to Glenda, who by then had learned to shrug it off or mock him right back with his own words.

"Towels. Soap. Sheet," she said back to him. "Will there be anything else?" she chuckled.

"Toilet paper." was his sonorous reply.

• • •

"Bob Hope" was one of a small handful of "regulars," regular customers who had established enough credibility with Daddy that they could just call ahead and leave the money in the room when they left, bypassing the check-in process and the registration chitchat that went with it. He had been given the name Bob Hope because, back when he was still registering and showing his face, I noticed he looked like the real Bob Hope. At first it was only me who called him that, just as I called a Mr. Fontenot from Mamou "Fats Cadillac" simply because he was fat and drove a green Cadillac, and a certain Mr. Finkleman from Opelousas "The Judge" after the *Opelousas Daily World* reported he was running for city judge. The shorthand made more and more sense as the years passed, so everyone, even Daddy, took to calling them by their motel names, including The Judge, even though he'd lost that election. We even went so far as to write their motel names on the registration cards, because we had soon forgotten their real ones.

Room 9 was situated in the former elbow of the L-shaped motel building. Before the fire three Christmases back, it had a narrow entryway notched out of Room 8's floor plan, which gave the room a sense of charm, of mystery, and even romance, as it provided a prelude of two additional steps before entering the actual room. After Room 8 was destroyed in the fire, the new Room 9 was reconfigured with a flat-front entrance like all the other rooms, and now, instead of being the unique elbow room, its door faced a row of new rooms on the opposite side of the parking lot. No more prelude.

Nonetheless, the new Room 9 was indeed one of the nicest rooms in the old section of the motel; its furniture, TV, bath fixtures, and air conditioner were all new, purchased along with the furniture, TVs, bath fixtures, and air conditioners acquired for the new rooms across the parking lot. The new beds all featured a simple, sleek mahogany headboard instead of the spindled, knobby oak frames of those of the 1930s and '40s. Matching nightstands, side tables, and squared-off chairs replaced the round-cornered furnishings of the earlier period. And though the rooms in the new section were all more modern than any of the old rooms, including Room 9, Bob Hope seemed to have a sentimental attachment to that room, and Daddy, if he could, always tried to accommodate his customers' wishes.

This eagerness to accommodate did not extend to his black customers, however. Instead of making the registration process nonexistent or, at the very least, easy for them, he often made it more of a challenge by chatting with them and greeting them with overtly racist (although he denied he was in any way racist) remarks.

"Look who's out of the penitentiary!" was one Daddy's favorite greetings to black men. Most black customers, the regulars anyway, had grown over the years to expect him to say something offensive under the guise of being friendly and comical, and were prepared to shrug it off, so they obliged him a chuckle to keep the transaction as brief as possible. It was just part of the price they had to pay for a room.

Every now and then, however, an uninitiated black customer would walk thorough the office door, be greeted with something completely offensive, and actually take offense.

"What'd you say?" one such customer asked when Daddy greeted him with, "They let you out?" Sensing the man's discomfort, Daddy let it drop, but the man was having none of it.

"What kind of bullshit place is this?!" the man asked. "You ain't getting a thin dime offa me!" he said as he did an about-face and slammed the door behind him.

We all had witnessed a version of this spectacle more than once, and it gave me a secret thrill to see Daddy lose a customer because of his bigotry. Perhaps the one most effective way to make a point with Daddy was to hit him where it hurt most, his wallet.

• • •

Thousands of customers would come and go over the three decades our family ran the motel. Most of these people were quickly and easily forgotten. Shortly after they turned in their keys and drove off to places near and far, someone else would arrive to take up residence, if only for an hour or two, in the same room.

There were more than a handful of others, however, who left a lasting impression, whether because they become regulars like Bob Hope, the Judge, or Fats Cadillac, or because, through their check-in revelations about themselves, or the evidence they left behind in their soiled rooms, their stories lived on.

There was the tall, dark, and handsome man who, after years of regular patronage, turned out to be a woman. Glenda discovered this quite innocently when she opened the door to the room thinking it vacated, to find two naked women, one of them clearly the "man" who had been checking in all this time. In the nothing-surprises-me environment of this business we operated, the revelation from Glenda seemed to embarrass her more than tickle her, as it did the rest of us, and it inspired only a shrug from Daddy.

"It takes all kinds," he said when Glenda told him. "As long as their money's green, what they do is their business." We'd never know if it was because of sheer mortification at being found out or just coincidence, but this would be the couple's last rendezvous at the Stone Motel.

Then there was the couple who left behind a red tabby cat; they called from a phone booth a hundred miles down the road to say they'd pick her up on their return, but never did (we named her Orphan). And the woman we suspected was a self-managing prostitute; when asked how long she needed the room, she responded, with a hoarse giggle, "Oh, we won't be long. In fact, we'll just be in and out, and in and out, and in and out." Mr. Wilkes, the middle school industrial arts teacher, was clearly mortified when he realized upon check-in that I, one of his pupils, was part of the family that ran this motel. (I would never know if the straight A's I made that year in his class were because I was so good at drafting or because I was even better at discretion.)

And of course there was the man who never made it home after his night at the motel: Momma pulled out of the garage on the way to church that morning when Gilda, in the backseat, commented on the man, who looked to be just getting into his car to take off. An hour later we were returning from Mass, and it was clear that the man was in the same position, half in and half out of his car. Dicky was dispatched on Glenda's banana bike to go have a look. The man had managed to get halfway in, with one leg at the pedals and the other propping him up from the driveway. He had turned his ignition switch just enough to engage the radio and apparently died then and there of a heart attack. "There's a dead man listening to his radio!" Dicky reported excitedly when he returned after having made a few circles around the car.

We came to know these people without judgment. Their lives were varied. Their needs—for an hour, or a day, a week, a month, or longer— were at once none of our business, and all of our business. It was our job, simply, to serve them. Daddy said that if we couldn't understand and fully accept that, then we were in the wrong business altogether.

23 | Zanny: The Souvenir

When Eliza and I got married, we really didn't plan to have all these kids, but we did and it makes sense to get them learning the importance of work early on. Work is good for them. They don't know it now, but learning how to work when they're young is gonna carry them throughout their lives. I know it did me.

But these kids, they wanna stay indoors all day and play cards. They'd watch TV all day if I didn't put my foot down. So they play cards sometimes for several days in a row, and just leave their cards right there on the dining room table overnight and then pick it up the next day. This happens all summer long. I guess that's better then watching that damned TV.

Eh vieux Long Jowl! Where you been? I haven't seen you in a few weeks! Now look, I'm not going to warn you again, but that woman of yours has a habit of "borrowing" a few towels now and then. It's not a big deal, but I'm gonna have to charge you for two towels. This time. No. No. I'm not looking for no argument. You know I'm telling you the truth. We have to watch all that. My daughter cleans all them rooms, and she come tell me the last time you was here that the two big towels was gone. So you tell your woman she can't do that. Them towels ain't cheap. That's gonna be another ten dollars.

I've been thinking a lot about my second boy, Morris. He's all mouth, that boy. And soft. And he sure is sassy. I know I do not handle him well at all. But to me, that boy is headed for a lot of trouble. He needs to be trained. I've seen it coming for years now, since he was little. He liked playing with the girls, not his brothers. He wasn't interested in any of the things most boys are interested in. He wanted to play house.

Eliza says she doesn't think he knows *how* to be a boy. I tell her that then we are just gonna have to teach him. One way or another, because he sure as hell is gonna have a hard life if he don't change his ways. Those kinda boys grow up to be troubled men. They're soft. There's all kinda words for that kinda soft man, and there's no way one of my sons is gonna be one of those.

I have tried with him but nothing seems to penetrate. Finally I really lost all control with him. It happened a coupla days after I lost half my motel in that fire. I watched as one by one, my motel rooms all went up in flames, just a few days before Christmas. Some joker left a cigarette burning in Room 5. He was long gone by the time the whole side of the building was up in flames. Burned half my place to the ground. I'm standing there and looking at that building burn. Everybody's outside at two in the morning watching them firemen fight them flames.

One of the worst days of my life. What the hell was I gonna do? I didn't know what to think. For a long time after that, I wasn't in my right mind. None of us was.

But me and Eliza and the kids got right back into it. Started cleaning up the place and doing whatever we could to get back on track. There was a big a family to feed, and everybody was on deck helping out.

And lo and behold, Morris was out there in the back yard chipping away at one of the stone columns I had salvaged. I grabbed him and started whipping him and something came over me. I just couldn't stop myself. If Eliza hadn't jumped on my back, I mighta killed that boy.

Well! Look who's here! How you doing, Cauliflower Ears? Weren't you just here on Monday? Sorry about barging in on you like that. Looked like you was about ready to pop too. Sorry 'bout that. But your car wasn't in the right place. I thought I recognized your car, but since it wasn't there in the right place, I thought maybe I had made a mistake, so I just unlocked the door. You know I gotta go around and keep an eye on things. When somebody checks out, I'm usually the first to inspect the rooms. Glad it was me barging in and not my daughter that cleans them rooms.

Anyway, you're here again already! Well, good for you. But you gonna need to park that car right in front of your room. That's how we know when you're gone, if your car ain't there. If you park in front of another room, we can't tell.

I can't tell you how many times I stopped myself from going off like that with him lately. To tell the truth, it coulda been any one of the kids, but

I was particularly concerned about Morris. It worried me a lot because I know I have the capability to kill someone with my bare hands. But when them kinda situations happen, something goes off in me, and I'm not myself anymore.

Some things you just can't know. I didn't know that Morris only wanted a li'l piece of that stone column for a *souvenir*. Eliza told me he told her that he thought I was gonna throw them columns away, so he wanted a li'l piece before they disappeared.

That hit me hard. A got-damned souvenir.

But I can't stand here and tell you that I woulda acted any different if I had known that at the time. I had just lost my business. I'm scrambling to get things up and running again, and there's this boy, this soft boy, deliberately doing more damage. I know there's people like me who'da done just what I did, but I also know that there's a better way than that.

I sure do know that now.

I know I was hard on Cassie, too. Our firstborn. We had no experience at all, and we learned the hard way how to handle a child. But she grew up intact, and before you know it she was asking for a prom dress. I shoulda noticed the look on her face. She was scared to death to ask me for the money for that dress. But I didn't see that. In my mind, what I saw was that she was asking for something frivolous at a time when we couldn't spare it. Something she and Eliza coulda made themselves. So what do I do? I hauled off and slapped her. And as I'm standing here, I can tell you that by the time I realized what I was doing, before my hand ever hit her, it was too late. She was on the ground, and then Eliza was out the door and hollering at me. She was mad and I was mad at myself. And I did not have the presence of mind to even imagine everything that had gone on in her mind before she got the courage to ask me for that money.

And I was hard on Andy, too. He came next after Cassie. Our first boy. Andy was tough from the get-go. You know, that boy had a touch of epilepsy when he was young. He grew out of it in a few years, but during those years with epilepsy, he had a few spells, and so it wasn't a surprise that he didn't do so good in school. He was quiet most of the time. Very shy. I think that epilepsy set him off on a path that would set his personality for life. He knew there was something wrong with him, so it made him self-conscious around people. It was hard to get him to understand that to deal with people you just gotta stick your hand out to them. Gotta look 'em in the eye and introduce yourself right off the bat. I tried to get him to understand that but could not get through to him. The one thing that made him perk up was being outside. Being in nature. Mention hunting and camping, and he'd perk right up. You'd see a whole different side-a him. We'd go hunting and he would be right by my side. That, more than anything, attached him to me. He was loyal and eager to please.

But that boy. I'm not proud of the way I pushed him. Sometimes too hard. And dammit, no. He set me off one day, too; he was a teenager by then. He set me off, and there I was, punching him. He just held his fists up to his face and closed his eyes. And I knocked him left and right. I don't even remember what the hell that was all about, but I remember punching him like he was a man, like me.

He just kept saying, "Why, Daddy? Why?" as I was knocking him around. That finally got to me, and I dropped my fists and walked away. No, I'm not proud of that.

After that, he shut down with me. We've never been the same after that.

Well, then. If it ain't Mister Escaped Convict! Oh, no. Not you. Not today. Look, the last time y'all rented one-a my rooms, I had to call the police on you. Had that woman running half naked screaming. Everybody seen that. Whatever you had going on between you and that woman of yours, well, that's your business. But you can't do that kinda thing here. No way. You got to go. No. I can't rent you no room. And don't you come back here, or I'm gonna call the police on you again.

I tell you, that was some hard times to go through. I'm just starting to get everything lined up to make a good business. We're meeting all the bills, keeping on top of the mortgage, and all the stuff that needs to be updated. All those rooms needed new furnishings, new carpets, paint jobs, and the like. But just as it was looking like we're making some headway, we lose half the business. And still have to pay for that half that was now ashes.

So we all get up and just got to it. There was no real plan, really. Each day we did what was right in front of us. It had to get done, and I had no earthly idea about how long it would be before we'd all get back to normal. It ultimately took us the best part of a year. By then, the burnt side was all demolished, and the side that was not fully burned was repaired and refurnished. By year's end, a new section of rooms was under construction, so finally I was able to let myself imagine coming through this okay. But I have to tell you, it was touch-and-go for a long, long time.

Vintage postcard of the Stone Motel, Eunice, La., circa 1955.

The Ardoin family, Chicot State Park, Ville Platte, La. Andy, Glenda, Cassie, Daddy, Gilda, Morris, Momma, circa 1964.

Daddy as a teenager, breaking a horse, Tate Cove, La., circa 1939.

Morris, first communion, 1966.

Dickie, Scotty, Morris at home with the Apache and motel building in the background, circa 1972.

Momma and Daddy, wedding portrait, 1951.

Momma and Alisa, back door of the house at the Stone Motel, Eunice, La., circa 1980.

Eliza's Beauty Shop

340 East Vine   Phone 457-4795
ELIZA ARDOIN, OWNER - MGR.
Open Tuesday through Saturday
Expert permanent waving
Hair coloring - Hair shaping - Manicures
Wigs - Wiglets - sold and serviced
CALL FOR APPOINTMENT
ELIZA ARDOIN   SUE LEWIS
STYLISTS

Business card, Eliza's Beauty Shop, 1968.

Momma, when she was a bookkeeper at G. Ardoin's Department Store, Ville Platte, La., circa 1948.

Momma and her brothers, Paillasse and Florence, circa 1940.

Pépère and Mémère, DeJean and Ortense Thompson, Ville Platte, La., circa 1965.

Wedding portrait, Ortense and DeJean Thompson, Ville Platte, La., 1920.

Pépère, DeJean Thompson, *forgeron* (blacksmith), Ville Platte, La., 1943.

Top to bottom, L-R: Andy, Cassie, Glenda, Gilda, and Morris, Easter, circa 1963.

24 | Grass, Carpets, Weeds

Every day from mid-July to mid-August much of south Louisiana gets a short break from the oppressive summer heat when clustering clouds, groaning with moisture wicked from the rivers, bayous, and lowland sloughs and swamps below can no longer hold their cargo, and so, accompanied by a series of thunderclaps, release a very welcome downpour that renders the air steam, and then burns away, having sliced a degree or two off of the thermometer. All in under thirty minutes. This daily phenomenon creates a perfect ecosystem in which the abundant, aggressive, and relentless Saint Augustine grass that grows wherever it can get a roothold thrives.

Keeping up with the grass so it didn't flourish to the point of returning our property to wilderness was a never-ending summer battle. The twins were both happy to drive the little red tractor to cut the grass, especially since doing so allowed them some tanning time that didn't involve the boring ritual of lying outside on a towel. They also loved commandeering the truck for a trip to the dump every now and then. But to Daddy, that kind of work was decidedly "boys' work," so it was we boys who were, for the most part, responsible for those chores.

Andy was Daddy's personal assistant, helping him do heavy labor around the property. Typically, once a week during the summers, it was he who got to drive the tractor to mow the large areas of grass that grew so fast and thick, owing to those reliable downpours.

Daddy decided that for me, a "too soft" eleven-year-old, the most appropriate job that he said would "help me grow into a man" was cutting the thick grass with the push mower wherever the tractor couldn't reach, and hand-pulling the tall weeds that grew under the wire fence lining the back of the property. There were a lot of places where Andy could not maneuver his tractor nimbly enough to reach, especially in between all the trees. So I push-mowed most of the patch of green surrounded by the front driveway that we called *the island*, a quarter-acre cluster of trees. I then mowed the lawns directly in front of the house, around the kitchenette apartments to the side of the house, and in the back of the house between the buildings—all places where the tractor was too big and clumsy to do the job. Then there was mowing to be done along the ditches and driveways, in places where the tractor missed, and around each of the twenty-eight trees and bushes that lined the motel access road to the highway.

Pushing that mower in the sticky summer heat took me the better part of two full days each and every week of the summer. Dressed in cutoff jeans, a tee-shirt, and tennis shoes, and taking advantage of the cooler morning hours, with a short break at the hottest part of the day, and then pushing on, to when the crickets began their nightly serenade at sundown, I mowed and mowed and mowed. By the time the thermometer reached ninety degrees around ten in the morning, I was soaked through with sweat. I could push on for about an hour before midday lunch break, then get back at it, with even hotter three o'clock peak temperatures nearing one hundred on many summer days.

At the end of such a day, I was the definition of exhaustion. My hands were blistered, my chest heaved. I coughed hoarsely, expelling a bouquet of mown grass and gasoline exhaust, and my lungs felt bruised and tight, a soreness in my chest that stayed with me for at least another couple of days after the cutting was all done. This easily was *the* most dreaded thing I had to do.

But my work was not all misery. I also was the designated vacuumer on Sundays. Each of the motel rooms had to be vacuumed at least once a week, since they were only swept with a broom between rentings. As I pushed the big black industrial Hoover methodically back and forth over the carpets, singing along to songs still in my head from the little kitchen radio, the hum of the vacuum gave me the opportunity to escape into my thoughts for a few hours.

Lately, I'd been distracted by the disappearance of one of my personal notebooks. For the last year or so, since Mrs. Fuselier, my seventh-grade English teacher, assigned us the task of keeping a journal, I kept up with writing notes every now and then. Until very recently I had four filled notebooks, starting with the one for Mrs. Fuselier's class. But a week earlier I was reaching over to my stack of notebooks to enter some thoughts in the newest one when I realized there were only three where I'd left them, in a desk drawer next to my bed. The second notebook, the one that had the notes about my summer between seventh and eighth grades, and then into the fall term, was gone. Of course I turned the area upside down in search of the missing book, but still only three remained. Had I mistakenly taken one to school? That didn't make any sense. I never took a notebook out of the house. The thought that someone had taken the book crossed my mind, but who would do that? That anyone would find the contents of these books of any interest was hard for me to believe. I asked the twins and Dicky about it, and they each shrugged. Could it be Daddy? Should I ask him? What would he say, even if he'd done it? Would he be angry? And, more horribly, what was *in* that book? What would he have discovered about my thoughts? There was plenty there to read, I'm sure, but I had no way of knowing. The idea that someone was reading my personal thoughts was upsetting and made me feel a bit vulnerable.

I finished vacuuming the old row of rooms, then moved across the parking lot to the new row. The change of location did me some good. I stopped obsessing about the notebook and thought of less worrisome things. I'd seen a recipe for Orange Spice Cake in Momma's *McCall's* magazine and wanted to make that. Mémère said she was coming for a weekend visit soon, which would be a good time to do another one of the series of interviews I had started with her—a project I decided I should do regularly enough so that I'd have her full life story down before she got too old and then left us. I mentally designed a new hotel that I would run someday (if I could only grow up before Daddy finished me off), a place all contained in one tower instead of a spread-out business like ours, and that had a built-in vacuum cleaning system so the vacuumer wouldn't have to haul around a heavy Hoover.

Because it gave me some time with my thoughts, I actually came to love the vacuuming job, the worst part of which was emptying the cloth bag, a process involving dust flying everywhere, no matter how careful I was to contain it. Vacuuming was light work compared to the hell that was mowing.

At nine, Dicky was too young to do much of anything, but he could be enlisted to help out any one of us so long as we don't expect too much from him. As he matured he would take his turn behind the mower and the vacuum, as well as at cleaning rooms and folding sheets like those of us before him.

• • •

Our chores centered on cleaning rooms, doing laundry, groundskeeping, and dealing with customers, but there were other, more interesting tasks to be done as well. Daddy insisted that the variety of work we were exposed to at the motel would teach us how to approach pretty much anything, no matter how difficult, or stinky, or simply odd. His assertion would be validated years later when we each would take for granted the ability, for example, to maintain an impeccable lawn, install a toilet, plaster a busted wall, or rewire a light fixture, and have no qualms about removing a used condom stuck to a TV or from under a bed, or pulling a rotting animal carcass from under a building, without puking.

25 | Croquet Sunday

On a sleepy Sunday afternoon in September, I was stationed at the registration desk. Gilda and Glenda had started a game of croquet on the lawn at the side of the house. Momma, Dicky, and Andy had joined the game. Daddy was having his Sunday nap after being up for most of Saturday night, the busiest night of the week. This would be his normal routine for three decades.

All quiet inside the office. I could see through the big picture windows the edge of the croquet game just off to the left. I was holding my head up in my hand, about to fall asleep myself.

Suddenly, out of the corner of my right eye, I saw movement that roused me to full attention. It was a woman I estimated to be somewhere in her late thirties, her black hair bobby-pinned down to her head, making it look like she had on a skullcap. Wearing only a pink bra and matching slip, she was running and flailing towards the office. Towards *me*.

Oh, my.

"Halp! Halp!" she screamed. "Call the po-lice!" she continued as she came barreling through the office door. "Call the po-lice! He's tryin' a kill me!"

The "he" in question was her companion, about twenty feet behind her, hopping from foot to foot on the gravel that stabbed at his bare feet. Wearing nothing but white boxer shorts, he was striking at the air with what looked like a dead cat.

"Hurry! He gonna kill me!" the woman screamed.

Meanwhile, on the lawn, heads were casually turning up and away from the brightly striped wooden balls and matching mallets. Glenda, who was in a semi-squat and shaking her butt in preparation for taking her strike, paused in mid-shake when she heard the commotion traveling towards me in the office.

"Go on," Gilda commanded. "Whatever that is, it can wait till after my turn."

I was scrambling to dial the phone. The woman was quickly inside the office, her cat-wielding companion had one hand in the door, and she was banging it against him to get him to back off.

"She two-timin' me!" came a shout from the man. "She a two-timin' *ho!*" he yelled, still waving the dead cat in the air, which I could now see was actually her wig. She banged the door against his arm, and he dropped the wig and recoiled. She quickly dead-bolted the door and picked up her wig.

Out on the lawn, Gilda was now at her ball, but the continuing disruption in the otherwise quiet day had the other players standing in place, croquet mallets in hand, looking up at the scene, mouths hanging open, and apparently still not in any particular mind to help.

There was nothing I could say or do but wait, since it was obvious that no one outside felt compelled to come to my rescue or get involved in any way. This was what struck me as the most peculiar thing. I was guessing they believed I could handle it alone.

"Hurry!" the woman screamed. "He gonna kill us both!"

When the cops arrived, Daddy, who had awakened and donned his coveralls, which he always removed for a nap, walked casually to the office, looked at me, beaming like the moon, and said, "Moy? You got this under control?"

"What?" I said, still not believing any of it. "Oh—um—the police are coming."

"Have a seat," Daddy said to the lady, as if she were there for a cup of tea and a friendly chat. "I'll take care of him," he continued, unbolting the deadbolt and heading outside.

"I ain't two-timin' him," said the woman. "He two-timin' me! He crazy."

A minute later the cops were pulling in. Daddy and the man talked to them, and the woman, now on her feet again, her wig back on her head, joined them.

"He crazy," she said softly, shaking her head.

They told her to go back to her motel room and collect her things. They were going to take her home and instructed the man that he needed to get his stuff and get in his car, and that he was lucky she was not interested in pressing charges. They all drove off.

From the lawn, a loud, crisp POP! pierced the renewed calm as Andy's mallet made a clean strike at a red ball, sending it hurtling towards the front ditch.

26 | Advance Token to Oatmeal Avenue

In terms of its capacity to keep us engaged and out of the heat for hours, or even days, Monopoly was the closest game to canasta, which was why we play it second-most often. That we lived at and helped to run a motel gave the game some functional familiarity, what with its hotels and property management issues, and we each had a favorite token piece, a feature you couldn't get from canasta, no matter how engaging. Glenda was partial to the Scottie, Gilda the top hat.

The dice-roll ceremony to see who would select his token and go first in the game filled the room with tension and could predict trouble ahead. When she rolled the highest number, a skill for which she had a certain knack, Gilda relished pissing off Glenda by selecting the Scottie, even though it had no appeal for her.

"Four," I said after my roll.

"Five," said Gilda after hers.

A betraying look blossomed on Glenda's face. "I want the *racecar* this time," she announced before rolling the dice, fooling no one.

"Um hum," Gilda said as Glenda threw the dice.

"Ugh. Three," Glenda said.

"I'll be the dog," Gilda said giddily, picking up the Scottie and placing it on the Go square.

Glenda's eyes darted from her to me, impatiently.

Because I liked the racecar, the iron, and the thimble equally, I didn't mind letting Glenda have that consolation. "I want the iron," I said.

Saying nothing, Glenda grabbed the car and put it on the Go square.

"All right, let's play," Gilda said, throwing a four and a two. She moved her token to Oriental Avenue.

"Oatmeal Avenue," she proclaimed, calling it by the name we had reassigned it, as we had done with other properties in the game. "I'll buy it," she said, putting the money from her personal stash into the bank, and fishing out the deed from the deed pile.

In addition to "Oatmeal" Avenue, we had re-named B. & O. Railroad to "Body Odor Railroad," Pacific Avenue to "Specific Avenue," Boardwalk to "Aardvark," and Park Place to "Fart Place," and Gilda had made some custom cards for the Chance pile: *You woke up Daddy from his nap, so pay Dicky $100 or you'll be sorry.* And so the game went; we exchanged practical game-related conversation but mostly wandered into discussions about the family happenings around us.

"So whatever happened when you told Daddy about Mrs. Oakley?" Glenda asked. I had gone over to the neighbor's house just a week before.

I started to explain.

"I picked up the phone, and it was her, Mrs. Oakley. She said, 'Please come help me,' and didn't wait for a reply. She just hung up the phone."

"So of course I had to go over there," I continued. "When I told Daddy—he had just walked in when I had hung up with her—he said it wasn't any of our business and that I should just forget about it, but I said I thought it sounded like an emergency, so I wanted to just go check it out. He said to go ahead, but not hang around there too long. So I walked over. When I got there, I could see Mrs. Oakley through the screen door. She was lying on the kitchen floor."

"Wow," Gilda said. "That musta been freaky."

"It kinda was," I said. "She said, 'Come in, please.' Very faintly. I could hardly hear her. '*Please*,' she said again. So I went in. She is sooo skinny, y'all. All bones. The veins in her hands were bulging out. It made me wonder how she was still alive, even. She looked like one of those Holocaust corpses in Daddy's box of pictures in his closet. Way different from how she used to look. Remember when they first came over when we moved here?"

"Yeah," Glenda said. "We never really saw them much after that, though. The only time we ever hear from them is when the electricity goes out and her or Mr. Oakley calls us to see if we have any electricity. But that's about it."

"So, what happened?" Dicky asked.

"I walked in and it occurs to me that I've never been in their house before, even though we've lived right next door all these years. The floors were cold-looking. Linoleum. Cracked. A red diamond pattern. All the furniture's dark, and old. Lots of varnish everywhere. The room smelled sour, like feet. I really wanted to just leave. It was spooky. I was only there because, well, when she called, it was me who picked up the phone. Anybody would have done. She was desperate. She didn't even know who she was talking to—she just said, 'Come help me,' and then hung up, so I went.

"When she saw me, she asked me to put her back in her bed, so I picked her up off the floor. I'm guessing she weighed about seventy-five pounds at most. She felt clammy. She didn't really have what I thought should be a human temperature. Know what I mean? Anyway, her dress was three times the size of her. It was a dingy, dirty cotton."

"And it was all very weird. The house was dark and damp, and kinda chilly, even though it's so hot outside. So she asks me to feed her some soup, from a pot on the stove. The only thing on that stove was a green enamel pot that was beat up—full of chips in the enamel. I wouldn't make soup in that. But apparently that's what it was. Some clearish water and little bits of turnip or potato in it; but barely anything else. It sure didn't look like any soup.

"As I'm looking for a bowl, she calls out to me, straining to speak. 'You don't need to heat it up, *cher*,' she says. 'Just put some in a bowl and feed me. Please.' So that's what I did."

"I coulda done that," Gilda says. "I think I'd be a good nurse."

"Shhh!" Glenda says. "What else happened?"

"Well, she was trembling as I brought the spoon to her mouth. She took in only a little. I waited a little bit before giving her another spoonful, so she could take it in.

"And then I noticed she was crying, silently. Poor thing."

"I'm sure there's all kinds of reasons for that," Gilda said. "But Daddy's right. It's none of our business."

"Well, that wasn't even on my mind. It wasn't important. She really just needed to eat something," I said. "Finally, after about five spoonsful, she said she'd had enough—that I could go. 'I'm gonna be okay, *cher*,' she said. 'Thank you for coming, *cher*.'"

"That's it?" Dicky asked. "She only wanted five spoons of soup?"

"It was all very spooky to me," I said. "When she said I could go, I asked her if she was sure, thinking that she might really want me to call an ambulance or something. Something was definitely not right. Not in my mind, anyway. But she said, 'No. I'm gonna be all right. Mr. Oakley is gonna be home soon, and he'll take care of me.' I didn't believe that for a minute, but what was I supposed to do? So I started to get outta there."

"That's it?" Dicky asks again.

"No, she said one more thing as I was walking out. She said, 'Don't tell anyone. Please.' And that just made it all more freaky. Something's definitely not right over there."

"That's so terrible," Dicky said. "Maybe we can go help her. Bring her some real food or something."

"No, we shouldn't interfere. If she needs something, she'll call again," said Gilda. "Besides, what if she's already dead?"

"Yeah, if Daddy said to mind our own business, he's probably right," said Glenda. "And it would just piss him off if he found out we were interfering with them. It's none of our business. We really don't know them that well."

"I tell you, as I walked back here, I couldn't help but wonder how long she'd be alive. I'm sure it won't be long," I said.

• • •

Gilda had just passed Go and collected another two hundred dollars. She owned the light blue monopoly she'd started three hours before with the purchase of Oatmeal Avenue, with hotels on each of them; the orange monopoly, also with hotels; and the most coveted, Aardvark and Fart Place, with two houses on each. Glenda owned BO Railroad, and the green monopoly, the second-most valuable real estate on the board, outfitted with hotels as well. I had somehow collected the fuchsia and yellow monopolies, with hotels on the yellow and houses on States Avenue and St. Charles Place.

"Yeah," Gilda said, handing the dice to me. "You don't want to set him off again. You never know when he'll turn mean again."

"He gives me nightmares," I said.

"Yeah, he's got something out for you," Gilda said.

"When he's beating me, where do y'all go?" I asked. "I mean, when it's happening, I am usually not paying attention to anything else. That time he whipped me with that wire, all I could do was try to imagine it being over."

"I just get out of the way," Dicky said. "When he's jumping on you, I'm afraid he's going to get me too, so I run."

"Yeah, pretty much me too," Gilda said. "He really doesn't know how to handle children."

"He's not that bad," Glenda said. She was the only one of all of us who never had a backhand to the face, or worse. "Y'all just are always doing stuff that pisses him off."

"Yeah, right," Gilda said, rolling her eyes.

• • •

In that game, we also discussed the Sunday afternoon cleanings of Momma's beauty shop in town. How it took three changes of soapy mop water to get the week's worth of TRESemmé hairspray off the linoleum floors; how we loved to be lulled to sleep by the hum and warm air blowing down on our heads when sitting under one of her big dryers; and we all wondered what was actually inside the canisters of blue liquid used for sanitizing the combs and brushes between uses. Turns out, none of us had ever actually changed that blue water.

"I thought you did it," Glenda said to Gilda.

"Not my job," Gilda said. "But I wouldn't let her touch me with one of those brushes."

"Y'all shut up and pick fig!" I said out of the blue, interrupting the recollection, as if it were the punchline of a joke. For us it kind of was a punchline, a way to close, and it sent snickers through the room.

27 | Y'all Shut Up and Pick Fig

Instead of joy, there was a dread that came over me each year when summer approached Louisiana. As early as May, temperatures in the mid-eighties were the norm, and by June, when the stifling heat had fully descended into the bayous, sloughs, and swampy flat terrain of much of the state, a day when it was *no more than* eighty-five degrees was seen as a blessing. So when Momma told Gilda, Glenda, Dicky, and me that we were all going to pick figs at Miss Dorothy Ledoux's back yard, we groaned. Hadn't we already picked enough figs in our own back yard? Apparently, Momma explained, Miss Dorothy could no longer eat figs, and she had four trees full, and they'd all turn to mush and go sour and stink up her yard if we didn't go get them.

The thought of picking the figs from four full trees in that July steam made us twitch just thinking about it. To make matters worse, Momma told us that, no matter how hot the heat bearing down on us was, we needed to wear long pants and long-sleeved shirts to keep the oozing, itch-inducing fig sap off of our skin. To complete our torturous outfits, we'd each be wearing a pair of Momma's hair-dyeing gloves, the better to grab the figs while maintaining hands that wouldn't stiffen and ache from the dried sap.

With it the heat brought bugs, particularly mosquitoes. Millions and millions and millions of mosquitoes. But, if the windshields of all the cars on the roads were any indication, the other state insect, the *plecia nearctica*, or *lovebug*, so-called because they seemed to be in a perpetual state of copulation, took a very close second. Though not as much of a health hazard as mosquitoes, when you were faced with the daily task of

126

having to somehow wash off the sun-cooked crust of a couple hundred lovebugs creamed on the glass and smeared further by the windshield wipers in vain attempts to see the road, you were hard-pressed to pick which of the two bugs was the bigger nuisance.

Up in the fig trees, a third, though not as abundant, nuisance insect joined the party: the fig wasp. Less for the likelihood of being stung, and more for the fact of them flying around you, freaking you out, the fig wasps added another layer of misery to our fig-picking expedition.

Miss Dorothy's back door opened onto a patch of grass no wider than three feet. Beyond that patch of grass was a fenced-in chicken yard with four ancient fig trees, weighted down with fruit. Beneath them, chickens, chickens, and more chickens, their chicken shit, and the flies that love it.

So, as we were up in the trees, filling our buckets, sweating like pigs, swatting mosquitoes and shooing wasps, lovebugs, and chicken-shit flies, and inwardly praying to not fall flat into the shit and mashed figs below, we somehow managed to take this adventure on as another summer game. So, as we picked figs, we talked.

"Momma didn't tell us about the chickens and all this shit," Gilda complained.

"I'm so miserable," said Dicky, his long-sleeved shirt sticking to his skin with sweat. "I don't even like figs."

"My hair has chicken shit in it," Glenda said. "Who put chicken shit in my hair? Gross."

"I love figs," I said earnestly. "I could eat them every day."

"Then you should pick them all," Gilda snarled.

It wasn't lost on us, the overwhelming unfairness of Momma and Miss Dorothy inside the air-conditioned kitchen having coffee while we sweated and swatted. So when the two old friends came out to check on us after an hour, it was really galling to have Miss Dorothy order us to keep working.

"Y'all shu-tup and pick fig!" she croaked in her swamp-lady patois. "There's a lotta fig over there y'all not gettin'," she continued, pointing unhelpfully to the tree at the back end of the yard.

"No, *y'all* shut up and pick *fig*!" Gilda mocked, accentuating Miss Dorothy's omission of the S on figs.

"Yeah, y'all better shut up and pick fig!" Dicky echoed.

"Y'all be nice to Miss Dar-ti," Momma said. The two ladies made weak attempts to stifle their chuckles and started to go back inside.

"Y'all shu-tup and pick fig!" Miss Dorothy bellowed once more for good measure before ducking inside, sending squeals throughout the chicken yard.

After another half hour of picking, we had filled four, five-gallon galvanized buckets and three cardboard boxes that Miss Dorothy fetched from her carport.

"I'm soaking with sweat," I complained. "My hands hurt."

"Me too," said Gilda. "This is so gross."

"These were a total waste of time," Glenda said, pulling off her gloves. "My hands are itching like crazy. I can't wait to take a bath."

"I'm full of bug bites," Dicky said. "And I don't even like figs," he repeated.

"Yeah, tell us something we don't already know," Gilda said with a raised lip. "Let's hurry and load all these figs in the truck and get outta here, or Momma's gonna talk all day with Miss *Dar-ti*."

Once loaded, the figs took up most of the room in the bed of the truck, but we squeezed in for the ride home, too dirty to be in the cab, and relieved beyond words to be done.

Momma would spend the next two days canning figs in the kitchen. The haul yielded seventy-three quarts of figs in syrup; the finished mason jars were stacked and created a wall of golden-brown preserved figs in the pantry. They'd be consumed on white toast with butter (my favorite way to eat them), in Mémère's fig cakes, over vanilla ice cream, and just by themselves, served in a bowl, for years to come.

A little more than two decades later, after all of us children had long moved on, Momma and Daddy were dead and buried, and the house was being cleaned to show to prospective buyers, there would still be a couple of quarts of figs in that pantry.

28 | Menfolk

Roy Ardoin was the sixth-born of Leonard and Earnestine Ardoin's fifteen children. Tall and hefty his whole life, he was strong and resolute, and possessed a bottomless capacity for joy. Though he grew up to witness plenty of things that would make many people sad and even bitter, he instead saw the world as a *fais do-do* and he was determined to sing and dance his way through it. Our dad, Zanny, like his older brother, was tall, but lanky instead of hefty, and clever. Cleveland, born between Zanny and Roy, wasn't tall, strong, or particularly clever, and we would never get the chance to meet him.

"It was me who finished raising Cleveland," Uncle Roy had explained to me one summer night at a campout. "That was right at the beginning of World War II. He was drafted as soon as he turned eighteen." I remember thinking that eighteen was only eight years difference in age from me at the time. And I was not in the least bit able to imagine myself in the army.

"Poor little Cleveland," continued Uncle Roy. "That boy died just three months shy of his nineteenth birthday out there in that Gulf of Mexico. There was a ship out of Port Arthur carrying a big load of sulfur in its hull on its way to Europe. That ship started taking on salt water, and POW! It just blew up. That's what they suspected at first, anyway. They never proved that, because that whole ship just disappeared in the Gulf. There was no one who survived to tell what happened. But I think that one-a them German U-boats was hiding in those dark waters all around there, and took advantage of that sinking ship and finished it off."

It was that kind of story that had me looking forward to being in any situation involving Uncle Roy. Now, *he* was a man to emulate. By thirteen I had already developed a strong distaste for hunting and camping, and just could not get excited about being out in the heat or the cold, itching or freezing, and smelling of musk and fur and squirrel blood, topped off by the pleasure of sleeping in a mildewed army tent on the hard ground, which was especially illogical to me when I had a perfectly good mattress at home. But when, on this particular Thanksgiving-week trip to the Red River area in north Louisiana, about a two-hour drive from the motel, Daddy said Uncle Roy was meeting us there, I perked up.

It was already dusk when we pulled up to the campsite, and Uncle Roy, still tall and hefty as ever, but now in his mid-sixties, wearing khaki trousers, a matching khaki shirt, big brown work shoes like Daddy's, and a wide-brimmed beige cowboy hat, was indeed there waiting for us. He had arrived an hour before to pitch his tent and get a catfish *court bouillon* bubbling away in a cast-iron pot over a solid campfire.

Reaching in his cooler for some 7-Up, Uncle Roy said to Andy, seventeen, and me, "You two pitch y'all's tent and then y'all can join me and your daddy for a highball." He looked right at me and said, "You about ready for your own highball, no doubt."

"Yep," said Daddy. "It's time this one grew up and joined the menfolk."

For an instant that word "menfolk" kicked me right in the gut, but I had gotten good at pretending not to notice it and others like it. As a teenager I was then at the age where Daddy felt that the need for a *course correction* in my development was getting urgent, so words like that came more frequently. And more frequently, I did my best to blink them away. I knew very well what he was doing, what he was driving at: I was not a proper boy, so I would never be a proper man. There were many words he and others used to emphasize their belief that any male who did not possess their idea of masculinity was not only less of a man, but less of a human.

• • •

The tent was big and simple to pitch. It stank of mildew and sweat, and had a few small holes in it, but looked like it would mostly do its job. When we were done, I was handed a highball from Uncle Roy's makeshift bar. It wasn't as bad as I had assumed it would be. The 7-Up sweetened the Old Crow just enough to make it sippable.

The sun completely disappeared behind the cypress trees, and Daddy and Uncle Roy talked out their hunting plans for the next morning. I sipped my first highball. After a while, I didn't notice the Old Crow in it at all any more.

"I'm gonna plant myself out over there where that big slough starts, right at the base of that ridge," Daddy said, pointing north.

"Then I'm gonna go in the opposite direction," Andy said. "We don't need to be on top of each other."

"Y'all are gonna wear y'all-selves out with all that walking," Uncle Roy said. "It's wet in there. I'm gonna stay right around here to keep an eye on things."

"You could come with me," Andy said to me. "I'll sit you down in a good spot and let you stay there and come get you when it's time to get out."

What? Am I being punished? I can't just have a walk along the levee and have a look at the terrain? I have to sit in a damp spot somewhere in the middle of the woods for a few hours, cold and bored? Again?

"Yep," I said. "Fine with me."

I finished my highball and was feeling somewhat more relaxed. Andy prodded me to have another one.

I really didn't want another highball, no matter how manly it was supposed to make me. "I'm already drunk," I protested.

"No, you ain't," he said. "Uncle Roy made yours with more 7-Up. You didn't drink enough whiskey to be drunk already."

"Leave him alone," Daddy said to Andy, as he poked the fire. "If he says he's drunk, he's probably drunk."

Unfortunately, at my age, I was not wise enough to have figured out that Uncle Roy could see right through to the core of any situation.

"That sure is a big tree," he said in my direction, pointing to an enormous cypress behind me. "You think you could climb that tree?"

"Oh, no," I said. "I'm too drunk to do that."

"Well, that's a good one," he laughed. "You probably right."

Later, Andy nudged me and said that I had failed Uncle Roy's test.

"If you was really drunk, you'da said you could climb that tree any time and then try to climb it. That would mean you were really drunk. You idiot."

"Oh," I said. "Really?"

I was embarrassed mostly, but also disappointed in myself that I'd revealed to Uncle Roy that I was full of shit, and I would have a hard time looking him in the eye for the rest of the trip.

• • •

But there was no avoiding him.

"Slept okay?" he asked as I came out of the tent in the morning. He was already fully dressed in his outfit from last night, complete with the big work shoes and beige cowboy hat, but had added to this hulking khaki scene a bone-colored pipe onto which his lips were pinched. A curl of white smoke wafted upward from the pipe; a calming cherry tobacco scent mingled with the oak, pine, and cypress around us as he talked. "You sure you're gonna be able to shoot all them squirrels?" he laughed.

I decided to try to salvage the remnants of my dignity by saying as little as possible and dutifully followed Andy into the woods, where I passed the day poking around the undergrowth near the tree where he left me. In the three hours I sat there, I saw a couple of squirrels a few trees away but couldn't be roused to pick up my gun.

I was fully aware but could not take comfort in the fact that general awkwardness is one of the universal curios of adolescence. I developed a plan: Around "menfolk" I would continue to keep my head low; I would smile when appropriate so as not to seem unfriendly and let my imagination take me through those awkward years until that period of my life was behind me.

29 | **Relief**

Wednesday morning, Thanksgiving Eve. We packed up and said our goodbyes to Uncle Roy and hit the road home for the holiday. Between the two of them, Daddy and Andy had bagged eleven squirrels. Uncle Roy had gotten only four, but he was happy with that. I managed to shoot one myself on our second excursion in the woods the afternoon before. And although I was instantly repulsed at the fact of killing the little animal, I was also very relieved to have earned a "badge" on my way to validating my masculinity.

The temperature dropped to about twenty-five degrees, and, even bundled up between Daddy and Andy in the Apache, with its rickety little heater rattling at full speed, it was hard to stay warm.

About thirty minutes down the road, Daddy pulled into a Sinclair station just outside the town of Colfax to fill up and use the bathroom. It was sleeting. Daddy went to pee first. Andy pumped the gas, then he went to pee.

I was beginning to feel the tightness of a nearly full bladder, almost to the point of a burning need, and was quite happy when my turn came. As I ambled out of the Apache, a hunter in a green Ford pickup pulled up and stepped quickly ahead of me in the line to the toilet.

As I waited for him to go, a little boy half my age got in line behind me and was squirming. Daddy tooted the horn for me to hurry; the man took his turn and exited the restroom.

Finally my turn. I looked at the little boy, and he was looking up at me, pleading silently for me to hurry. I thought about letting him go ahead of me, but Daddy was tooting the horn again, and I was waffling. *Should I just let him? How long could he take? He's so little.*

I bit my lip and let him go ahead of me. His relieved smile was all I needed in thanks. Daddy unrolled his window and yelled, "Let's go! We gotta get on that road before it ices over too much!"

I was thinking the little boy was gonna be out any moment, but no. He was in there, probably having a shit. I did not imagine he'd do something like that to me after I was so generous to him. Shit!

"Hurry up, gotdammit," Daddy yelled. I saw his face burning, glaring at me like I just kicked his dog.

The sleet was coming down harder and faster. It was freezing and I figured I'd rather be warm than have an empty bladder, so I got back in the truck.

"About time. What took you so long?"

I didn't answer.

• • •

I didn't know how I was going to survive another hour in that truck without getting a chance to pee, so I closed my eyes and tried my best to think it away.

I was envisioning anything besides pee or water or a swelling bladder as the truck bounced, unhelpfully, along the road.

The smells of Uncle Roy and Aunt Rose's kitchen in Tate Cove: gumbos past, Pine-Sol-ed floors, cherry pipe tobacco, aged varnished bead-board, rubber boots by the door, and a musty deer head mounted and hung up above the hearth, which divulged its own particular history of cottonwood logs, charred stone, layers of dried smoke, and new fire.

I was thinking of Christmases long gone: Momma's beauty-shop fruitcakes, silver tinsel, construction-paper looped garlands made in school, the brightly colored spinning child's globe I got from Tante Versie one year, Mémère's twin red Yorkies under the tree, one each for Gilda and Glenda; Dicky singing "Christmas is com-ing to-day!" into the new mini reel-to-reel tape recording machine that Santa had brought us all as a family present.

I thought about Pépère, whose whiskers scratched me when he scooped me up in his arms; his sweet voice assuring me my stomachache would go away if I lay still on the living room sofa and let him pray away the pain with his *traiteur* gifts; how he died one night in that same room, with Mémère standing over him panicking when the Coca-Cola and peppermint she tried to heal him with weren't powerful enough to stop a heart attack.

I looked at Andy, now in his mid-teens, and wondered what it must have been like for him as a young boy with epilepsy, not knowing when another episode would strike, or what to do about it; and about Daddy's mean streak, my constant fear of another violent beating from him set off by any number of possible triggers. I wondered what would happen to Dicky, whose mind always seemed to be veering off in some other direction, resulting in him watching helplessly as the rest of us had long digested the moment and moved on to something else.

• • •

A rut in the road jolted the truck and my bladder, ending my reverie.

I was aching. We had another fifteen minutes at least, and I couldn't take it any more. I was going to burst. There would be pee everywhere, and Daddy was gonna haul off and pop me.

The cold and wet outside were not helping. The windshield wipers were feverishly swishing back and forth. And my bladder was in crisis.

"I have to pee!" I finally said to Daddy.

"Didn't you go back there at that station?" he asked.

"I didn't get a chance," I pleaded.

I wanted so badly to explain. The man who got in line ahead of me, then the little boy squirming behind me who needed to poo, not pee. And had I known that, I would never have let him go ahead of me. I couldn't find the words to explain why I didn't pee.

"You're gonna have to wait till we get home," he said. "We're not far. I can't stop now."

My eyes were watering. I was not sure if it was from the sheer pain, or that I was just crying at how absurd it was that we couldn't just pull over so I could pee on the side of the road or something. I was bouncing up and down on the seat; the steel coils squeaked loudly.

"Sit still, gotdammit!" Daddy yelled.

I stopped bouncing, but bent forward, holding myself, my legs were wobbling wildly, faster than the windshield wipers. I closed my eyes again and tried to find more things to think about. But this time it just was not happening. My whole right side was aching. Sweat dripped from my forehead. I was sure I would literally split in two, and the pee and blood and my organs would fly everywhere. This went on and on. The cruel reality was that I could see that we were getting closer to home. The familiar houses and barns and occasional businesses passed us by, which

I would have thought would comfort me but instead seeing them had the opposite effect. The closer we got to that toilet at home, the more urgent my urgency.

Mercifully, and finally, we were pulling into the driveway.

"Let me out!" I screamed to Andy, who seemed to be enjoying taking his time to get out of the truck.

"Let me out!" I screamed again.

He finally got out of my way, and I stumbled out the door, onto the ground. *I am not believing how hard this is.* The toilet was just moments away. And I would be delivered from this agony, from this indignity, from this torture.

My bladder had other plans, however. It felt the earth right beneath it and, with a mind of its own, released a gush of piss, soaking my pants, impossible to contain it all any longer. I peed. And peed. And peed some more. I was on the ground and soaked in my own pee, and more pee was coming out.

And I was happy.

Andy was squealing with joy and pointing.

"You pissed your pants!" he laughed. "You pissed your pants!"

I didn't care. The pain in my side was finally only a bruise that would take a little while to disappear. I was convinced that my bladder would forever be stretched beyond recognition. But the relief was momentous. I was lying on the ground, soaked in piss, looking up at the blue and white Thanksgiving-eve sky, and was happier than I had been in all memory.

30 | **Pigs and Rats**

As I entered my early teens, I wanted to like what Andy liked, or enough of what he liked to be liked back by him. Mémère recommended this as one of the ways I could keep Daddy away from me. I tried to acquire Andy's love for the "great outdoors," especially hunting and camping out in the woods. For me this was much easier imagined than accomplished. It was, in fact, never accomplished.

On a not-terribly hot June morning, Andy talked up the idea of having a campout with Dicky and me out at "the barns," which were located in a remote area a couple of miles from the motel, down a gravel road that veered off the back road to Ville Platte. It was the same quiet area where, three years later, Glenda and Gilda would give me my first driving lesson in Daddy's stick-shift-and-clutch-operated Apache.

It didn't matter that none of us knew who owned the three barns and a little outbuilding near them, or that each time we went exploring out there, we were trespassing. Without a house on the property to indicate anyone actually living there, the barns looked perfectly welcoming to us, and in all the years growing up near them, none of us had ever been yelled at for being on the property. All that did matter to Andy was that the wooded area that included the barns, a nearby creek, a clearing of a few acres of soybean fields, and an abandoned graveyard not too far down the same road, made for a great destination to escape to, with lots of potential scenarios for keeping us entertained.

We would leave right after lunch.

"I know there's a wild hog that lives in the field out there next to the barns," Andy said. "We could catch it."

"What are we gonna do with a wild hog?" Dicky, who was about to turn eleven, asked.

"Cook it," Andy said matter-of-factly.

"Hmmph," I said. "We better bring some other food, just in case."

"Don't worry. We'll get some weenies and stuff at Bed-nah's on the way out."

Andy was old enough to drive but didn't yet have a license, so we would be traveling by bike. Andy would double Dicky and haul two tightly rolled sleeping bags on his old Schwinn, and I, not having a bike of my own, would borrow Glenda's green banana bike to pedal myself and, strapped to the back fender, more gear, including another sleeping bag. And to catch that wild hog, a burlap sack that once held fifty pounds of onions. When I asked to borrow her bike, Glenda, ever the tomboy, said she wanted to come with us, but Andy persuaded her that if she cooperated this time, she could go camping another time.

"My butt hurts," Dicky complained as we pulled into Bed-nah's, not a mile from the motel.

"At least you don't have to pedal," I said, huffing from the weight of the cargo on my fender.

For Andy, who was muscular and fit from years of heavy labor with Daddy, it was a breeze to pedal the two miles to the barns.

"Don't be pussies," Andy said. "We're not even halfway there."

At Bed-nah's we bought weenies, buns, mustard, chocolate-covered graham crackers, and some cans of orange pop and cream soda. No Cokes or Sprites, because we had those all the time; the machine at the motel offered only those two items.

Then back on the bikes and off to the barns we pedaled.

The afternoon sun began to beat down harder. We were all sweating, even Andy, but pushed onward for the remaining mile or so to the barns. I struggled a bit with the banana bike and the gear, and the grocery bag from Bed-nah's, and with the heat pounding down had fallen a bit behind.

Ahead, Andy and Dicky turned down the gravel road to the barns. I was still a hundred yards or so behind them, quite relieved all the same that we were nearly there. When I arrived, they had already taken down their gear and spread out their two sleeping bags in the biggest of the two barns. Later we would make a fire in a shallow that had formed near the front of the smaller barn.

"What took you so long?" Andy asked.

"Yeah, right," I said, soaked in sweat and not appreciating the hassling.

"Put your stuff in the barn with ours," he said. "We're gonna go find that hog. Bring the sack."

He had it all figured out. In his warped estimation, he, being the biggest, was best suited to stand at one point at the far end of the soybean field to scare the beast out, with Dicky positioned at the opposite side. I, being the next biggest, was perfectly suited to scoop up the pig in my fifty-pound burlap sack.

"We'll scare him out and all you gotta do is catch him in that sack," he said. I was not as confident as he but would do as instructed.

When he reached his desired point, he motioned for Dicky to take his position, and yelled, "Whoop whoop whoop!" as he did jumping jacks.

If I were a wild pig, I don't think that would do the trick.

"Whoop whoop whoop!" Dicky echoed, mimicking the jumping jacks Andy was doing.

"Whoop whoop whoop," I said flatly, holding my burlap sack open and ready for action.

Nothing happened.

The sun had become shielded by a cloud. I was hoping for rain, so we could stop all this foolishness.

"Whoop whoop whoop!" Andy continued.

"Something's moving!" Dicky shouted. "Over there," he continued, pointing to a rustling in the field between them and me.

Andy started lunging towards the rustling and ordered Dicky to do likewise. They were bounding through the field, but the rustling moved faster than they could leap over the soybean plants. The rustles continued in my direction.

Can this really be happening? I'm not believing this.

Oh, it was really happening. As Andy and Dicky met in the field, I followed the rustling to a row where I could see a pig, a big pig, very definitely running towards me, with Andy and Dicky flailing behind it.

"Whoop whoop whoop!" Andy continued. As he got closer to me, he yelled, "Get it! It's coming right for you!"

Dicky trailed a little, but he too was caught up in the excitement.

"Whoop whoop whoop!" he yelled.

And here came a wild pig.

From the first glance, at that distance, it looked to be only about twenty-five pounds at most. And it was indeed coming straight for me. From that position it looked as if I might actually be able to grab it up in my onion sack.

But then it kept coming, and as it did, I could see it was a lot bigger than twenty-five pounds. It was at least two hundred pounds if it was an ounce. As it approached, I could better make out a sizable head, and an even bigger body attached to it—its red eyes wild, its snout wet and shiny, hooves pounding the dirt.

Thrump thrump thrump thrump!

What had a second ago looked like a manageable pig was now the size of a washing machine as it came into better view.

"Get it!" Andy screamed. "Get it!"

So I was hunched, legs spread to shore up my position against the barreling animal.

"Grumph! Grumph! Grumph!" it growled as it trotted towards me. Thrump thrump thrump! its hooves pounded the ground. I was directly in its path, and it was not about to stop.

Or to let me catch it, for that matter.

"Get it!" Andy continued to yell.

As the beast barreled towards me I could see that there was no way that two or even three humans with a mere fifty-pound sack not big enough to fit the pig's head, let alone its body, would ever be able to capture this animal, and I dove out of its way as it bounded past me and down the road, where it quickly disappeared into the woods.

• • •

"I can't believe you let it get away," Andy said, as he turned his weenie over to scorch its other side. "We had him right where we wanted him."

"You didn't get a real good look at him," I said. "That pig was huge. No way could I have got him with that ridiculous little burlap sack. No way all three of us coulda gotten him, even if we had a bigger sack."

He was not convinced but let it go after I looked right into his eyes and said, "Piss off. The only way to get that pig was to shoot him."

"Yeah, you probably right," he finally conceded.

Dicky said nothing. I think he was just happy that he wasn't the one designated to grab the animal.

We ate our hot dogs and the chocolate-covered graham crackers and washed them down with orange pop.

"I love being outside at night," Andy said. "Look at all those stars up there."

"So when you grow up, are you gonna find a job where you can work outside?" Dicky asked. "That's what I would do if I was you."

"That would be good," Andy said. "But I wanna be a mechanic, so I'll be working inside in a garage, mostly."

Mostly, Andy said very little around us, or anybody. It took him a while to warm up to the notion of conversation for conversation's sake. It wasn't that he didn't have a lot to say. On the contrary, I think he had a lot going on in his head, but it took him a while to unbraid his thoughts.

"What do you want to do when you grow up?" he asked Dicky.

"I don't know," Dicky said. "Being a grownup is kinda scary to me. They have so many things to worry about. I don't like thinking about it."

"I'm gonna be an architect," I volunteered, since no one had asked. "I love to draw buildings. When I found out you could do that as your job, that was it for me. I could see myself doing that forever."

I didn't really know what I wanted to be yet, but I wanted something to say. Because of Daddy's repeated, unpredictable attacks, I had not been able to envision being an adult. I had accepted what I believed to be my fate: he would one day go too far with his fists, or his boots, or his belt, and actually kill me. I had accepted this like I had accepted my auburn hair and freckles. So, mostly I was simply relieved that the pig adventure was over, and I wanted us to steer clear of any more conversation about it.

And I totally understood Dicky's worries about growing up. When I was his age, before Daddy began attacking me and I actually could imagine a future, I worried to the point of distraction that I would not be able to survive if I had to speak French like all the adults around us did. They just *knew* French. But no one was teaching us French, except Mémère, and only a few words. How would I possibly function in society? Of course, I would come to realize over time that I could live in a place, pretty much any place, where English would be enough to survive quite adequately, and that French wasn't much spoken in the US outside of Louisiana, anyway.

• • •

After the hot dogs, cookies, and pop, we played a game of *bourré* as we watched the fire a bit more, then took turns peeing in it, and then literally hit the hay. We slept on piles of the pungent yellow grass in the same musty sleeping bags Daddy had acquired for squirrel and deer hunting trips. The sleeping bags emitted their own aged musk of gunpowder, campfire smoke, and squirrel fur and would soon acquire a dash of fresh hay. The combination was a not totally unpleasant odor, and after the bike ride, the wild pig party, the weenie roast, and the slow conversation around the dying campfire, it was easy to fall asleep.

Naturally, I had a pig dream.

I am on a bike, not Glenda's, not Andy's, but a shiny new red bike with playing cards attached to the spokes with clothespins so they create flapping noises when the bike is in motion. Flapflapflapflap! go the cards as I pedal towards home. Running behind me is my second first-grade teacher, Miss Betty Lavie, who took over our class when Mrs. Bello left to have her fifth baby. With a face that was permanently scrunched up on one side because she fell asleep in front of a blowing air-conditioner as a girl, Miss Lavie is now flailing her hands and yelling, "Whoop whoop whoop!"

I turn around to look at her, but she is now the pig, barreling down the road, grunting and staring me down. I lose control of the bike and end up flipped over in the ditch. The pig trots up to me and begins kicking me in the head. I push it away from me with repeated brushes of my arm.

I was awakened by Andy, saying in a loud whisper, "Don't move! Just don't move!"

"Wha'?" I said, still half asleep but startled, my arm still shooing away the pig.

"There was a rat on your head."

"What?!?" I said again loudly, sitting up, now fully awake.

"It's gone now. Go back to sleep. If you want I could zip you in so it doesn't bother you again."

"Um, no. I'm not gonna be able to sleep now."

Dicky, who had slept through the whole thing, grunted and turned over in his sleeping bag.

Years back, on my first day of first grade, when he walked me to my class and sat me down at my desk to make sure I would not feel lost and on my own, I didn't really appreciate Andy as a protector. Indeed, in the years since then, he had instead become a typical big brother. He made fun of me when it amused him and lost his patience with me pretty quickly. But that night at the barns showed me that he, despite his own struggles—in school, with our dad, with his own self-doubts—had been looking out for me, all along.

31 | A Kiss in the Remnants

awny Lynn Brown had just turned twelve. She was nearly five feet tall, athletic, and pretty. Blue eyes, curly blond hair, an over-eager disposition. She shared Apartment 19 with her mom, Phyllis, a Virginia Slims Menthol Light chain-smoker from Hattiesburg, Mississippi, whose favorite drink, day and night, was Boone's Farm Strawberry Hill wine. Late thirties, bottle-black hair, an affinity for animal-print tops paired with tight-fitting, stretchy black slacks, shiny gold or silver slippers, and cat-eye glasses that she refused to give up, even though the rest of the eyeglass-wearing world had moved on. The man in this scenario, Greg, Phyllis's second husband and Tawny's stepdad, was seldom around, owing to his job out in the Gulf, like so many of the men who parked their families with us at the motel while they roughnecked their way to a paycheck.

It was the end of the summer of my freshman year in high school, I had just turned fourteen, and I was interested only in building my science fair project for the fall. I was not interested in a twelve-year-old girl who would be gone in a few months.

"What's all that about?" Tawny asked, pointing to the timetable chart I had drawn up and colored in to illustrate the trajectory of the evolution of humans. "Looks like a bus-station schedule," she continued. "I've been on lots of buses with my momma."

"It's my project for the science fair this year," I told her, hoping she'd go away or glom on to Dicky, who was her own age.

"You already doing your science fair project, and it's only July?" she asked. "I hate science. I never do any homework till the teacher makes us."

Dicky came to the rescue, showing up just as I was about to ask Tawny to go back to her apartment and leave me alone.

"Hey," he told her.

"Hey," she replied.

"Let's go ride bikes," Dicky suggested.

"Okay."

I was relieved that for a while at least, I would be able to focus on finishing what I was doing. When I got involved in something, I didn't like distractions.

Dicky and Tawny become pals over the next few weeks. Thank God for Dicky.

• • •

On Saturday it was pouring rain again, so there was no mowing to be done, no outside anything that we had to do. Daddy had disappeared into town, Momma was at her beauty shop, and Gilda and Glenda were at basketball practice.

I was not interested in working on my project, so I agreed to play hide-and-seek with Dicky and Tawny. It was Dicky's turn to be the Seeker. We limited the game territory to the living room, the big bathroom, Andy's room, and Momma and Daddy's room. Momma and Daddy's room was clearly the best, because it had the most good hiding spaces. A large bed with plenty of room underneath, big billowy curtains with lots of child-concealing folds in them, and wall-to-wall closets with louvered doors, so the Hider could see out when someone was coming. The closet was an excellent choice, because it had some shelves up top if you could get up there, and lots of fabric remnants stacked in boxes on the floor.

As Dicky counted down from a hundred, Tawny and I darted in opposite directions at first, but we each dove into the louvered closet as he counted off the last few seconds.

"Five. Four. Three . . ."

Tawny entered through Daddy's side, and I entered through Momma's, which was closest to the hallway door, and usually the first place the Seeker would seek. We all knew this but also knew that the Seeker would typically look in all the other places in the other rooms first to build the suspense. In fact, the spot had been used so many times that only a fool would hide there, so it was often deliberately ignored by the Seeker altogether.

" . . . Two. One! Ready or not, here I come!"

I was not exactly sure where Tawny had crawled, but I crawled to the center of the closet, where Momma's and Daddy's stuff met. Tawny had also snuck to the center from her side of the closet and had covered herself with fabric remnants. When we discovered each other, we each muffled a squeal and instinctively held hands.

It was the first time since Mary Belinda Fontenot that I had held the hand of an unrelated female. Six years earlier, before we moved to the motel, we lived in a neighborhood in town where all the back yards were connected by alleys. Mary Belinda's back yard was on the opposite side of the alley from ours. She was two years older and had an obvious crush on me.

One afternoon she invited me along with her for a walk in the neighborhood. Even though she made me nervous, I agreed to go on this adventure with her.

After we strolled a few blocks away from our neighborhood and into the next one, totally foreign to both of us, Mary Belinda took my hand. I jerked it away.

"It's okay to hold hands," she said. "You have to hold my hand because of the cars."

That seemed to make sense to me, even though there wasn't much traffic, so I let her have my hand. As we walked, she talked about growing up and having babies and wanting a nice house and stuff. I don't remember what I was thinking about those things, but I do remember feeling awfully self-conscious about the handholding. I began feeling I was not gullible enough to really swallow the traffic explanation, but I continued to let her hold my hand anyway. After a while, I joined in her grown-up fantasy and considered the idea of all those things.

"What do you want to do when you get big?" she asked.

"I guess I'm gonna get married and have kids, like you," I said because that seemed to be what she wanted to hear.

"Then you and me should get married," she said. "Let's kiss!" she exclaimed.

"No way!" I said, pulling abruptly away from her.

Startled and embarrassed, she changed the subject.

"I want to be a beautician," she said, "like your momma."

We had already gone several blocks but after that awkward moment had turned back towards home. And no more handholding. We got to the block before our houses, where I could see Momma and Mrs. Carol, who lived across the street, and some other neighborhood ladies, out on the sidewalk.

"Where have y'all been?!" Momma demanded, looking wildly alarmed at me, then sternly at Mary Belinda. "We have been calling all over the neighborhood."

"We just went for a walk," Mary Belinda said. "We didn't go that far."

Not only did I get a serious lecture from Momma, I was completely turned off to this handholding and kissing business. And that pretty much ended Mary Belinda's crush on me.

• • •

In Momma's closet that day, as Dicky searched for us all over the living room, taunting, "I'm getting closer. I'm gonna get you," Tawny and I were still holding hands.

Our suppressed giggles turned into tense anticipation as Dicky got nearer and nearer. Just as we heard his voice turn in toward the hallway, we jerked simultaneously and again suppressed our giggles. I saw her eyes, only inches from mine. I was bewildered at the feelings racing through me. I had never had an urge as strong as I had at that moment as I stared at Tawny's bright, excited face. For only the slightest of moments, I closed my eyes, puckered my lips and moved my head towards hers. She didn't move. I didn't know if she was keeping her eyes closed, but we kissed, lips to lips. A quick, cool, dry brush of the lips. Nothing more. That was enough for me.

"Gotcha!" Dicky screamed, throwing open the louvered doors.

I thought I was having a heart attack. My face was burning, and my heart was racing. Tawny had already tossed off the fabric remnants and darted out of the closet.

• • •

A month passed before Tawny and her parents packed up and went back to Hattiesburg. In that time I avoided her, and we never discussed that kiss. I was relieved to see them go.

Despite the fleeting titillation that came with it, the kiss in the closet with Tawny would be one of only a handful of such kisses I would have with those of the female sex. I soon would become quite comfortable with this reality.

32 | The Meat Man

Momma asked me what I wanted for my fifteenth birthday, so I said without hesitation, "I want a job at the National."

"For your birthday present?" Momma asked.

"Yes," I said. "That would be a great present. You know all of them there. Could you come with me to ask them if they'll give me a job?"

"Okay," she said. "That's a good idea. And you're right. I know Mr. Sonnier and Mr. Fontenot, and all of the ladies on the registers. Let's go."

And that's how I landed my first job outside of the motel. I was too shy to just go ask them myself, plus I knew that they knew Momma well, because she was in there practically every day, spending most of her beauty shop money on food for us. And that's a lot of groceries. It was funny, because I think I got my initial shyness from her. And like her, once the ice is broken, once I know somebody, I may be a little awkward at first, but I'll be fine.

• • •

On my first day, a Saturday, the manager, Mr. Gabriel Sonnier, a sincere, nice-looking man in his mid-fifties with a head of thick, still-black hair, calming blue eyes, and a friendly disposition, introduced me to the other people up front.

"This is my assistant manager, Jimmy Fontenot," said Mr. Sonnier. "Keep an eye on him. He was the class clown."

Mr. Fontenot was a skinny, nervous man in his mid-forties with a habit of shifting from one foot to the other, almost like he was dancing. He came across to me as a game-show host.

"Well, well, well!" he said. "Who's the new victim? Ha!"

"Don't mind him," Mr. Sonnier said, pointing me onward with his hand on my back. "He talks to himself a lot. And that's because most people tune him out."

Next up, Miss Jesse Dickson, the chief cashier and bookkeeper, a woman no older than her early forties, who was hard to read right away because she looked reserved, like a librarian. But I was told later that she was really not as stuffy as all that when she was not wearing her National Tea Company name badge.

And finally there was Mrs. Ann Rousseau, the second cashier, early fifties. Blue-black rinse job, sharp features, sassy mouth.

"You gonna join the union?" she asked right off the bat. "You don't have to. This is a right-to-work state." I had no idea what that meant.

"I'll tell you all about it later," she said as Mr. Sonnier pulled me toward the back of the store.

"She reminds me of my Aunt Rose," I told him. He said nothing.

He then took me over to meet Mr. Anthony Jordan, the produce manager, a fireplug of a man with a mostly bald head and a pencil mustache, late forties. His produce section was impeccable. "I keep a clean department," he said to me. "One day I'll show you the ropes if you're interested in produce."

From there we went all the way back in the store to the meat locker to meet Jacques Babineaux, an athletic man about six feet tall, no more than thirty years old. Green eyes, thick blond hair. Wearing a fitted white shirt with a National Tea Company–issued solid orange necktie, and tight khakis that accentuated a firm, round butt.

"Nice to meet you," he said with a voice so smooth it made me think he should work in radio. "You got a great head of red hair. I bet you get all the pussy you want." I felt the blood rush to my head. I couldn't believe he just said that.

"Hey, Jacques," Mr. Sonnier jumped in for the rescue. "You gotta give this young man some room."

"Sorry. I'm just so damned horny all the time," Mr. Babineaux said, grabbing his crotch to give his dick a good squeeze. "I work around this pink meat all day, and all I can think about is pussy."

I couldn't help but notice he had quite a bulge in his tight khaki pants. I quickly looked away. My eyes darted from side to side, then up to the ceiling, anywhere but at the man's crotch. *He has me figured out before I have myself figured out.* He patted me on the shoulder and gave my neck two firm squeezes as Mr. Sonnier ushered me back out into the main store.

"See you around," he said.

I was *smitten*—a term I had just learned in English class at school. Like Orsino was for Olivia, I was completely *smitten* with Jacques Babineaux. It was the first time I had lost all my senses on the spot because of meeting someone like Jacques Babineaux. Nothing in my life before had prepared me for it. Not that handholding episode with Mary Belinda, or that awkward kiss in Momma's closet with Tawny Lynn.

This Mr. Jacques Babineaux was something else. It was also the first time in my life that I knew for sure that I wouldn't be getting married and having babies. Not me. That was not gonna be my life. I didn't yet know exactly what my life was gonna be, but I knew then what it was *not* gonna be.

Happy fifteenth birthday to me.

• • •

Mr. Sonnier initially put me on stock duty. In addition to an official orange National Tea Company vest, I was issued my own box cutter and pricing gun. I liked stock duty right away, because I could stick to myself and not have to deal with people. I spent the four hours of my shift getting food out of boxes from the back warehouse, priced, and then on to the shelves where it could sell.

My crush on Jacques Babineaux lasted the entire two years I worked at the National. But he made me so anxious I made every effort to avoid contact with him, and that was pretty easy to do because I had nothing to do with the meat department, except that I had to pass near there on my way to punch my timecard. Now and again I would bump into him, but I kept my eyes averted, was always polite, and got out of his path as quickly as possible. His obsession with sex was endless.

So I was punching my timecard one day and encountered Mr. Babineaux, who had Miss Dickson, squirming, in his arms.

"I need you so bad right now, Jesse," he said to her. "I'm so horny!"

"Then ask me out," she said with a laugh and pulled away from him.

It was obvious to me then that his very sexual personality not only did not bother her in the least, but that she in fact seemed to enjoy the attention, and that this was not an isolated incident.

"We'll see where that goes," she continued, with a big smile and a wink for me as she headed back to the front.

He had a big grin on his face, looked at me, grabbed his crotch, and said, "She wants it bad. I can't let all this go to waste."

I couldn't control my face. I felt it glowing with mortification.

I smiled and said, "Then ask her out, like she said."

As I made a move to head back to the warehouse, he grabbed me from behind and enclosed me in a tight bear hug. I could feel the heat of his entire body against mine, his swollen bulge pushing up against my butt. He said in his smooth radio voice into my right ear, "One day soon you're gonna know what it's like. You redheads have something in your blood like we blonds do." I tensed up. He sensed my discomfort, released me from the bear hug, and spun me around to face him, his hands squeezing my shoulders.

Is he gonna kiss me? I was not sure what I would do, but the thought wasn't repulsive to me. On the contrary, I was completely titillated. *Do it! Kiss me. I want to know what that's like. Do it!*

He didn't. Instead, he grabbed my face in his hands, forcing me to look directly into the quicksand of his green eyes. I was trembling. A bead of sweat rolled down my right temple where seconds ago his lips had brushed up against my earlobe.

"Remember this day," he said sweetly, softly, and then released me once more to let me get back to work.

"How could I not?" I asked him, stumbling out the swinging doors to the warehouse.

• • •

Mr. Fontenot instructed me in the fine art of "fronting" the merchandise. "Every night before we lock up, we go through the whole store, aisle by aisle to make sure everything is positioned right up to the front of the shelf," he explained. "The merchandise always needs to start each day at full attention."

"I can handle that," I assured him. In fact, fronting became my favorite part of the whole stock-boy experience. It gave me an outlet for my need for perfection. Not that I was a compulsive person, but seeing the merchandise all perfectly stacked and aligned to the edge of each and every shelf, aisle after aisle, after aisle, gave me a sense of serenity.

Cans and boxes and more cans and boxes: Libby's Vienna Sausages, Dinty Moore Beef Stew, Heinz Ketchup, Hamburger Helper (*the fat white glove printed on the box enticing shoppers to pick it up and take it home*). Hellmann's Mayonnaise, Lawry's Seasonings, Stove-Top Stuffing, SPAM, Del Monte Pork and Beans, Folgers Coffee, lots and lots of Campbell's

Soups. Veg-All Mixed Vegetables, Armour Potted Meat, Betty Crocker Cake Mixes (*rumor has it she is having a steamy affair with that Duncan Hines fellow*), Kraft Salad Dressings, Jell-O Pudding in chocolate, vanilla, banana, lemon, and butterscotch. Pillsbury All-Purpose Flour, Kraft Macaroni and Cheese, Green Giant Niblets, Premium Saltines, and Chef Boy-ar-dee Spaghetti and Meatballs (*the chef looks like a scary pervert— probably best friends with that Quaker man on the oatmeal*).

The product-logo-printed cardboard boxes that held all of these smaller boxes and cans of food items needed to be taken off a pallet from the back warehouse, where they were kept after delivery, but not for long. Mr. Sonnier and Mr. Fontenot did not like to see pallets of stock sitting in the warehouse. As soon as there was room on the shelves, out to the front they went. And that's where I came in. I got one of the dollies (*Miss Dickson said the name for them where she came from was "hand trucks"*). My favorite was the green one, because its wheels weren't crooked like the wheels on the red one, which wobbled when you pulled it. I stacked as many as six of the cardboard boxes on it, then rolled it all out to the front.

Exactly as I was taught by Mr. Fontenot in my first week on the job, I glided my handy box cutter along the very top of each box, careful not to slit any of the contents, especially if it was something like packages of Rice-a-Roni, or plastic-wrapped four-packs of toilet paper inside. Next, like a pistol, I pulled my labeler from its hoop on my apron and quickly labeled each item, according to that week's pricelist, which was printed up on Monday mornings by Miss Dickson. It was then that the stocking and fronting could begin in earnest. I was pretty efficient at this part of the process, owing to my need for order. I made sure to keep each line of product within its designated territory on the shelf. I didn't want to invite any complaints from Mr. Fontenot.

Once stocked, the cereals made for a city wall of brightly animated boxes: General Mills offered Cheerios; Lucky Charms, with its happy but clearly mischievous leprechaun smirking; Count Chocula's smiling, friendly-ghoulish face; and Frankenberry, Boo-Berry, and Cap'n Crunch (my favorite stick-to-your-teeth cereal). From Kellogg's it was Frosted Flakes, featuring Tony the Tiger's happy lemon-shaped head; Corn Flakes, Apple Jacks; and Special K. Post, meanwhile, supplied America's breakfast tables with Sugar Smacks, Honeycomb for kids, and the boring Raisin Bran and Grape-Nuts for the constipated grown-ups.

I didn't get to stock the bread, which was done by the traveling bread man, who was only ever referred to as Mr. Joe. The magazine rack, cigarettes, and toiletry and candy shelves were handled by Miss Dickson and Mrs. Rousseau.

When he was not around, I filled in for Mr. Fontenot in the dairy case. Gallons, half gallons, quarts, and pints of milk, cream, half-and-half, and, during the holidays, eggnog. Cracker Barrel cheese blocks, Kraft Singles, Cool Whip, yogurt, cottage cheese, lots of butter, and several varieties of margarine.

• • •

A few months into the job, Mr. Sonnier tried me on a register to see if I had any facility there. Turned out, despite my shyness around strangers, I was pretty fast with the keys and actually good with the customers, so I would get assigned a register on occasion. I developed a rapport with the regular customers, and in no time, I began to spend more of my hours at the registers than anywhere else. This was fine with me, because it helped me get over my shyness, and I learned to enjoy it. Plus, it kept me away from the back most of the day. Away from Jacques Babineaux.

The awkward titillation I experienced at the first real brush with my sexuality would stay with me as I fumbled my way into it, one experience at a time, for years to come. At fifteen, although I was smart enough to know I didn't know enough about the world in which I would belong, I felt a sense of dread that my life was not going to be as easy as it was for all those other people in the world who, since time immemorial, have had this aspect of their lives neatly laid out before them. Was Daddy right? Would it be easier for me to simply accept this and contort myself to abide by society's prescribed plan? My inner Ayla Jane Sanders, the little kitchenette guest who peed on Dicky's head, said intuitively, "Nawww."

33 | Chilled *Lagniappe*

Tante Estelle had plastic curtains. She lived in an unpainted clapboard house on a gravel road on the northern edge of Ville Platte. I was in my early teens before I realized Estelle was her given name, and not "T'tell," which was how Mémère said it and, furthermore, that she wasn't actually Mémère's *tante*. Estelle was in fact the elder sister of DeJean, Mémère's long-gone husband, my *pépère*, who suffered a heart attack and died before I started first grade.

Ville Platte, a little prairie town where French was still the dominant language well into the 1980s, Main Street had four traffic lights, and nothing moved very fast (except chickens on Mardi Gras morning), was full of *tantes* and *n'oncles*, mostly belonging to nieces and nephews who lived in larger towns and cities that had more to offer. For every *tante* in Mémère's social circle, there was a *n'oncle*, dead or alive, to match. Couples were often called Tante and N'oncle (the N' pointing out the smashing together of *mon* and *oncle*) regardless of whether they had any actual nieces or nephews.

When other kids were trying to outgrow their grandparents, I genuinely looked forward to *passer la vie* with Mémère, especially in the summers, when I could take her up on an offer to "come pass a big week with me, *cher*," by which she meant a full week plus an extra weekend. Part of the attraction was being taken for rides in her black 1952 Bel Air, a big rounded car with stiff vinyl seats and windshield wipers that, moving out of sync and in opposing directions, feverishly waved away the frequent summer rains. The Bel Air, which by then had survived nearly two decades gently lumbering around Ville Platte, took us to the public pool, or to Chicot State Park or, most often, to drop in on any one of the people in her life who might have been home at the time. As was the custom, no advance warning or express invitation was required.

Of all the *tantes* and *n'oncles* populating Ville Platte, Tante T'tell was at the top of Mémère's favorite-people list. When Mémère and I visited T'tell, I'd sit quietly, watching her plastic curtains rustle gently in the dusty, gravel-road wind while she and Mémère chattered away in Cajun franglais as they slurped strong hot Seaport coffee from chipped, mismatched demitasse cups.

The house smelled of stale coffee, spent cigarettes, linoleum tar, and old paper. The curtains were a delicate, gauzy, tissue-like translucent plastic, with big pink and red camellias printed on them. It seemed they would tear very easily if yanked just right. Of course, I never really knew for sure, because I wouldn't dare yank on Tante T'tell's curtains.

A bulky, aged, brown four-poster bed that emitted a sour varnish odor absorbed a corner of the front room. Odd to have a bed right in the front room, but there it was, covered grandly with a red velveteen bedspread that matched the red of the flowers in the curtains. In the corner opposite, next to the kitchen entryway, a foot-powered Singer sewing machine, just like Mémère's, stood idle, as it apparently had for years. She had been a seamstress in her youth; her husband, Clarence, a mailman. But T'tell's sewing days were over. It served instead as a home for various curios and family pictures. Women and babies on crocheted blankets, and yellowing images of men in their military uniforms, pristine from head to toe.

The wallpaper was also yellowed and puckering and cracking. Several pieces had long fallen away; some to the floor, where pieces still rested; I imagined others must have landed between the wall and the wallpaper.

The two ladies usually sat on rocking chairs by the window or, sometimes, on the front porch if the weather was not too stifling. Tante T'tell's thick, wispy blue-gray hair shot out of her head, going in all directions. Like porcupine quills. She wore loose-fitting sleeveless house dresses that fell a few inches below her knees. In all the years I was privileged to visit her with Mémère, I never once saw her wearing shoes. Maybe it was because her big, corroded feet were too hard to shoe. Gnarled toenails, protruding bunions.

The thick horn-rimmed eyeglasses she wore had lenses so strong that they had the effect of shrinking her eyeballs to the size of field peas when you looked right at her. My favorite thing about Tante T'tell, however, was that she rolled her own cigarettes and was rarely seen without a yellowed butt either dangling from her lips or pinched in her hand. It was a thrill to watch her flip the lid of a Prince Albert tin, scoop out just enough of the chopped tobacco, then roll her cigarette effortlessly between her thumb and two fingers, allowing the crumbs to fly about, fall onto her lap, and then onto the floor when she stood. In a few seconds, she licked the gummed edge of the rolling paper, scratched a match, and began puffing anew, without missing her place in the conversation.

Mémère was fiercely loyal to her family and friends. It was obvious that she dearly loved Tante T'tell. They were more than in-laws; they were best friends. As they caught up with each other's lives since the last visit—just a week or so before—one woman took her turn to talk, while the other intently interjected a *Pense donc!* or *Cher, pitié!* Their repartee was like a tennis match, back and forth, back and forth. Often there was some overlapping, both women cackling at once. Unfortunately, I understood only a little French. I was able to pick up on some of the key words, but understanding those two, at the rate they rattled, was possible only by interpreting the inflections in their words or the nonstop fluttering of their hands. Because they used their hands to communicate as much as or more than words, *observing* a conversation was often more informative and entertaining than listening to one.

Estelle Thompson Vidrine, born in 1900, four years ahead of Mémère, raised two children, Katherine "Catin," a twice-divorcee raising her own daughter, Roxanne, and a son, Ernest, who was eventually killed by a German who shot him point-blank in the forehead during the war. Ernest, looking earnest, was one of the men in uniform atop T'tell's Singer. He looked too slight to be in a war. More like an algebra teacher than a foot soldier.

Catin was a hairdresser, an advantage for her because she loved keeping her own hair up in lacquered, tube-shaped curls, which were pinned gymnastically on top of one another, forming a half-foot-high crown highlighted with silver edges that were sprayed on with a Streaks 'n Tips can. Mémère and I ran into Catin and the ever-mischievous Roxanne sometimes when they all had the same *envie* to visit T'tell.

I was not fond of Catin, because every time we met, she grabbed me and marked me for the day with her cloying Charlie perfume. "Coco Chanel said that a woman who doesn't wear perfume has no future," Catin said when I screwed up the nerve to ask why she wore so much of the stuff. She didn't grab me any more after that.

It didn't take long to figure out that Roxanne, who was three or four years older than me, was quickly becoming her mother. She, too, was fond of Streaks 'n Tips and tube curls. And like her mother, she was probably destined to go through a mess of husbands before she reached the age of forty.

"Maw-maw Estelle has a whole new house up there in her attic," Roxanne told me, pointing to the attic's access panel cut into the kitchen ceiling. "There's a brand-new stove, a brand-new ice box, and new curtains all around the house up there. It's beautiful!" she said, poking a finger into one of her frosted curls.

"Why doesn't she just live up there, then?" I asked, allowing my eagerly gullible mind to picture the whole new place.

"Because it's too hard for her to climb up into that little hole," she said authoritatively.

"Well, I wanna see it," I said.

"You can't. It's locked up."

The thought of a beautiful home just above T'tell's decaying surroundings, sitting up there unused seemed to me like a terrible waste.

On the drive back, I asked Mémère, "How come Tante T'tell doesn't live in her attic?"

"Well," she began, somewhat bewildered, "that don't make no sense, *cher*. Nobody lives on their attic."

"Roxanne said she had a whole new house up there in her attic."

"*Mais*. Well! That's why!" she chuckled. "Roxanne is *brigand*. Don't listen at what she tell you, *cher*."

"What's 'bree-gon,' Mémère?"

"*Roxanne* is *brigand*," she insisted.

I knew not to persist. Like everyone around her, Mémère's first language was French, not English. It was up to those who wanted or needed to understand her to make sense of her. If she'd had her way with Momma, all of us kids would have learned French and English at the same time. Part of the charm and intrigue of Mémère was that she'd cut off all English words when she felt like it and then use only her native tongue. That was when I listened closest. This was her way of teaching the language.

When I was still a boy, she'd scoop me up in her arms and rock me while she whispered French sentences in my ear.

"*Ouvre la fenêtre.*"

"*Ferme la porte.*"

"*Mange d'la merde.*"

And, except for that last one, Momma always seemed pleased to hear the new things Mémère had taught.

One of the conditions of being Mémère's pupil was the ability to accept that many words in French just do not have a singular English translation. I would therefore have to trust that *brigand* was probably French for sneaky, dishonest, or mischievous, because Roxanne was definitely all of those.

• • •

One fall Saturday morning a few years later, when I was finally old enough to drive Momma's car, I went to Ville Platte to take Mémère grocery shopping and driving around to visit her friends. As much as it irritated her, her age and the expense of car upkeep had put an end to her driving days. Her 1952 Bel Air and the car that finally replaced it, a tuxedo blue 1967 Ford Fairlane, were both long gone. This was a solemn handicap she felt, because now she was relegated to asking for rides, walking everywhere she needed to go, or staying home. When I arrived, Mémère was trembling with anxiety.

"Get me off this damn house!" she said, scuttling to the car.

So off we went. First stop, the A&P on Chicot Road.

At the A&P the prison in which poverty holds people like Mémère became crushingly apparent to me for the first time. And nowhere in the store was it made more obvious than at the meat counter.

"*La viande, là*," she said, pointing out a piece of chuck to the butcher.

"*Combien?*" she asked discreetly, her eyes darting around her to make sure no one else heard.

"*Cher, pitié!*" she gasped with a hand to her chest when he told her the price of the meat. She knew that such a cut of meat would not fit into her cruelly limited food budget, but she asked anyway, as if to validate her instinct to buy some nice "grind meat" at only seventy-nine cents a pound.

Before she selected the ground beef, I watched with a thick lump in my throat as she eyed the other nice cuts of beef, pork, and links of andouille sausage with a longing in her face that seemed to hark back to the days when she didn't have to watch every dollar, when the rewards of *la boucherie* provided her family all the best of whatever animal had been slaughtered.

At the produce section, I watched silently while Mémère removed most of the outer leaves on a head of iceberg lettuce, rendering it the size of a croquet ball.

"*Combien?*" she asked, handing the lettuce ball to the produce man for weighing. "*Dix cents*," he answered automatically as he wrote the new price on a sticky green label. The kindhearted man's wink to me indicated that this was not the first time he'd experienced this kind of thing and that Mémère most probably was not the only old woman in Ville Platte who managed to buy less than a full head of lettuce from him.

As we walked out of the A&P towards the car, Mémère asked if we could go for a quick visit to Tante T'tell's new studio apartment in the housing projects. Catin had decided her mother should live out her days in a clean place, surrounded by other people her age, and where she could be looked after by the nurses on staff there.

T'tell smiled warmly when she saw us at the door and welcomed us to her new home. She was wearing another one of her big, sleeveless house dresses. The skin below her arms dangled like a turkey neck.

"*Allo, mes cheries!*" she said, kissing Mémère on the cheek and then taking my head to her bosom for a big hug. I had no concerns about being hugged by T'tell. She only ever smelled of mild perspiration and cigarettes, neither of which offended me.

I had the bag of groceries with me to keep them from melting in the hot car, and T'tell motioned for me to put it on the little kitchen table. Mémère told her we couldn't stay very long.

The studio apartment was a sterile beige box with a tiny kitchenette and bathroom. Sheetrock walls, harvest gold appliances, and beige drapes. I wondered what had happened to the camellia-splashed plastic curtains. T'tell and Catin had managed to cram some of her belongings into the room, but the plastic curtains didn't make it. I imagined those big red and pink flowers still back in that house on that dirt road, wilting from the shame and disorientation of abandonment.

The big four-poster bed with the red velveteen bedspread had been replaced by a cold metal rollaway that had been positioned in a corner. Butting up against the foot of the bed was a dressing table with some of those pictures that once stood on top of the silent Singer. The unused sewing machine, for some reason, did make it in the move but had been tucked into a white louvered-door closet on the right wall, which divided the living-bedroom and the kitchenette. The louvered doors probably irritated T'tell, I thought, because they were both opened all the way, a position that seemed permanent, revealing the machine, several cardboard boxes, some hanging clothes, and a couple pairs of swollen shoes.

In the move she had somehow acquired a brand-new pear green Naugahyde sofa, on which she and Mémère now sat and caught up. The new sofa was positioned in the only place left in the room to put anything, against the entry wall. Above the sofa hung a new plaque T'tell had recently received for winning an accordion-playing contest in Port Arthur, Texas. I have never witnessed a stronger accordion player in person, nor have I ever enjoyed watching anyone play as much as I did Tante T'tell.

When she played (she was partial to "Les Maringouins Ont Mangé Ma Belle" [The Mosquitoes Have Eaten My Sweetheart]), she kept time with her be-bunioned right foot, and as her head bobbed with the rhythm, her upright wispy hair undulated to and fro like rows of rice stalks in a wind.

I sat in a ladder-back chair next to the front door. That same chair, spindled oak with a scratchy cowhide seat, had survived the move from the old house. From that position, I could watch the two women, sitting an arm's length away on the couch, and still appreciate the graduated bronze hues of the harvest gold appliances in the kitchenette. It was then and there that I decided that my own kitchen one day would also be outfitted with harvest gold appliances.

I glanced over towards T'tell just in time to see her wet tongue glide across the gummed edge of a rolling paper, sealing her cigarette with one smooth lick. Her sunken eyes were diminished even more by the thick lenses of her glasses, but she sure could see enough to roll a fresh cigarette in only a few seconds, Prince Albert tobacco crumbs flying around her. I was in heaven.

Mémère got up to make some coffee. From her position on the sofa, T'tell was not able to see the goings-on in the kitchenette.

"How about some good coffee-milk, *cher*?" Mémère asked, tapping my knee as she passed me on her way to the refrigerator.

"Okay," I said, shifting my eyes from T'tell to Mémère.

The refrigerator was almost bare. There was a bottle of something yellow, a pint jar of what looked like preserved figs, and a small can of evaporated milk. Nothing else. No eggs, no bread, no meat. Mémère's tiny frame shrank as she stood stunned, staring at the near-empty refrigerator.

"Them coffee grinds, *c'est dans le cabinet*," T'tell said loudly from the sofa.

Maybe the cabinets would have some food? Not so. The cabinets were as bare as the refrigerator. A bag of coffee and a box of saltines. Cups, plates, drinking glasses. Nothing else.

Mémère put some water boiling, then prepared the cotton sack for the coffee grounds. She worked quickly and silently. When she turned, I saw she was crying. Clearly, the empty refrigerator and cabinets devastated her.

Like Mémère, T'tell lived on a barely-enough income but was not about to complain. She'd been through harder times in her long life.

Mémère glanced at me, her always affable face reduced considerably by the disparity of the situation: T'tell with an empty refrigerator, and us, with a bag of groceries. Her eyes landed on the bag, in which sat the items she had negotiated, item by item, at the A&P not thirty minutes before.

"Bring that over here, *cher*," she said to me, pouring a cup of boiling water into the sack of the hand-drip coffee pot. I did as I was told, then sat down again, watching quietly as Mémère took the ground beef, the croquet ball of lettuce, and a little loaf of Sunbeam bread out of her bag and placed them on the top shelf of the harvest gold refrigerator, where T'tell would be sure to find them.

"Shhh," she said softly, an index finger pressed to her lips. T'tell would simply find this *lagniappe*, a little surprise—a little something extra—after we'd gone. Another lump formed in my throat. I swallowed hard, breathed in deeply, and blinked away my own tears.

• • •

Back home in Eunice, when I began making enough as a stock boy at the National to buy myself a car, a navy blue 1968 Volkswagen Beetle, trips to Mémère's would become much easier for me. The National was my first real job outside of the chores I did at home at the motel.

As I turned into the driveway of the motel for the first time in my new blue bug, Gilda came running.

"Wow!" she said when I pulled up. "Let me take it for a spin."

"I wanna go to Mémère's," I said. "If you come with me, I'll let you drive back."

"Deal."

"Bring your guitar. She's gonna want you to play."

Gilda was too *honté*, embarrassed, to play in front of anyone but family. Acquiring her guitar, an Ovation with twelve steel strings, was her first major life accomplishment. It represented to her much more than a mere possession. When Cassie first got her Ovation and played for us, every song previously played on a regular nylon six-string bloomed into a whole new sound experience. The extra six strings rounded out and enriched each chord and give every song a more vivid, floral timbre. Our guitar-playing icons—Cat Stevens, Paul Simon, Glen Campbell, and many other musicians who inspired countless wannabes across 1970s America to begin playing and singing—all played Ovations.

Once Gilda had fixed her mind that she was going to have one of her own, she aggressively saved what she made running the machines and folding the towels and sheets in the motel laundry. It took her nearly two years to get the six hundred dollars. "The Ovation is a guitarist's guitar," she liked to say, authoritatively, parroting Cassie, whose approval she had sought since early childhood.

At night, upstairs in her room, just down the hall from mine, which I had inherited from Cassie, Gilda played for me and had begun teaching me a few chords. She had soon convinced me to buy a guitar of my own, a hand-me-down, her old bulky Epiphone, nothing like an Ovation, but a decent starter guitar nonetheless. At fifty dollars, it was my next major life purchase after the Volkswagen. While I ultimately was able to figure out picking patterns by ear and learn a handful of the chords required to play "Leaving on a Jet Plane," "How Could I Tell You?," and "Landslide," I was not in possession of the patience and dedication required of a true player.

My interest in the guitar was an asset, however, when I asked Gilda to come with me to Ville Platte. And, on this particular Saturday, she was in a mood to play. She knew I was right when I said that Mémère would want to hear her play. Mémère loved nothing more than when one of her precious grandkids showed interest in music.

It was fitting, therefore, that for my virginal road trip in my new, old Volkswagen, I headed out to Mémère's in Ville Platte, with Gilda as my first passenger, and her prized Ovation securely lying on the backseat in its custom-made crush-proof case.

"Ooh, this car is so cute," she said after about five miles. "I wanna drive now," she said excitedly, lifting a chunk of her dark auburn hair back away from her face.

"Okay, but I haven't had a real good chance yet either. You can drive halfway there, then I get to take over."

"Deal," she said. "Now pull over."

After a few miles, when Gilda's initial excitement about the Volkswagen had evaporated, I asked, "Why don't you come with me to Mémère's more often?" I had been going regularly since I got my license.

"It's too depressing," she answered. "There's too many old people living in Ville Platte. And everybody's so poor. Besides, I don't like Billy Joe. He gives me the creeps."

"Even with him around, she gets so lonesome if we don't go see her enough," I said. "Momma said she'll probably die from the loneliness."

"I knowww," she droned. "It's just that everything there is so depressing. She should come to see us at home more often. But every time she comes, she can't wait to get back to her house to keep an eye on Billy Joe. I think Daddy makes her nervous too."

"Everything makes her nervous," I said. "Do you know how poor she is? I don't understand why she has to be so poor. Why don't Momma and Daddy give her a car? She wouldn't be so lonely if she had her own car like she used to."

"I don't think she'd accept it," Gilda said. "She's too proud. I think she gets insulted when Momma offers her anything. You have to be very careful not to offend her."

"I know. I tried to give her five dollars once, but she almost had a stroke," I said.

"She's so damned stubborn," Gilda said. "If I was her, I'd have taken your money. You make more at National than she ever did in her whole life."

"Yeah, I know," I said. "Isn't that pathetic? Once, when I went to stay with her, I noticed her fidgeting with the curtains in her bedroom. She stopped whatever it was she was doing when I walked in. It looked pretty weird to me, so when she wasn't around, I checked it out. Know what she does? She hides her money in the hem of those curtains. She folds the bills just right so she can slide them in and out easily. I checked all the other curtains in the house, but she only uses the ones in her bedroom. Poor thing. She's probably gotta hide the little bit of money she has from that drunk. Anyway, when I found that out, I started slipping in a few bucks."

"You think she knows you're doing it?" she asked.

"I'm not sure," I said. "I don't put in any big bills, just some ones and fives. I think she'd figure it out if I put in anything bigger. Besides, I think it's best if it's only a little at a time. A little surprise once in a while was always better than having it all at once."

The trip to Mémère's normally took about thirty minutes, but it seemed to go faster with someone to talk to.

When we got there, Gilda stepped out of the Volkswagen, her Ovation in tow. The knocks at the big green door to the kitchen of Mémère's house went unanswered.

"She must be at Miss Hadley's," Gilda said, cocking her head toward the neighbor's house. "Go see if she's there."

Like Mémère, Miss Hadley had been widowed for a while. Apparently, the two women got into regular spats concerning local gossip or, when Mémère was still single, an eye for the same available man. When they were fighting, Mémère would never say exactly why, especially if their feud did indeed concern a man. And, even though they were next-door neighbors, they could go for weeks without speaking to each other.

But when Mémère and Miss Hadley were on speaking terms, they were inseparable, with a genuine affection between them. I had witnessed their sisterly bond on many occasions. One Sunday afternoon, when Miss Hadley popped in to Mémère's for a chat, Mémère peeked into the coffee pot and found there was only enough for one cup, so she gave that to Miss Hadley and had none for herself. When Miss Hadley mentioned it, Mémère fibbed and said she had just had some. She was not about to let her think she was imposing.

• • •

I trotted through the bushes to Miss Hadley's. As I approached the screened porch, I heard them rattling off about something.

"*Allo*, Madame Hadley, Mémère *est là*?" I asked, as if expecting a possible "*Non, cher.*"

Normally, Miss Hadley spoke with what sounded like a throat full of phlegm. It was only when she was excited or surprised that her voice broke out of the phlegm long enough to be understood.

"*Aw, cher, bon dieu!*" Miss Hadley answered. It was rare to hear her speak so clearly.

"*Gardez donc ça!*" Mémère said, poking her head through the window.

"Me and Gilda came to visit you, Mémère," I said over Miss Hadley's subsequent phlegmy incoherencies.

"Okay, *cher*. I'm coming."

Back at Mémère's front porch, Gilda was just closing the clasps to the Ovation case. "She's on her way," I said.

"Aw, you brought the gee-tar!" she gasped excitedly as she approached her front porch, totally ignoring my new car. "Now we gonna play some mu-zeek!"

Once inside, Gilda played a few songs while Mémère made some lemonade. After a while I got a chance to strum a few of the notes I had learned. Mémère was delighted.

Gilda seized the opportunity to check out the bedroom. I knew what she was up to.

A few moments later, she emerged with an accomplished smile on her face. "Get your accordion," I requested, keeping Mémère's eyes on me and not Gilda.

"She's broke," Mémère said, her dentures clacking as she talked. "But I tell you what. Let's go visit Tante 'Ya. She just got her a new one."

. . .

Illya Guillory had been widowed since 1973, when her husband, Illiad—they were only ever referred to as "'Ya and 'Yud"—died after having a stroke. I had not seen 'Ya since 'Yud's funeral. Since then, a terrible disfiguring skin cancer had attacked her forehead and nose. The doctors had to remove half of her nose to clear away the deadly tissue. While they were successful at stopping the cancer's spread, they did a lousy job of rebuilding the nose, having used a graft of skin taken from her leg. The resulting face was hard to look at directly.

Like her sister, Estelle, 'Ya wore big, billowy house dresses and was most comfortable barefoot. There was much more of a resemblance between T'tell and her sister than between T'tell and her daughter, Catin. For every Streaks 'n Tips–lacquered banana curl atop Catin's coif, 'Ya had a countering wisp of bottle-black mane, going in all directions like her sister's. For every new pair of patent-leather pumps in Catin's closet, 'Ya had a new corn or bunion in progress.

'Ya also shared her sister's appreciation for the ease and versatility of plastic curtains. Hers had big yellow tulips and were cinched at the center with braided yellow crocheting yarn to match.

The house was small. We all sat in the yellow-curtained front room, which also featured framed photos of the same men in uniform. Several religious images—a glittered Jesus, illuminated by a heavenly halo and displaying his stigmata; Mary and her newborn, immaculately conceived baby, done as a mosaic; Our Lady of Guadeloupe standing in front of a radiant waterfall encircled in a garland of roses—awaited the due reverence of all who entered the room. A stringy yellow-green fern hung in one corner and shiny new ashtrays from Astroworld (from a recent trip to Houston, no doubt) dotted the room at various intervals. Behind the peach colored vinyl couch hung a large printed tapestry depicting some cowboys on horses in a desert. The floor was carpeted, but scattered on top of it were several multicolored carpet remnants. Two empty outdoor plastic swan planters flanked the coffee table, while a large ceramic Irish setter guarded the Zenith.

"I didn't know y'all was comin', *cher*. I don't got nothing for *lagniappe*," 'Ya said to Mémère, unable to conceal her regret and self-inflicted embarrassment. Of all the days not to have something to offer us prized redheaded grandkids from out-of-town, seeing how the thirty miles that separates Ville Platte and Eunice qualified us as "out-of-town guests."

"Don't worry yourself, *cher*," Mémère answered. "We just come to pass a li'l visit." That didn't matter to 'Ya. It was just not acceptable to her to have company, even drop-ins, and nothing to offer them.

Gilda, who was sitting next to a three-shelved metal knickknack case, knocked over a small ceramic figurine as she reached for her guitar. 'Ya pretended not to mind that the figurine shattered when it fell, but we could tell that it did bother her a bit by the way she gingerly picked up the broken pieces. In her mind, this was her comeuppance for not having any *lagniappe*.

"Mémère," I said, drawing attention away from the broken figurine, "are you still gonna play the accordion for us?"

"Okay."

"Lemme get it then, *cher*," 'Ya said, scooping up the last broken piece into her palm. She disappeared into the kitchen, then returned moments later with her new accordion and handed it to Mémère, who immediately started squeezing it, searching for a note that would inspire a song choice.

While Mémère was in the middle of "Jolie Blonde," Gilda, who was tuning her guitar quietly, popped the E string. Its recoil snapped the base of her thumb.

"Yeow!" she shrieked, shaking away the pain.

It seemed as though 'Ya was getting more irritated by our presence. "Are we making her nervous?" I mouthed, almost aloud, nudging Gilda with my elbow. "Are we interrupting something?" Gilda shrugged and shook her head.

'Ya leaned in and told Mémère something in French, then started to leave the room again. Just as she approached the threshold to the kitchen, a man in his late thirties or early forties entered and brushed up against her.

"Oh, there you are. Y'all, this here is Pierre," she said, explaining that he had been staying there for a while. Pierre's black hair had been chopped bluntly, as if he'd taken the scissors to it himself. His face was flushed, and the skin above his nose was dry and flaking off. His eyes bulged, his nose leaked. "How y'all do?" he sniffed, rubbing his nose with the sleeve of his oversized and faded madras shirt. He, too, was barefoot.

"What kinda geetar is that?" he asked, pointing to the Ovation.

"I just got it a coupla months ago," Gilda said.

"Well, I play geetar too, me. Lemme go get mine," he said as he turned and followed 'Ya out of the room.

"Should we leave?" I asked Mémère. "Where's 'Ya going? She looks upset about something."

"Don't worry, *cher*. She's gonna get y'all some *lagniappe*."

"We don't need anything," I said. "It's okay, really."

When Pierre returned a couple of minutes later, he was carrying a beat-up red and white electric guitar. Affixed to the instrument's glittery lacquered front was the word *"ibson"* spelled out in chrome. The "*G*" was long gone. He had just the guitar, no power cord, no amplifier. He perched the guitar on a raised knee and began strumming, creating a shrill, flat noise that had no resemblance to anything musical.

"Cost one hunnerd dollars," he said, to validate its worthiness to be in the same room as Gilda's immaculate Ovation. Droplets of spit flew as he spoke excitedly about the shiny Gibson. "All it needs is some new strings," he continued, his dark teeth spewing forth more saliva. "Got it at the pawn shop over there by Teet's fruit stand," he said, caressing the guitar's neck with stubby, tobacco-stained fingers.

It was hard for us to look interested. Pierre's right eye was twisted in such a way that it seemed he could see us from every angle. His fuzzy beer belly poked out of his unbuttoned shirt when he sat down and continued plucking the remaining strings of his hundred-dollar find. The noise he created bleated excruciatingly and bounced from every corner of the room. Jesus, Mary, and Guadalupe cast sideward glances at each other.

As soon as he finished, he looked around, expecting applause. We didn't know what to do, so we clapped. Gilda nudged me in the rib, indicating that she was more than ready to leave before things got any more surreal.

"We'd better be going before it gets too late, Mémère," Gilda said.

"But we need to wait for 'Ya," Mémère protested.

"We have to get back. I told Momma we were going to be home in time to help her with the dinner."

"Oh, okay, then, *cher*," Mémère said, resigned.

As we said our good-byes and thank-yous, Pierre was very anxious. "Don't y'all wanna wait for 'Ya? She'll be right back," he said, almost pleading.

"We really need to get home," Gilda said quickly. "Tell Tante 'Ya we said thank you and that we'll come back real soon. Okay?"

"Uh, okay," he answered nervously, his eyes shifting to and fro, his head ducked a little, as if he'd be scolded for letting us leave.

Back in the blue bug, Gilda said, "Oh my God, I thought we'd never make it outta there alive!"

"Aw, don't be silly. Pierre was just a li'l *coullion*," Mémère said, revealing to us what we had already figured. "He's not right in the head."

"Was that why he still lives with his momma?" I asked.

"That's not his momma," Mémère said. "That's his girlfriend."

"That's disgusting," Gilda said.

Just as we got down the road about a block from 'Ya's, I glanced up into the rearview mirror, where I saw 'Ya standing out in the middle of the blacktop, feverishly waving to us.

"Look, y'all. 'Ya's waving bye to us," I said, rolling down my window to return the wave. Gilda and Mémère also turned to wave. From that distance, it might have appeared to someone who didn't know her that she was grimacing, that she looked distraught. But I was sure it was only the facial disfiguration from the cancer. Clutched in her other hand was something that looked like a red box. A piece of Pierre's electric guitar gear, I thought. I kept driving.

But in a phone call to Mémère after we'd returned to her house, 'Ya revealed a different reality: As we drove away, she was indeed waving excitedly. She had just returned from where she had earlier disappeared to, the little grocery store three blocks from her house. Her face was, in fact, further distorted by disappointment as she watched the Volkswagen become but a blue speck in the distance. In her left hand she had held the Christmas-red carton of Coca-Cola she had just bought for us. Six glistening bottles of chilled *lagniappe*.

34 | Take the Bug for a Spin

To get to and from work in the first few weeks of my job at the National, I had relied on rides from Momma in her big maroon Chrysler Newport, or from Daddy in the Apache, or one of the twins in their sweet Rambler, but even with all this rotating chauffeuring, that plan quickly got pretty tiresome for everybody. My self-consciousness about this burden on them all helped me make my first big Life Decision: I must buy a car. Not *should* buy a car *one day* after I've saved up for it, but I *must* buy a car *now*, and Daddy would have to lend me the money.

Since it turned out he was doing most of the chauffeuring, Daddy had not only agreed to lend me the money but decided to take the lead on this project. He found me the 1969 navy blue Volkswagen Beetle and then fronted me the eight hundred dollars to buy it. After years of treating me like a nuisance, I was kinda blown away by this sudden helpfulness, but I questioned nothing. Took it all in. I got me a car, and nothing else mattered.

What struck me most about the design of the VW Beetle was that there were very few straight lines on it: from the outer rounded fenders, roof, trunk, and hood, to the interior, where the dashboard, knobs, seats, and even the windshield had rounded corners. The car's compactness was comforting instead of claustrophobic to me, which was surprising because I did have a touch of claustrophobia in most situations. I liked the feeling of its roof and outer walls hugging me with its closeness as I drove. In fact, if I stretched out my arms in any direction, I could touch something—the opposite door, the backseat, and practically even the back windshield.

And that little car changed my fifteen-year-old life. I no longer had to rely on anyone else to get me to and from work. And no more standing out there on the side of the road to catch the school bus every morning. The freedom the blue bug offered was all new to me, and actually kinda scary to me, but I managed. I could for the first time just decide to go somewhere and get in the car and take off.

The blue bug let me be the chauffer for friends at school who needed or just wanted a ride home. I had a newly discovered sense of possibility: I really could just get in my little car and *go*. And, though mostly confined to trips to work, to Mémère's, and within Eunice and its environs, that was exactly what I did.

• • •

In the fall, a more challenging road trip opportunity arose: to the parish science fair at Opelousas Senior High School. I knew how to get to Opelousas, had passed through it on the way to Lafayette, but was not at all familiar with the interior of the town. Wayne Arceneaux, a friend in the freshman class who had bummed a ride to the fair with me, said he knew how to get to the school.

"Yeah, it's no big deal," he assured me. "It's just a coupla turns off the main drag."

We each had qualified for the parish fair by earning blue ribbons at our school's fair. My project was in the anthropology category, on the history of Louisiana's architecture. It was a bulky affair, involving *papier-mâcheé* models of a traditional Cajun house with a galley wrap-around porch; the phallic thirty-two-story State Capitol building where Huey P. Long was shot down; a diorama of a section of the French Quarter; the brand-new Louisiana Superdome, including its spaceship-like parking platform; and a folding tri-paneled backdrop to box it all in. It pretty much took up the whole back seat of the blue bug.

Wayne's project was in the geology category, on the physical structure of the Earth and how it culminated in the creation of oil, Louisiana's biggest export. He and his brother had built a box with Plexiglas windows to illustrate the Earth's inner core, core, lower mantle, upper mantle, and crust, each layer with a different color and texture to highlight their distinctions. My favorite part was the miniature derrick poking out of the crust near the top of the box.

Turned out at the end of the judging, neither of our projects was good enough to get us to the state competition in Baton Rouge. We piled everything up in the backseat of the Volkswagen and headed back.

Fifteen minutes outside of Opelousas, it began raining just enough to slicken the smooth concrete road to Eunice. I was aware that the tires on the bug needed replacing but thought that if I watched my speed, we should be okay.

"Go around that guy," Wayne said, pointing to a green International pickup truck in front of us. "He's going too slow."

"I can't right now. There's a car coming on my side."

The car on the side passed us, so Wayne figured it was a good time for me to switch lanes and decided to take matters into his own hands. He grabbed my steering wheel and gave it a sudden tug to the left.

The little car abruptly jerked and jolted us into a full 360-degree spin on the wet road. A fast, clockwise spinning, spinning, spinning in the road. Through the planted median we went spinning and whirling. A spray of grass, leaves, mud, all flying. For a second we were suspended in a snap of shock and horror. Then a fleeting, twirling nightmare of pure disbelief, and finally, simultaneous bug-eyed awareness, and humbling, overwhelming confusion when the spinning, spinning, whirling, and more spinning, just as abruptly, stopped.

Silence. The car had not flipped over. We had not been plowed under by an oncoming car or worse. And we were not dead.

I breathed out. Without looking at Wayne—I would strangle him if I did—I exited the bug and had a look around. Nothing had fallen off. Nothing was damaged. There was mud everywhere, and we were facing the opposite direction of traffic. But we were upright. And alive.

I got back in the car, and Wayne was brushing off his white pants and straightening himself out.

"Did I get anything on me?" he asked.

Project parts were all over the backseat. I imagined that, as the car spun in the road and into the median, my little Cajun prairie house with the wrap-around porch had gone twirling in the air like Dorothy's house in *The Wizard of Oz*. It was now sitting upside down, on its roof, in the foot space behind Wayne. The phallic State Capitol building had come apart at its three main sections; the heavy Superdome seemed to have remained in the same spot I placed it, but the spaceship parking platform had cracked away from the rest of the building.

Wayne's Plexiglas box was busted open, and the layers had all merged into a colorful heap of sand on the seat.

"What?!" I said to Wayne, my face throbbing with blood. "Did you get anything *on* you?"

"But . . .," he tried to explain.

"Shut up! Just shut up!" I yelled.

I turned the ignition and was extremely relieved when the car started. The last thing I needed was to have to call somebody to come pick us up and find us in this condition. Car in the median, facing the wrong direction, our projects all jumbled in the backseat, and Wayne Arceneaux smoothing over his white pants and worrying if he'd gotten anything on him, with me ready to explode.

I drove out of the median and carefully, slowly, and silently, toward home. Nothing was said between us for a full ten minutes. Then, as the ridiculousness of it all displaced our shock and my anger, I looked over at Wayne, who shrugged and held it. He was not sure he should be looking back at me. My face, which had turned to cold stone, cracked. And our fits of laughter in that little blue mud-covered bug propelled us the rest of the way home.

35 | Someone Else

"Ooooh-wee! Taffeta's back in town!" she said, fingering a bolt of the shimmering teal fabric. She was alone or, on the surface of it at least, not accompanied by any *corporeal* being. I was standing not ten feet from her, looking at men's shoes. Loud enough to be heard all the way in the back, she continued, "Sure is pretty. The nicest thing in my chifforobe back in the day was a gold taffeta dress I wore to graduation. Still have it. Hmmm."

Her fitted beige-on-beige brocade suit segregated her torso from her hips and bottom, cutting her into sections. Like a dress form. She pivoted dramatically from the fabric area and headed towards the crafts and notions area, her undergarments swishing—shhwish shhwish shhwish—as she walked. With a white-gloved hand, pinky out, she picked up a Butterick pattern featuring a nurse's uniform—*who would make themselves a nurse's uniform?*—examined it like a menu, front and back, and then put it down again.

"Yes, ma'am?" a petite redhead in a green-and-white summer dress and black Mary Janes said as she approached the woman. "Can I help you find something?"

"Oh! Thank you!" the dress-form lady said to the salesgirl. "I'm looking for opera-length gloves for my niece for her cotillion," she said. "White, like mine, but opera length. She thinks they're old-fashioned, but I told her they are all the rage again in the big cities, and she'll be ahead of the trend here in Ville Platte."

"Hmmm. Don't think we have those *yet*," the salesgirl said as if the G. Ardoin and Company Department Store in downtown Ville Platte had plans to get them any time soon. "But let me go ask Mr. Willie to be sure."

"Hold on. Before you go, I'm also looking for pipe cleaners," said the dress-form lady. "I looked around the housewares stuff but couldn't find anything. It's a long story, but nothing works like a pipe cleaner when you're trying to get the tarnish out of the crevasses of a cigarette case. I have a collection of cigarette cases dating back to the early eighteen hundreds."

"Oh. Hmmm. I've never seen those here, but I'm sure Mr. Willie would know if we have those," said the salesgirl, walking to the back of the store, then through a doorway draped in burgundy velvet curtains, like those in a movie house.

With her begloved index finger, the dress-form lady lifted her oversized white sunglasses back into place on the bridge of her nose, discreetly straightened her Eva Gabor wig (I had the notion she was fully aware her wig was in need of a good wash but figured when she left the house that morning, "Nobody's gonna care. Not in this town"), and followed her to the back, stopping just short of the burgundy curtains.

Just about a minute passed before the salesgirl emerged from the velvet to inform the woman that the store had neither of the items on her list. "But you can get pipe cleaners at the tobacco shop in the next block," said the girl.

"Y'all just ain't got nothing that I need in here, then," she said with a friendly laugh of feigned disappointment. "Guess I'm gonna have to go all the way to Lafayette!" she said pertly as she clasped shut her white patent-leather purse with a loud Snap! and theatrically oscillated this way and that, as though the whole store were her own private runway, and finally out through the aluminum-framed glass front doors in a blur of beige and white.

· · ·

I had moved over to the stationery and office supply aisle to join Mémère and Momma. The three of us, as discreetly as possible, had been witnessing this little scene as if it were a stage play. I didn't know what Momma and Mémère were thinking, but I half expected a chorus of shoppers to break into a rousing musical number as the dress-form lady pirouetted through the store, pinkies out, without a care in the world outside of her shopping list.

"She's the kind of customer who holds up the line at the register," Momma whispered to me. "The kind that asks a bunch of questions and is loud so all the *ordinary* people who have to wait behind her can hear." Indeed, every extravagant proclamation the lady made seemed to be whatever mundane thought popped into her bewigged head.

"Y'all know when the next Cotton Festival is?" she had loudly asked the room before leaving the store. "Maybe I should think about some shoes for that while I'm here."

Thirty years earlier, before Momma, Eliza Mae Thompson, became Eliza Mae Ardoin, she herself had worked in this very store. She was exactly that salesgirl waiting on the dress-form lady—down to the red hair, the cotton dress, and the Mary Janes—and was also the store's bookkeeper when things were quiet.

"She seems to be handing her about as well as she can," Momma said to me of the salesgirl. "Glad that for her sake it didn't get to the point of actually having to check her out, with her carrying on and on like that."

I was well aware of the story of Momma's first job. Family history was the kind of thing she and I talked about regularly, because my budding reporter's mind had been at practice since I was a kid.

At twenty, when Momma had begun working behind the counter at the back of the store, things were not so different from that morning I spent with her and Mémère there. Even though Mr. G.—the G. was for Guillaume—had long since passed away, and Mr. Willie, his son-in-law, had taken his place in the store, nothing much had changed. The prices had changed, of course, but only gradually. In the fabric and notions department, taffeta was available on bolts in three colors: sunset gold, robin's-egg blue, and a peony pink. And they did not carry ladies' opera-length gloves back then, either—only the short ones, and only during the Easter season. The store was pretty much the same. Same layout and same smells of old wood floors and musty fabrics, and the same overall peculiar, but comforting, scent of nutmeg that had been ingrained into everything, probably a combination of the woodwork, cleaning products, and commingled perfumes. And in many cases, the same merchandise, untouched for at least twenty-five years. But they had never, ever, carried pipe cleaners. With a tobacco shop in the next block, which had been there since the turn of the century, there wasn't much sense in carrying anything to do with products for smoking, a habit that Mr. G. had frowned upon anyway.

So there was Momma, a third of a century later, shopping with Mémère and me at that same store on a beautiful April Saturday morning. Ten-thirty on the dot, according to the big Seth Thomas clock up on the wall behind the back counter where she once stood waiting on customers when she wasn't in the office reconciling the month's income-versus-expenses.

We were in the store to pick up a bathrobe and maybe some pajamas for Billy Joe, who was going to be living on his own, finally. On our drive from Eunice to pick up Mémère in Ville Platte, Momma said she didn't want to feel sad about the turn of events that led to this development.

"Those muckety-mucks at the Evangeline Parish courthouse are just doing their jobs. Even though I already know it, it is better if they make the official call that Momma would be better off without Billy Joe always dragging her down."

For Mémère it had been years of living in the hell that Billy Joe created around him wherever he went. His antics had become very predictable: he drank day and night, he stole money from her, and he disappeared for days.

But after ten long years of that, at long last, she couldn't take him any more. His value to her, principally as a companion, something she prized above all other comforts, diminished considerably when he routinely spent the night in the parish jail for drunken disorderliness or whatnot. Plus, he had alienated everyone she loved: her children—my uncles Paillasse and Florence, and momma—and all us grandkids. No one liked being around him, the fact of which saddened her because it also meant that we weren't spending as much time with her as we had before he appeared in her life that fateful night at Snook's. And after ten, nearly eleven, years, she just couldn't take it any more.

"We can get him put on disability," Momma explained to me in the car. "I talked to the lady yesterday on the phone, and she said all we have to do is sober him up enough to take him to the office at City Hall, and they'll show us through the paperwork. Once that's done, he'll be their problem, not Momma's."

The lady at City Hall had recommended a robe or at least some pajamas, so Billy Joe would have something on when the care worker came by to feed and check in on him. And this necessitated the trip to the department store.

"I agree with their decision entirely," Momma said. The Parish had decreed that Billy Joe was to stay away from Mémère's house and could see her only if she initiated a visit to see him, and only in the small clapboard house three blocks away from hers, where he would be living for the rest of his days. He would have a care worker visit him three times a day, provide him with meals, see to it that he stayed away from the bottle, and had a weekly bath.

"Pretty sensible deal," Momma said. "A lot better treatment than many other people get, under the circumstances."

During the drive from her house to the department store, Momma told Mémère, "Momma, it's not for me to tell you what to do, but I want you to know that I think this is the best thing for you, and for him. And I'm going to be here with you as much as possible so you won't be going through this all by yourself."

"I know, Mae-Mae," Mémère responded. "That's fine, *cher*. But you know how lonesome I get, me, when you gone and I'm all by myself. That's the hardest part for me."

"I know, Momma."

• • •

We were in the store for about thirty minutes, Mémère in the Men's Department, unable to decide on the dark blue or the light blue robe for Billy Joe, and Momma in the crafts area looking at the yarn, when the fussy dress-form lady swished in, flailed about, and disappeared again through the front doors.

"*Mais regarde donc, ça, cher*," Mémère said to Momma, cocking her head toward the redheaded shop girl attending to the lady. "She look just like you when you work here."

"That's funny," Momma said. "I was thinking the same thing."

• • •

And, I would learn later, Momma was also thinking then about meeting dark, handsome, and lanky Zanny Ardoin from up the road in Tate Cove one Saturday in March of 1951, a day that would change her life forever, even though she didn't know it at the time.

"Yes, sir, can I help you?" she asked him as he stood there grinning.

"Sir?" she said a bit louder when he didn't respond right away.

"Oh, yes. Um. How do you do?" he said clumsily. "I don't know if you remember me, but we met at a party a few years back. Before I went into the army."

"Ohhh, yes," she said, hoping not to appear too eager. "I thought you looked familiar. Wasn't quite sure. We see a lot of people in this store, especially on Saturdays. You were wearing your uniform that night if I remember correctly. I'm gonna assume you got yourself a few medals and ribbons to pin on it since then."

In truth, she knew exactly who he was and had thought about him more than a few times over the years since that party. At the party he informed her he was going into the army, going to do his duty, then come back, find a girl to marry, and settle down. Then he told her she was the prettiest girl there, but she figured he was saying that to anyone who'd listen.

She wasn't sure if she liked him. He was cleaned up all right, but listening to him talk, she imagined he was probably going to be a man who made his living getting dirty. Maybe a farmer, or a blacksmith, like her daddy, which wasn't so bad, or an auto mechanic. Not sure about any of that, she had yet to piece together a full picture of marriage, let alone the type of man who would be her husband. The little bit of thought she did have about it leaned toward finding a professional man, like a doctor, or a lawyer, or a banker. That way, getting out of Ville Platte would be the next logical step.

But that night there was something she liked in his face, and it was that face she had thought about when she thought of him in the years since. Handsome, but not overly so. Lean features, dark hair, and a dark tan that tipped her off to his likely vocation as a laborer of some sort. He looked serious and at the same time had the remnants of a boyish streak that would probably disappear in the short term, she thought. And something else. Something so slight in his personality, but noticeable enough to be off-putting. He looked *mean*.

"Oh, yes, I sure did," he replied, thankful for the opening. "I got myself one for service, one for them special operations I was on, and another one for leadership."

"Well," she said. "That's very impressive. So what can I do for you today?"

"Oh, um, I thought you might want to go out with me."

"Excuse me?" she said puzzled. "You didn't come here to buy something?"

"Um, well, yes, but then I saw you all the way back here when I walked in the front of the store, and now I can't remember what it was I wanted. So that tells me that I'm supposed to ask you out."

"Oh."

"So is that okay with you?"

She had been dating, and in fact was engaged to marry, Jimmy Bergeron, who was away in Lafayette attending Southwest Louisiana Institute studying accounting. They had that in common, an interest in bookkeeping, and, frankly, not much else. She knew it, but she also knew that she had to be practical about these things. Jimmy Bergeron was a perfectly fine man, and over the years since meeting Zanny Ardoin at that party she had come to figure out exactly what marriage would look like, and the kind of man who would make a good husband. And that was Jimmy.

"Well," she hesitated. "You'll have to ask my daddy," she said, reaching for some way to stall. "He insists on meeting anyone who asks me out."

She wasn't about to mention Jimmy Bergeron, or the fact that both DeJean and Ortense Thompson had already given her their full blessing to marry him.

"All right, then," Zanny said. "When's a good time for that? I'll go over and ask him."

She wouldn't let him get to her house before she could to explain to them that he was only being polite and friendly after running into her at the store, and that anyway, she had been having second thoughts about marrying Jimmy Bergeron, because, well, he was just really boring, and that it might be good for her to meet other people before rushing into anything.

There was not much they could do. By then she was twenty-five, had had a job for five years, and could make these kinds of decisions for herself, so they pretended to accept.

So Zanny Ardoin from Tate Cove, Louisiana, an unincorporated patch-quilt of fields and farms and country houses far enough away (by ten minutes anyway) from the "city" folk of Ville Platte, stunning in his full army dress uniform, resplendent with two shiny medals and a colorful ribbon bar on his chest, knocked on the door of the house on East Jackson Street, politely asked DeJean Thompson for permission to ask his daughter out on a date, and was granted it on the condition that he behave himself and get her home by ten.

"I can do that," he said to DeJean.

"Make sure you do," chimed Ortense, who was standing in the doorway right behind her husband.

On their first date, Zanny told Eliza Mae about his travels during the war and the kinds of things he'd like to forget: shooting German soldiers the same age as him, bodies piled up in ditches, the stench of the battlefields, the bitter cold of Normandy, the restlessness his buddies felt knowing that many in their midst would not make it back to America.

"One day I'm gonna go back there and see Europe the way you should see it, not under such god-awful circumstances."

He talked about marriage from the get-go. It was his plan to get married and start a business in town. He didn't mention children, so she asked him about that.

"How many kids you want?" she asked.

"I hadn't thought about that," he said. "I had so many around me in my family growing up—there were fifteen of us—that I'm not sure if I want kids at all."

When he saw her blanch, he tried to cover his tracks. "Well, maybe one or two would be okay."

But it was too late. He had shown his cards. She could not possibly know that what was cooking in Zanny Ardoin's subconscious was that he'd already seen too much horror in the world and was himself a survivor of a truly bleak childhood, and that having his own children might not be such a good idea. But he wasn't in a position to fully understand all this himself, either. It was just an instinct to him that bringing children into the world, especially since he'd only recently begun to live a full life without a constant dark cloud over his head, was not a good idea.

But what he saw in her face was a very plain message that a marriage needs the souls of both parties fully functioning together to succeed. She hadn't experienced all the horrible things he had, and although she suffered, as most people did, during the depths of the Depression, she was still quite optimistic that life could be better for the next generation.

"Yeah," he continued. "The more I think about it, it would probably be okay to have a kid or two."

It was the second time that she sensed in him something that was not part of the checklist of ideals she had come to expect in a potential husband. She hadn't forgotten that nagging sensation about him having a mean streak that was part of her first impression the night they met at that party.

• • •

"Is that you, Eliza Mae?" came a voice from over Momma's shoulder. The three of us turned to see a woman holding a department store bag containing the items she'd just purchased. It was a face Momma knew from her school days at Ville Platte High School.

"Anne Marie Jagneaux?"

"It's LeJeune now," said the woman. "Don't you remember I married Halley LeJeune?"

"Oh, well, yeah," Momma said.

"I know you too, *cher*," said Mémère. "I used to know you momma before she die, her, *pauvre bête*."

"Well, hello, Miss Thompson," said Anne Marie. "So glad to see y'all again after all these years!"

By then, Anne Marie, like Eliza Mae, had had a houseful of kids, was now in her mid-fifties, and had managed to keep herself trim and tidy. She had on a black sweater over black slacks, and a red scarf wrapped around what looked like a neck brace.

"What happened there?" Momma asked.

"Oh, what a nightmare," said Anne Marie. "I was in a car accident a month ago in Eunice. Surprised you hadn't heard about it. I was on my way to pick up my daughter-in-law for a shopping trip in Lafayette, and this girl in a van runs through a stop sign and plows right into me. Spent a week in the hospital."

"No! I hadn't heard about that at all. That's horrible."

"Well, I'm okay now. The doctor said I'm gonna have to wear this thing for another month or two. How y'all been? How's that motel and all y'all's kids?"

"Oh, we're making it," Momma said. "You know I married Zanny Ardoin from Tate Cove . . ."

"Oh, I remember Zanny!" she interjected.

" . . . and he didn't want any kids at first, but thank God for *them*," she said, putting a hand on my shoulder. "I don't know how we coulda made it without them helping us out."

"Oh, you are so right," said Anne Marie. "My boys help their daddy run his trucking business and I don't know what I'd do without my girls. Oh, my. I gotta get. I hate to chat and run, but I'm in a hurry this morning. So good to see you all!"

• • •

A few years after this trip to the department store with Momma and Mémère, long after they and Daddy had all passed away, I would learn the full story, from Cassie.

Eliza Mae Thompson had indeed married Zanny Ardoin forty years before. Not long after he knocked on the front door of the house on East Jackson Street in his full army dress uniform, she realized she really had no deep interest in marrying Jimmy Bergeron. She told him as much in a letter, and though he fired off a reply right away to protest, he finally accepted the news when he was able to hear it from her own lips when he came home after his finals.

"So you gonna marry that army man?" Mémère asked when Momma told her.

"No. Not at all," Momma replied. "But he has helped me see that I haven't had a chance to be sure about anyone, including him and Jimmy. And I just want to be more sure."

Daddy proposed in May, not quite two months after meeting her again that Saturday at G. Ardoin's. She said, "No," that it was way too soon for her to agree, but that she was happy to continue dating him.

"I need some time," she insisted. "I need to be sure."

"Well, you take all the time you need, then," he said. "I'll wait."

She had real concerns about Zanny Ardoin. He was great at making her feel special and desirable, but even after dating a few months, she couldn't shake the notion that he wasn't the right man for her.

In another few months, she learned she was very likely pregnant and didn't think too much about it before she accepted her fate: despite his lack of interest in children, and that nagging idea that, deep down, he had a mean streak in him, she would marry him.

"We gotta do it," he insisted when he found out. "There's no way you can have a baby in this town without being married. We gotta do it."

It wasn't at all how she imagined things would play out for her. In fact, the big issue for her was that she felt she hadn't yet taken enough time to imagine her life at all. Things were happening all around her, and she didn't know how to stop long enough to make a plan for herself, or even that she should allow herself to *have* her own plan. All around her, women didn't get to have a plan. They just did whatever came up. Well, *this* came up, and she was going to have to do it.

And that was that.

Once she had fully accepted the notion that she was going to be married to Zanny Ardoin and have a baby with him, she struggled to prevent any further doubts from penetrating her thoughts. She stepped, one by one, through the proper stages laid out for her until she was married, then had a husband, and a new place to live, and would focus on making sure the baby inside her would be healthy and cared for with all she could give it.

When the baby, Cassandra "Cassie" Marie, came eight months after the civil ceremony, Momma and Daddy acted surprised that she had "come early," and another word about the whole situation was never uttered. Not aloud, anyway. She would bear this secret her whole life. For her, the deception was a burden; for Zanny, something to be shrugged off and forgotten. He had what he wanted. And if that meant he had to have a baby to go along with it, then so be it.

. . .

"I think he would like the dark one best, *cher*," Mémère said to Momma. "I almost pick that light one, but then I think to myself, 'That's not for me.' I like that light one, but it's not for me. So let's go with that dark one."

"Good. I'm sure he'll be fine with the dark one," Momma said. "Let's get out of here and get you home. We need to get on the road."

On the ride back to East Jackson Street, Momma's mind was racing.

"Momma, do you remember when Paillasse and Florence and I were little, when we tried to tame that wild momma cat?" she asked Mémère.

"Not sure, *cher*," Mémère replied. "Tell me about it."

"We wanted to be able to pet her, and for her to be friendly so all her babies would be friendly too. So we caught her in a burlap sack and tied it up so she wouldn't get out and would calm down. She was wild and jumping around in that sack so much that we just left her there under the fig tree in the back yard, hoping that after a while, she'd be calm enough for us to pet her and teach her that we were friendly and then she would be too."

"I don't think so, *cher*. That was too long ago."

"Well, I wish I could say it had a happy ending, but I can't. It has a sad ending. We had left her out there in the shade under that tree, but after a while, the sun moved, so she was in the direct heat. By the time we remembered to check on her, the sack was calm, so we opened it up, and there she was, covered in sweat. Poor thing. Soaked in her own sweat and breathing real hard. But it was too late to save her. She died after a little while, even though we tried to cool her down. It was too late."

"Why you telling me that, *cher*? That's terrible."

"I know, Momma. It was terrible."

"But I was thinking about that momma cat today when we were in that store. How scared she musta been. She didn't know what was happening to her, and no matter how hard she clawed, she was trapped. Sometimes I feel just like that momma cat. I feel trapped. Like I'm suffocating. You know what I mean?"

"No, *cher*, I don't," Mémère said softly.

Our ride back to Eunice was quiet at first, but I broke the silence.

"Are you okay?" I asked, sensing that she was somewhere else, deep in her thoughts.

"Oh, yeah," she replied flatly. "I was just thinking at how different my momma's life turned out from mine, but also how similar it has been."

"I'm not sure what you mean," I said.

"Well, neither of us had set out to have the lives we ultimately had. Both of us simply went with the flow of things. Neither one of us ever had the notion to actually plan our lives for ourselves. Girls didn't do that. Girls got married. There wasn't much out there for us to do."

This made sense to me. Outside of housewifing, or maybe housewifing and teaching, or housewifing and nursing, or as in Momma's case, housewifing and hairdressing, women seemed to have far fewer options than men.

"I wasn't exposed to many choices. It wouldn't have crossed my mind to be a doctor, or a lawyer, or a banker like the men were. And that was the way of the world."

It was quite a common story, after all.

"Every now and then a woman is able to assert herself, like that lady looking at the fabric at the store. But where does that get her? I don't know for sure, of course, but I would bet she was pretty much alone in her life, except for her relatives."

More silence in the car.

I wondered if Momma ever knew what it was she was *supposed* to have been, if things had been different for her. What might have made her feel fully alive, completely her own person. Instead, she had become someone else's spouse, someone else's threadbare momma, someone else's invisible maid and exhausted cook, someone else's reliable ear, someone else's tireless caretaker, and had lived someone else's idea of a life. *Someone else.*

36 | Gilda, Glenda, Alice

The early 1970s became the mid-1970s. For the twins and me, a world outside of our motel lives quickly opened as we matured. I suddenly had a "real job" that paid real money, an unheard-of four dollars and seventy-five cents an hour, versus one dollar for several hours of work at the motel, which I continued to do as well. Daddy was not about to release any of us from our motel work, as long as we were "under his roof." And like me, the twins had taken on lives they had to squeeze in, in addition to their jobs at the motel.

Glenda tried out for and was selected as a cheerleader. It surprised and delighted her that this was even possible for her. Gilda joined the Green Jackets, the group of uniformed girls, who, waving green and white nylon flags attached to poles grasped in white-gloved hands, marched along behind the band to rally school spirit at sporting events and in town parades. She had a featured role among the line of girls with strapped-on parade drums, banging obediently as they marched.

Cheerleading and Green-Jacketing took plenty of time practicing and rehearsing, and would be quite enough for most girls, but there was more in the cards for these two redheads. Both were natural athletes. This became apparent first on the basketball courts, then on the tennis courts. Hours of time practicing were spent on each sport. They quickly became stars at both. So much so, that in my first year at the high school it soon became apparent to me that I would need to make my own way out from under their considerable shadows.

In high school I finally emerged from the years of stomach-knotted shyness I'd had since childhood, brought on, no doubt, from the mortifying shit-my-pants episode in Mrs. Bello's first-grade class. I became perfectly comfortable as one of a few class clowns, an occasional poet, and budding journalist. I even dabbled briefly in politics; first, as sophomore class parliamentarian, a position that for me existed entirely as a name-builder for my next role, junior class president, and then as a member of the vaunted student council. While these activities took some time outside of school, and my job at the supermarket kept me fairly occupied, my extracurricular life was nothing compared to those of the twins.

• • •

"What are you doing?!" Glenda screamed at me, grabbing *The Exorcist* out of my hands and flinging it violently across the room, where it hit the wood-paneled wall and dropped to the floor, its pages splayed out like a turkey tail.

"How can you be reading *that* at a time like *this*?!"

"Um, I was just trying to take my mind off things," I replied, startled by the outburst, although I was not sure the alarm in Glenda's voice was misplaced. None of us yet knew how Gilda's condition would play out. We were all on edge after the accident that afternoon that left her in the hospital with a concussion and Glenda in a tangle of nerves and an unshakable sense of dread. When they were competing against each other in a game of tennis or basketball, or, not so long ago, when we still regularly played, a few long rounds of canasta, it was all done with fierce competitiveness; each would stop at nothing to win. But they were each also fiercely devoted to each other, something this accident brought into full relief.

"Read something else! That book is evil, and your sister could be dying right now in that hospital!" she bellowed before storming out of the room.

• • •

It was another Saturday of many the twins had spent on the tennis courts inside the circle that separated Park Avenue East from Park Avenue West in town. After several hours of hard practice and play, they left the circle to make a run to the Sonic. Both girls were developing an impressive set of attributes required of formidable players of the game: they were fast on their feet, had keen observation skills and quick reflexes, had mastered precise swing techniques, and the capacity to deliver powerful, controlled backhands. All skills that came with hours of dedicated practice.

Also, it helps quite a bit to have a natural aptitude for sports overall. And that was indeed what each of the twins had: plenty of aptitude for all things sporting. During the summers, when Andy recognized this aptitude in Gilda and Glenda, he lent them gloves and enlisted them to play catch, then a game or two of football, then later, in a makeshift ring, compete in boxing matches, where he knelt to handicap himself against his sisters.

And it was with Andy that the twins' innate skill at basketball first emerged. After nailing a shiny new orange goal at the regulation height up on a tall pine tree, they played the game so much that the grass around the tree soon disappeared, leaving a smooth dirt court.

The twins had a frustrating experience in junior high, where the girls' coach benched them in favor of her clumsy, untalented pet students, but the dynamic twin redheads would nonetheless go on to take over the sport on the high school team, drawing crowds for both home and away games.

• • •

On the trip to the Sonic that Saturday, Gilda was driving. Glenda didn't yet have her license, because she wasn't interested in driving and preferred that others do it.

"I'm burnt," Gilda said, turning their little white, round-fendered car onto Ninth Street, heading toward Eunice's main drag, Laurel Avenue. "I'm craving a cherry 7-Up."

At first glance the little car, a 1960 American Rambler, something from another era, looked like it might belong to an eccentric stamp collector, or a scholarly botanist, or a mad taxidermist. A little less than a year before, Daddy had picked it up for $250 from an elderly couple on a farm off of the Chataignier Road. In the moment he spied her parked in their front yard, Daddy named the little car Alice. He had a habit of assigning random, sometimes rude, sometimes racist, names to people: Cassie was "Sweet Polly," Andy was "Long Jowl," and many a black customer was called "Reverend" whether or not they'd been ordained as such. In this case, for a change, Alice seemed to suit the car perfectly, and so the name stuck.

• • •

The stop sign at the intersection of Ninth Street and Laurel Avenue was completely obscured by a full tallow tree. Just as Gilda drove right through the intersection without stopping, Glenda saw the pickup truck, the second before it would hit them, prompting a reflex to lift her left foot up onto the dashboard to brace herself.

Traveling at the thirty-five-miles-per-hour speed limit, the truck slammed into Alice's front left fender. The blunt-force punch of the two steel vehicles colliding could be heard from blocks away. With a rubber-to-road screech, the impact sent Alice and the twins skidding completely across the avenue to the opposite side, where they came to a full stop in the parking lot of a Conoco gas station. Then all was quiet.

The force of the crash knocked the breath out of Glenda. She felt as if she had been kicked in the lungs. For a few panicked moments, she could not take in air. She could not breathe. She believed she was going to die. In the next instant, however, with a gasp, her lungs filled again, like a baby slapped into its new world.

In the impact, Gilda's head banged into the steel bar of the car's frame, where the side window and the windshield met. She apparently had lost consciousness, but her body didn't yet know it. Crying hysterically, she forced her way out of the car through the smashed door and slammed it shut behind her. She was disoriented but looked to be fully awake when the ambulance arrived to take her and Glenda to the hospital.

• • •

Dr. DeRouen popped into Gilda's hospital room. He was there to release her after a night of observation.

"You'll be fine," he said. "But be careful out there."

"Okay," said Gilda, eager to get out of that place. That hospital room made her skin crawl. She had a headache, but Dr. DeRouen said that was normal. That she'd be good as new in a day or so.

And so she would.

• • •

Afterward, Alice sat quiet in the back yard; her bashed-in parts would rust where the raw steel was exposed. She would never be driven again.

By the time 1976 arrived, Gilda, Glenda, and I had joined the world of young adults, with Dicky not far behind. We each had cultivated our own interests; the twins their sports and other school endeavors that continued into college; me, my job at the National, which exposed me to the business world outside of the motel for the first time. While our motel work still kept us connected to home, it became less of a binder for the four of us. With cars and some money we had means to escape and, whenever possible, we did just that.

. . .

Together the four of us experienced several summers and falls and winters and springs. And we were mostly intact as young people, despite the obstacles—the merciless summer heat, the never-ending chores, and violence at the hand of our daddy—or perhaps because of them. The crash in Alice coincided with the beginning of a new phase in each of our lives. "We are not guaranteed any tomorrows," Momma said to us when it was all over. She had used that expression before, but the accident revealed this stunning reality to us like nothing in our lives had until that point. Talking for hours and telling stories; playing cards in the dining room; making cakes from Momma's magazines; singing along to the little kitchen radio. Our canasta summers were behind us.

PART II

THE ELDERS DEPART 1989-1998

37 | Momma and Me at the Peacock

So there we were sitting at a little table at the Peacock. The *Purple Peacock*. Just Momma and me. Unlikely as that may seem, she was the one who suggested it. It was early in the evening, not yet seven. The crowds wouldn't start coming in till ten at the earliest, and we'd be long gone by then. It was pretty much just us, a quiet waitress, and the bartender.

For years I had been coming home on weekends from LSU in Baton Rouge, and then a few years after that, from grad school in Lafayette. I'd get my stuff out of the car, take my clothes out back into the laundry room, and if the washer was clear, start a load. Then I'd go inside the house and say hey to everyone, hang out for a while, gradually finish my laundry, and later head out again to go visiting friends in town. Pretty much every time I went in for the weekend, that was my routine.

"When you gonna take me with you?" Momma asked each time I headed out the front door for the night. Always assumed it was just talk, just a joke. It hit me one day that maybe she was not joking. Why *not* take her with me?

"All right, then, come with me tonight," I replied on a particularly warm April Friday night on my way to town to play cards with Wayne Arceneaux and his wife, Vicky. I had served in their wedding five years earlier.

That I was obviously serious with my invitation for her to join me caught Momma off guard.

"Oh," she said. "I can't tonight. I was just joshin' with you, anyway. You know I can't go and leave your daddy here on such a short notice."

"Well, let's do it another weekend, then. How about we make a date for next time I come in? That way you can prepare him for the shock of having to spend a few hours on his own."

"Okay. It's a date, then." There was a lilt in her voice; her eyes smiled. "How about we go to the Peacock for a coupla drinks? I haven't been there in twenty years."

"Um, sure. That sounds like fun," I replied, even though what I was envisioning was just having her come with me when I stopped in at Wayne's or the home of some other friend's who needed visiting that weekend. We'd have a drink with whomever, sit a while and talk, maybe play a hand or two of cards, then get back to the motel in time for Daddy to have an evening nap before the late-night customers kept him up.

I thought about this little turn of events on my way to Wayne and Vicky's. Lately, she had been feeling down. Like she was lonely. She was sad. She was tired. She was definitely not herself. There'd been a lot of ups and downs in her life. Seems she had been married for a million years. She gave birth to nine babies. She ran her own business for a decade. Now her children were all gone except for the youngest, Alisa, who herself would be on her way to college after she finished high school next May. Of course she was feeling off.

• • •

As planned, the next time I went home, Momma and I headed out for a drink at the Purple Peacock.

The waitress brought us our Tom Collinses. Though neither of us really smoked, to accompany our drinks we each had a lit Marlboro Light from a pack I bought at the cigarette machine near the bar.

"If only we could sell that place," she said before I asked how she was doing.

"What do you mean?" I asked.

"It's too much for us. Round the clock. All these years we had all y'all kids. I don't know how we're gonna keep it up by ourselves."

"You think he's really gonna sell it, then?" I asked.

"I keep telling him that we need to do it, that twenty years was a good run. That it's given us a good life and did what it was supposed to do. But now with Alisa leaving next year, we won't need to keep at it forever."

"He should know that," I said.

"I think he does, but he's also afraid that he won't know what to do with himself if we sell. His excuse is that the market's not good right now. He wants to get a good price for it. But the market hasn't been good for several years."

"So y'all are not likely to be able to get a good price any time soon," I said.

"That's what worries me. We have to get a good price, or we won't leave with enough to retire. We could live for another thirty years. Social Security won't be enough, that's for sure."

But that's not all there was to the story.

"Motel or no motel, if it wasn't for y'all kids, I would have left already," she continued, staring blankly over to a dark corner in the expansive, quiet nightclub—it would be throbbing with disco in a few hours, drawing people from all over the state.

"Really?" I asked, a bit shocked and not sure if I should press her for more. I didn't have to.

"He's been hard to stay with all this time. I've thought about leaving many, many times—especially back when he was so violent with you and the others. But I couldn't imagine making it work with all the kids with me, and I wasn't about to leave y'all with him. So I stayed put."

"Wow," I said quietly. "I wouldn't have—none of us would have—blamed you for leaving. We would have made it work somehow."

"You're probably right, but I was so scared of what could happen to us. It's never easy on the woman. The men always make it out of that kind of situation okay, but the women don't. Believe me, I've heard plenty of stories from the women in my shop. It's a common thing, unfortunately. So many women stay with men that aren't right for them because they have nowhere else to go, and especially if they have kids."

I took a long drag on my Marlboro Light, which made me cough. Even though I had a cigarette every now and then, I was not a practiced smoker, so I hadn't built up my inhalation skills like the pros do. She was even less of a smoker. She took a drag on hers, and like me, she coughed up a few clouds.

We talked about Mémère and her fear of being alone; about Pépère dying and leaving her behind way too soon; how that devastated her; and then how Mémère then endured Billy Joe Olberg for so long simply because he provided some company, and because she did not want to be alone in her little world. She told me about how she met Daddy all those years ago when she was the bookkeeper at the department store in Ville Platte, how she had a sixth sense that he was not what he seemed, how he in fact turned out to be mean and quite violent. How that violence affected their first five children, born before he mellowed enough to better control his temper.

She told me how hard it was to lose a child, Thomas, her fourth son. How that really surprised her and caught her completely off guard, especially after having six perfectly healthy babies before him with no problem. To then have one with encephalitis, who died after just two days. Having to bury that little boy without having had a chance to hold him in her arms.

We talked about her beauty shop. How she set it up from scratch after beauty school, how the ladies there became a circle of friends she may have never known otherwise. And how their lives, when compared to hers, were in many ways, much harder. And how that fact made her see her situation as more manageable. How, when she got to her shop each day she was in control, not only of a successful business but of her own life. About being able to travel a little by her own means, because Daddy never honored his courting promise to take her with him to see the world. The few parts of the world she did see were because she made those trips happen: trips to the Mississippi Gulf Coast, the New Orleans World's Fair, and the mountains of Tennessee.

I was intentionally steering the conversation to her life, because I wanted to know what was going on with her. But we did talk about me a little. She asked if I was happy, if I had an idea what would make me happy, and if I did, could I share that with her. How I approached romance and what I thought about *forever* love. She said she'd known since I was a boy that I would have a difficult life because of the gay thing. But that she had no idea that some of the hardest battles I would have to fight in my life would happen early on, right at home. That the man she married would show himself to be my biggest threat because of that, and how she tried her best to calm him down; to get him to accept that nothing he did could change me; that this was not something to fear, but rather something she believed I could learn to handle with strength.

"I saw early on, when you were just a toddler, that you could find ways to go around things," she said. "If something gets in your way, you have a knack for getting around it and coming out on the other side unfazed. I think that is pretty remarkable. I would wish that skill for all of my kids."

And then we talked about her, personally. About how she had lived her whole life fulfilling other people's needs.

"I have no problem whatsoever doing for my kids," she said. "But it took me a long time—years and years—before I figured out that I can be that kind of a momma, and I can *also* give myself some time to enjoy life. There's a whole life inside me that I haven't lived. That's what pushes me now. I want to live that life. I want to do things that interest me. That make me feel alive on this earth. Before I die. Before I am too old and it's too late."

"Alisa's about to graduate," I said. "When that's done and she's in college, you won't have that holding you back any more. You should come live with me in New Orleans. It's my turn to take care of *you*. You deserve a good life, and you're right: that needs to start now."

And I meant it. I was not telling her this to make conversation. She was at a critical point in her life where someone needed to help her see it was indeed possible to escape that man. I did it and was more than confident that I could help her do the same.

I could already envision having her living with me in New Orleans. During the day she'd keep herself busy with the many things the city has to offer: touring, shopping, or just reading in a comfortable chair on the back balcony. We would sit together on the front balcony in the evenings listening to the magical city's nightly performance: people laughing in the house next door, someone playing a saxophone across the way, the clanging bells of the streetcar as it went by every few minutes. There would be smells of seafood gumbo wafting up from the apartment below, enticing us to make our own pot.

On weeknights we'd cook and watch TV, or go out to dinner, to the movies, to hear live music in any one of the venues that punctuate each neighborhood of the city. And on weekends, we'd have beignets in the French Market, just like the tourists did, have a good long walk along the rousing Mississippi's banks, or take car trips to the malls on the outskirts.

"That sounds so good," she said. "But I'd not be able to visit Momma as often as I do now. You know, that's pretty much the only thing that keeps me sane. If I didn't have my Momma, I don't know what I would do. I can't imagine being in this world without her. But after she's gone, I can see myself getting out of this place and living in New Orleans. Wouldn't that be an adventure!"

It was approaching eight thirty. We'd had two Tom Collinses and smoked, or puffed and coughed through, three cigarettes each. The cocktail waitress asked if we wanted anything else. I told her no thank you. We had to be getting back.

"If only we can sell that place," she said once more, as we walked back to the car.

This oft-repeated lament my mother made in her last years on earth still haunts me as a cry for help that none of us—not my siblings, not me, and not our father—were fully able or willing to hear.

38 | The License

Momma emptied the contents of her purse onto the dining room table to reveal a messy pile of randomness that to her eyes looked a lot like her life. A set of keys to the boxy maroon Chrysler Newport, seven bobby pins, two unopened packs of Wrigley's Spearmint Gum and one nearly empty pack of Juicy Fruit, which made her think of her third boy, Dicky, who counted on her always having gum in her purse. He was partial to Juicy Fruit. A set of manicure tools from her old beauty shop—the little nail clipper, the big clipper, a file, a buffer, and the finishing scissors—all in a Ziploc bag, the fake leather case that once contained them now long gone. Exactly three dollars and eleven cents in coins: six quarters, twelve dimes, eight nickels, and one lonely penny. *The pennies seem to multiply everywhere else, but for some reason not in my purse.* Another set of keys, this one to Daddy's silver and blue Chevy pickup. A travel-sized bottle of Jean Naté body splash, the nub of Revlon Fire and Ice, her favorite lipstick color, though she rarely wore the stuff, and the skeleton key that she used for ten years to open the front door to her shop in the mornings and lock it up again at night.

But no driver's license.

She had already rifled through her snap wallet. She had of course looked there first, emptying its card slots, pockets, and photo sleeves, to no avail.

A bobbin of coffee-colored thread rolled off the edge of the table and onto the carpeted floor, landing snugly in a corner, where it would go unnoticed until weeks later, when the vacuum cleaner sucked it up, making an awful clanking noise as it moved through the innards of the machine before landing in the dirt bag. One of Alisa's yellow-sleeved report cards that was supposed to have been signed about two years ago. She had gotten four A's and two B's. And a C in conduct. *What's she doing that she's getting a C in conduct?* The anomalous C was why she had held on to the report card, with plans to call Alisa's teacher for an explanation.

There was a rosary made of hand-carved cedar, worn down by decades of her *traiteur* father's reverent rubbing as he said prayers over ailing "patients," this a fresh reminder that he had died without passing on his gift to someone else in the family. *Such a shame, really.* And finally, a deck of cards wrapped in a dry-rotting rubber band, to which was stuck the empty wrapper for a purse-sized packet of tissues.

But no driver's license.

"Zanny, I'm gonna need you to help me look," she called out to Daddy, who was in the half-bath off the TV room.

"Wha'?" he called back.

"I need my license, and it's not turning up anywhere," she explained. "That girl at the license bureau was just as nasty as you can imagine. Said I had to have my license if I wanted to renew it. Wouldn't listen when I told her the whole point of me being there was because I had lost it."

"You're gonna need to take my truck, then," Daddy said before flushing. When he came out of the half-bath, he said, "Andy and I are gonna take a look at the brakes on your car today."

"I hate driving that truck," she said. "But I need that license. I'm supposed to go to Momma's tomorrow."

Daddy had gotten used to Momma's frequent trips to Ville Platte to spend time with Mémère. He knew better than to suggest she put that off any time.

So they looked high and low, at first together, room by room, then separately. Throughout the downstairs, in the front office, the back office, the bedrooms, the living room; and she even thought about going upstairs. *But that doesn't make any sense. How would my driver's license get upstairs? Unless Alisa took it up for some reason. What the hell? I won't rest until I have a look up there too.*

She started to climb the steep stairs. It was the first time in years she'd done so. After three steps, she stopped. *Damn! I'm getting old.* Her knees ached. After ten years standing all day in her beauty shop, now she couldn't imagine doing this every day. *I guess this is what sixty-three is supposed to feel like.* She stopped at the top of the stairs to compose herself. She had a quick look around the little room. A single bed covered in one of the afghans she had crocheted. She'd made one for each child. This one was a design of alternating blocks of forest green, rust, and a deep plum, with touches of golden yellow. She didn't remember making that one. She also couldn't recall who slept in this room after Cassie left for college all those years ago. *Dicky? Morris?*

She continued through the short hall to the back bedroom, where the white lattice frames of the twins' matching canopy beds were the only evidence that the room was ever shared by two people with anything in common whatsoever. The walls of the room remained the same soft blue color with white trim chosen by the twins. They had hung posters of musicians they admired—Elton John in a close-up on one wall; and another John, Olivia Newton, on the abutting wall; then three of Gilda's absolute musical hero, Cat Stevens, the first showing his curly locks spilling around his face, and one with those locks chopped back to shorter than even a buzz cut.

The current occupant of the big room, Alisa, apparently was not interested much in changing anything. The walls were mostly barren. She had slept on Gilda's side of the room and piled clothes, stuffed animals, and her books on what once was Glenda's bed. Aside from one little bookcase that held long-abandoned knickknacks, there was not much else in the room. If there was a driver's license here, it would not have many places to be.

A quick walk through the bathroom revealed that the claw-footed tub was coated with soap scum. A skyline of variously filled and empty shampoos, conditioners, bubble baths, and even a spray bottle of window cleaner cluttered the shelves where towels were supposed to be. The wallpaper surrounding the tub was peeling, and the toilet was in an even sorrier state. All the years this place was a bathroom and bedrooms to four girls—Cassie and the twins first, then Alisa—and now it was just a place in waiting. Waiting for the next family to move in one day, perhaps soon.

The trip to search the second level of the house she had shared with her family for twenty years proved equally fruitless to the downstairs search she had done first alone, then with Daddy, but she was glad to have at least eliminated the upstairs as suspect.

Once back in the dining room, she started to gather up the contents of her purse but then stopped herself, deciding instead to leave the pile right there on the table. "I only need my wallet and the checkbook," she said to the empty room. "And the keys to the truck," she added, scooping up the keys, which were held together by a black plastic keyring with "ESSO" embossed on it in gold letters. She took a step toward the front door but stopped herself again. Wishful thinking! She knew darned well that she could not possibly leave her mess all over the table. Item by item, she collected everything, even the empty tissue wrapper that most people would have taken the opportunity to toss into the trash, neatly placed it all back into her purse, and snapped it shut. The crisp snap of the clasp gave her a sense of comfort, completion, and confidence. *I am NOT coming back here today without a new license!*

She stepped out, into the bright sun of that early May day, climbed up into the pickup, cranked it, and backed it out of its parking spot next to the garage. Before shifting to Drive, she paused a bit, looked at the big glass picture windows of the motel office. *Those windows are filthy. Need to ask Andy to give them a good going over, inside and out.*

Once onto the road, Momma first passed the Oakleys' little white and green house, and then the Fontenots'. In the curve after the Fontenots', the Thibodeaux house, and opposite them, the new Quick Stop convenience store, which seemed to have popped up overnight where once there was a rice field, right in the crook that joined the old highway that now fronted the Stone Motel with the new highway, that hugged the back of their property.

She came to a complete stop at the stop sign, exactly as she had done a thousand times before, and would have done had this been a driving test. She looked left toward oncoming traffic, and then right to the opposite lane of approaching traffic, and then left again, and directly up through the windshield and into the cab of a fast-approaching eighteen-wheeler. Then she pressed on the gas.

The driver of the eighteen-wheeler would recall later that day that in the split second of the impact, "Mrs. Ardoin's face looked blank to me, expressionless." He plowed right into Daddy's Chevy, splitting it completely in half, separating its cab from its bed, in a detonation of steel, glass, rubber, diesel, and gasoline. And blood. The blood of a woman who had seconds before "I could swear" looked right into the eyes of the man that killed her. He climbed out of his overturned and jack-knifed truck mostly unharmed, looked around in a state of utter disbelief, and vomited into the unmown clover.

39 | Eliza Mae: No Going Back

died in a car crash. Just a few yards from the motel. On the road right there at that intersection.

So close to home.

I wasn't paying attention.

It was my fault.

I was in Zanny's truck because my car needed some brake work done. Zanny said to take the truck. I never liked driving that thing. You sit up too high from the road.

The guy who hit me says he saw me stop at the stop sign. I came to a complete stop, looked both ways. Looked up to him like I saw him—stared right at him, in fact, and then looked straight ahead.

And pressed on the gas.

He couldn't stop in time.

He just couldn't stop.

He was in a big blue-and-white eighteen-wheeler. Those big trucks are hard to stop just like that.

He hit me and split Zanny's truck right in half. The front with me in it went flying into the median.

• • •

It was all like a spit-second dream, where I had disappeared, planning to come back, but then realized all at once that I wasn't gonna *be* coming back.

You know that feeling? How, when something horrible or just plain stupid happens, you imagine that, if you could just stop right there and jump back in time a little bit, and none of it would have happened? I remember once I had opened a bag of frozen strawberries that had thawed out. I wanted to separate the juice from the berries and use them both—but for some reason, I took out a colander, cut open the bag, and then poured the whole thing into it without a bowl underneath to catch the juice. And so all that juice went right down the drain. I stared into that sink and couldn't believe what I had just done. Right there, I thought, "Let's go back two seconds!" Two seconds and my mind would have correctly registered what I was doing.

And I *needed* that strawberry juice.

• • •

I can't believe how simple it would have been for me to just *stay put* at that stop sign.

But your mind's on something else. So you can't go back. It's done. All in an instant.

There's no going back.

I didn't feel any pain. If that's what you're wondering. It's what everybody says after an accident like that. At the funeral. And to themselves: "She died instantly. Didn't suffer. Didn't feel a thing."

That gives them comfort.

They can't know that I did indeed *feel* something. No one wants to think of such a thing. But I actually felt in that split-second as that big truck was crashing into me—splitting me and my truck in two, my body being thrown into the air—I felt very *cold*. My skin was crawling all over me. My lungs went empty. My eyes popped wide open. My bones. I felt in that second, every one of my bones.

But then, just as quickly, right away, I felt very *warm*. My heart was full. My head was clear. All my thoughts had flown away. Like startled birds. And my feet. For the first time in years, both of them were warm. Very warm.

And then, *nothing*.

So, yes, ultimately, I did feel *nothing*.

I feel nothing now. It's a feeling I had known for a long, long time before I ended up in that ditch.

So many years ago, it wasn't like that for me. I felt everything all around me, all the time. I had my kids, and my sweet momma. That should have been plenty for anybody, but on top of that I also had this beauty shop for ten years.

Those ten years, I have to say, were hard. You stand on your feet for nine or ten hours, five days a week, Tuesdays through Saturdays, then go home to a house full of hungry people. But those ten years? The best ten years of my life. It wore me out, but looking back, I *loved* it.

Thank God for my beauty shop. For me it was an escape. Outside of this shop, in public situations, I'd get so nervous around people, but here in this shop, I felt *safe*. I was in charge. This is *my* world.

And my beauty shop ladies—my customers, my friends—kept me laughing, kept me involved and *connected*. Happiest ten years of my life. All at once, running my own shop, then getting home to all those kids. When you have so many, like I did, the older ones are able to take care of the younger ones. That's why my beauty shop was even possible. They all grow up so fast, and in no time, it seems, they were old enough to take care of themselves. And run that motel too, when they weren't at school. That was a big help.

I'd get home from the beauty shop with two bags of groceries. Practically every day I worked in that shop, I had to stop by the National to buy groceries on my way home. Feeding ten people every day takes a lot out of you. And it's expensive. That's where most of my beauty shop money went. Mr. Fontenot at the National used to joke with me about that. "Miss Ardoin, you're keeping us in business," he'd say. "I see more of you than my own wife. Ha. People gonna start talking!"

Zanny and I had an agreement about the money. The motel money paid for the big stuff: anything to do with the buildings, equipment, insurance, electricity, the cars. And I bought the groceries and school stuff and was Santa for the kids with the money I made at this shop.

There was never any money left for a vacation to Europe, or hardly even a trip out of state. In fact, for most of my life, I had only been to two states besides Louisiana. Mississippi—we went to Biloxi a couple of times—and Texas. Zanny had a sister in Beaumont. We went there maybe twice in all those years. So I really didn't see much of Texas other than Beaumont, and Mississippi outside of Biloxi.

For most of my days, that was the extent of my exposure to the world. But then, during the 1984 World's Fair, I got on a bus and went to New Orleans. I did that three times while that was going on. Miss Weetsey Ledoux and Charlene François, ladies from the shop, came with me. Twice. It was Miss Weetsey—oily scalp and dry hair—who told me about that charter bus in the first place. For twenty dollars a head, they'd take you there and back. So I went twice with them, and a third time with that

Edna Fontenot—thin hair; sold her a wiglet. Maybe two wiglets. I don't remember now. She wanted to go before it left town. I loved that World's Fair. Right there in New Orleans, just three hours away. Close enough to go and come home in one day.

Now, the *farthest* I ever traveled beyond these three states was that summer when I went on a trip to Gatlinburg, Tennessee, with Alisa and Morris and his roommate, Cathy. He was living with her after he moved back from college. Cathy had a crush on him so bad. She came over to the motel one day and tried to convince Zanny and me to help her persuade Morris that they should be a couple. "A coupla what?" I asked, kinda gigglin'. We knew that wasn't going to happen with her, or any woman, but she didn't seem to be able to accept that. She was under the impression that she could *change* him. But that's a story for another day.

Anyway, we drove in Cathy's big orange Cadillac through Mississippi, then Alabama, then into Tennessee, then back again. Yup, a lot of people get to see the whole world. Europe, Canada, Mexico, whatnot. I got as far as Gatlinburg. In a big orange Cadillac we called "the pumpkin." Gatlinburg was nice, a little mountain town. Really cute. But mostly, I just liked being on a road trip.

• • •

So I guess I really saw the world through my beauty shop. I loved this little shop. It started out as somebody else's home right here on Vine Street, next door to our old house. Zanny bought it for me and fixed it up so that I would have my own place after I finished beauty school. I never worked for anybody else's shop. I went right into my own shop.

The little house was white with a front porch that was painted shiny gray, and enough of a yard in the back that we could put in a vegetable garden one day.

I only needed this front half of the house. The front living room and dining room became the shop area where I could have three ladies sitting in their chairs at the same time, and another two or three under the dryers. The little kitchen became my shampoo room, and they built me a little bathroom off of that room for the customers.

The back halfa the house was pretty much left alone, except they made a big kitchen at the very end of the house, where Zanny could cook his *sauce piquant* for his Lions Club friends when it was his turn to host.

So it worked out perfectly for both of us.

Every morning when I came in around eight, I opened the door using just this one skeleton key. That's all the security we needed in those days. One key.

Let's see: I had a coat rack on the wall on the right when you walked in, then along the adjoining wall, the four hair dryers with magazine pockets and ashtrays built in. All push-button controls built in on the right arm. It was funny. Those dryers didn't all match. We had gotten them all used from a beauty supply place in Jennings. One was pink with a glittery dome; the two in the middle were aqua colored with black specks, with clear domes; and the last one was done in a gold and black motif and a shiny metallic gold dome. That one was my personal favorite, because it was the newest. And I've always liked the color gold.

On the opposite side of the room, I had the wall of long mirrors where the customers could watch as I cut their hair, and the built-in counter where I had all my beauty supplies.

So much "stuff" goes along with the furniture and mirrors. You gotta have lots of combs, various kinds of hairbrushes, boxes of bobby pins, cans of TRESemmé—that's the hairspray I used—plastic gloves for doing perms, rollers, hairclips, hairpin papers, foil sheets for the perms. I even had the little manicure cart that rolled around on wheels. And that had nail polish remover, nail files, nail clippers, and fingernail polish in all kinds of colors.

And that blue comb and brush sterilizing liquid in the "Barbicide" jar on the counter over there. "Barbicide"—that sounds terrible, like Barbie killed herself. Ha ha ha! Anyway, that blue liquid? That was never changed. Just so you know.

Now my scissors, I kept my scissors in their sleeves, inside the drawers of the counters, because you can't leave those out. They get all banged up. And a beautician's scissors are her most important tool. They have to fit right and be the right length for your cutting style. If the scissors don't fit correctly in your hand, between your thumb and your index finger, you'll be uncomfortable all day. You could get blisters, and the last place you need a blister is on your hand when you cut hair all day. Scissors come in a lot of sizes, so once you find a pair that works for you, you should get more than one pair, so you have an extra one on hand if you have to send the other one out for sharpening.

I had no idea that there were so many things to know about scissors or, as they teach you in beauty school, "cutting shears." But I always called them scissors.

But there was something I hadn't thought about, though, in those classes in beauty school. You get the basics about how to set up a shop, or at least, what a shop needs to function properly. These hydraulic chairs that you could pump with one foot, to the right level to reach each customer's head. The sinks, the hair dryers, and all the supplies. So you get all your shop set up, and at the very end you realize something's missing. Magazines! It dawns on you. They're gonna need something to read while they're under those dryers.

So I got all these subscriptions. *Reader's Digest, Ladies' Home Journal, Redbook, Woman's Day, McCall's, Good Housekeeping.* I never had enough time to read them myself. But my ladies could tell me all about what was in them. If there was nothing to talk about especially, which was rarely the case, you could talk about what was in those magazines. Every month, you got something new. Gardening, decorating, sewing, romance advice, recipes. *Redbook* always had a cake recipe. Mississippi Mud Cake. Sock-It-To-Me Cake. Double Dutch Chocolate Cake. Orange Pineapple Cake. Every month a new cake. My kids loved making those cakes.

So really, there was always something to talk about. And that's the secret of a good shop. You need to be good with those scissors, but what you *really* need is the ability to listen. You have to provide a good ear if you are going to be successful.

And boy, did I listen. When those ladies sat in one of my chairs, I wasn't just doing their hair. I was their psychiatrist. Their priest. Their best friend. For that hour or so each week, anyway. And you can believe that over those ten years, standing on my feet all day, I heard some stories.

You wanna hear some? I really shouldn't say anything. Some of them are still around. But what the hell; I'm dead, anyway.

I got a call from Ellie Herbert. All in a panic because she had let her little niece in beauty school do her hair, and the girl made such a mess that when she walked through the door of my shop I let out a gasp that I couldn't control.

"Oh, Ellie," I said. "It's gonna be a while before you'll get back to normal with that one." It was so bad, I figure her niece had used acid or something on her head, because there were big patches of hair missing, and her scalp was chemically burned. Poor thing.

All I could do was cut away some of the burned hair and give her some skin cream to put on her scalp. And I sold her a scarf to wear for a few weeks. She wanted a wig, but I couldn't recommend that because the mesh would've caused her more irritation, and that scalp needed to heal.

That one was extreme. Most of the bad hairdos I had to fix weren't nearly that bad, once I clipped away the messy cut and focused on what was salvageable.

The most interesting stories had nothing to do with hair. What those women told me in this shop I often couldn't believe, or if it was believable, it was often so sad or heartbreaking that I figured, with all my troubles, my life was still pretty good by comparison.

Sheila Thibodeaux's husband was an *awful* man. The way she talked about him, he musta really hated her. He hit her at least once a week. Showed up at my shop more than once with bruises. He cheated on her with anyone who'd come along. And he neglected those two kids.

"I can't leave him," she told me. "We have no place else to go. We'd starve and he wouldn't blink." I felt so bad for her. With all my troubles with Zanny, one thing I have to say is that he always took his responsibility to provide for his kids seriously. Not in any very emotional way, actually. He definitely coulda stood some improvement in the emotional department, but he knew he had to take care of their basic physical needs. That's the thing that always came through: no matter how mean he could be, he always settled down in the end and realized that our kids were what held us together. And they were a big help in the business. There's no way we coulda had that motel and I coulda had my own shop if we didn't have all those kids helping out.

Most of the ladies who sat in my chair had kids, and as far as I can tell, most of them had their troubles like we did, but overall were . . . okay. But there were a couple of ladies who had some serious trouble at home with their kids, and my chair was the only place they could talk about it.

Alice Fontenot was like that. Her boy Farrell was having trouble in school, showing up at home with bruises and cuts. She thought he was getting into fights. It turned out he was getting those bruises at home. It was her own brother who lived next door that was abusing that boy and hitting and threatening him to keep control over him. They mighta never found out about it, except one night the brother got drunk and came banging on their door and blubbering all about it, confessing. Releasing his demons, as they say. The boy had never said a word, even when they were lecturing him about keeping away from the bullies at school so he could concentrate on learning. I hope that poor boy didn't grow up to be an abuser himself. But isn't that always the way?

You know, that's what I think was the case with Zanny. He had some stories to tell about how he grew up. Like we all had during the Great

Depression. Those were some hard times on people. Life was really cruel; everybody hadda deal with awful things. And that was just *normal*. People hit their children, made them go without food, didn't, or couldn't, take care of them properly.

So Zanny's daddy beat him and his siblings. The Depression came and went around the country, but was still hangin on in Louisiana, and Zanny's momma had died of pneumonia right after she had the last of her babies, Earnestine. So his daddy pushed him and two of his brothers out to go live on the farm across the field from them, because he really couldn't feed all his kids alone. So Zanny and his brothers worked on that neighbor's farm and lived in their barn till they could get out of there and join the army.

And what they saw during that war made matters worse. Those boys were only teenagers working on a farm in the middle of nowhere, and then suddenly they're in some foreign country with a gun, shooting people. Their minds aren't even fully developed yet, and they're seeing all that blood, day in and day out.

So he had his reasons, of course, but I wasn't going to let that be an excuse. A lot of time had passed since all that had happened to him. He had time to grow up and forget those things. But I know now that he was never able to put those years fully behind him.

One Saturday afternoon I had gotten back from the shop. It was right after Christmas, a coupla weeks after half the motel burned to the ground, and the only money coming in was from me and this shop. We were under a lot of pressure, cleaning things up, getting the business going again. It was a hard, hard time for us all. And it really knocked Zanny down. He took it the hardest. The night of the fire he watched his livelihood go up in flames. We were all still in shock about the fire. All of us on automatic pilot just to get through each day.

So I know he was in a bad way that Saturday afternoon. I get home, get my groceries out of the car, and before I could get into the house to put the bags down, I hear this terrible, terrible screaming in the back yard. So I run to look out the door at the back of the garage, and what I saw made my blood boil.

Right there under the big fig tree was Zanny, holding Morris down on the ground with his shoe and whipping at him with a piece of electrical wire. It was another one of his breakdowns. So there he was, going at Morris like a maniac. *Again.* And this time it was the worst I'd ever seen. The sounds coming out of Morris were horrible. He didn't even sound like himself.

I had held my tongue most of the other times, because Zanny would get furious if I challenged him on how he disciplined the kids. That was his area. His job as a parent, keeping the kids in line. And anything I had to say about it was only asking for trouble.

But this time it was different. I couldn't possibly look the other way. And I don't know how I got there from the garage, but next thing I know I find myself on Zanny's back and screaming, myself.

"STOP HITTING MY CHILDREN!"

And it was all over in a flash after that. We had fallen on the ground together underneath that fig tree, and then everything got really quiet. We got up on our feet. Zanny looked right into my eyes. He was trembling. He still had that wire in his hands. And I could tell he wasn't actually *registering* the fact of me, or Morris, for that matter. Like he was completely lost. Morris had run off into the house by then, and I looked around. My groceries were all over the place.

"That child's eleven years old! What are you doing!? What are you *doing*!?"

He was still in a fog, and he stayed that way for the rest of the afternoon. He went in and sat in his rocker and lit a cigarette. He didn't say a word. The whole night. Didn't eat dinner. Didn't make a peep.

I went into the house to talk to Morris in his room. He was still crying, and his whole body was heaving, like he was having spasms. I can't tell you what it's like to see your own child like that. I tried to hug him, and he jerked away from me.

"Don't!" he said. "Please. Don't! Just leave me be. Please."

My heart was breaking. I couldn't just leave him be. I wanted to tell him something that would make him feel better. That would help him calm down. I wanted to say something that would make him feel *safe* again. But I had no idea *what* to say. What do you say? What *can* you say? I decided it was best to leave him alone and try to have a talk with him later on.

We all needed some time to think. I know I did.

• • •

What do you do with a man like that?

Morris wasn't the only one of my kids Zanny had a bad way of showing his anger with. He beat Andy with his fists, like he was a grown-up, but he was no more than fourteen at the time. A grown man doesn't punch a fourteen-year-old. Andy had struggled in school, and Zanny's way of making him do better was to punch him? I just don't understand that. I told him he couldn't do that, and he nearly hauled off and hit me, too. It made me crazy to have to keep my distance.

Anyway, I think that growing up like that started Andy off on the wrong foot at a very young age. He never really got a break in life as a grown-up. He worked hard, but it took him a long time to get settled on what he wanted to do. He was really shy. Never comfortable around people. I know he inherited some of that shyness from me, but I suspect a lot of that came from him having any self-esteem he may have had beaten out of him by his daddy.

With Cassie, Zanny never let her have a moment of pride in herself, either. When she became drum major at the high school—that was a big deal because it had always been boys—he never said a word. She was so proud of that accomplishment. She got to wear a beautiful green uniform with brass buttons, a tall white drum major's hat, and white boots with tassels. All those years she had spent practicing and going to summer twirling camp had paid off. She was the best kid to come along for that drum major position in several years. There was no way they wouldn't have given it to her. And what did Zanny do? Nothing. He said nothing.

But a year later, when she had graduated and was named "Miss Eunice," and got home after the pageant still in her dress and crown, he looked at her like she was a movie star. He wasn't good at showing it—but he definitely was proud of her. He would tell anyone who would listen that his daughter had just become Miss Eunice, but he wouldn't tell her to her face that he was proud.

"You need to encourage her," I remember telling him. "She needs to hear it from you."

"She already knows what I think," he said. And he looked at me like I was from the other side of the moon.

I really don't think she did know what he thought of her. He could be gentle one minute, then cold and distant the next. He was hard to read that way. A year before that pageant, when she was not even eighteen, she asked about a dress for the prom, so I suggested she go outside and ask him for the money. I had the stupid idea that it would warm his heart to give her money for a prom dress. She was our firstborn; our little girl was all grown up. Going to the prom.

So I was watching from the kitchen window. And when she asked him, he turned his face toward her like some kind of a monster and slapped her so hard it raised her up off the ground. I couldn't believe what I was seeing. It didn't make any sense. I ran to her and got her inside. We were both stunned.

And I don't know what she was feeling inside, but I know overall it hurt her not to have his blessing, his support, his encouragement, to feel loved by him. Every daughter wants that from her daddy. I think that haunted her for years. Probably still does.

• • •

It's funny. I had no problem listening to the troubles of my ladies in the shop, but I never said a word about my own troubles at home. I was never one to talk about that kinda stuff with them, or anybody, really. They needed me to have somebody to talk *to*. There was no place for *my* problems in all those conversations. So I kept it all to myself all those years. The only person I could tell any of it to was my momma.

My parents had two boys, my brothers Paillasse and Florence, and then me. So I was their little girl. We were all children of that Great Depression. Daddy was a blacksmith, and Momma did odd jobs when she could find something. We were dirt poor, but I don't think that we children knew it.

Our momma, like all good mommas, had no limits when it came to making sure we had what we needed. She made us cornbread or, if we were lucky, *bouillie au lait* to take to school in our lunch pails. *Bouillie au lait* has three ingredients: flour, milk, and cane sugar cooked into a thick pudding. Sometimes, if there was nothing in the house to sweeten it, it would be just the cooked flour and milk. By lunchtime the *bouillie au lait* had formed a skin on top that you could lift with a pinch. That was my favorite part. Wasn't very nutritious, but it would fill us up and get us through the day.

When I was nine, Momma tore up bedsheets to make me a uniform, so I could play on the girls' softball team. Isn't that something?

When I was fifteen, my high school dance was coming up in a few months. During the war, it was mostly girls at school, so we'd still have our dance, but with no boys around, we'd dance with each other.

Of course there was no money to make me a dress so I could go, and sheets just wouldn't have been right, so over a coupla weekends, Momma and I picked the leftover cotton in the harvested fields outside of town and sold that to buy just enough fabric. She was whiz at sewing, using that old wrought-iron Singer. I can still hear the "clack clack clack clack clack," of her cranking up and down on that foot pedal. After some back and forth, the finished dress fit me perfectly. It was a blue-and-white floral print, with a fitted bodice and a full skirt.

And don't you know that after all that, when I went to press the dress for the first time, I took the iron off the fire on the stove and burnt a big old scorch right on the front of the skirt. My heart sank. Momma and I cried and cried. I wasn't going to be able to go to my dance. And it was another one of those times in my life that I wished I could just jump back in time for one split second. But no. There it was, a big brown burn mark on that cotton-pickin' dress. And don't you know that the vision of that iron mark burned into my new dress still burns in my head.

Anyway, it all ends okay. Paillasse was still over in Europe, but when he got word of it, he sent money to buy enough fabric to fix the dress. And I went to my dance.

All those years later, when I was going through my troubles with Zanny, my momma and I cried together again. She knew how helpless I was feeling. She knew my *disappointment*. When I married Zanny, Momma and I both had expected a very different life would come for me. He was so handsome and solid. He made a good impression on Momma and Daddy. Daddy saw something in him that gave him confidence that he would take care of me. I saw that, too. Zanny was going to take me out to see the world. The war had taken him overseas. And he had traveled all over, and that's what we had talked about in the early days before we were married. Seeing the world. He wanted to show me where he'd been, but this time under peaceful circumstances. And we'd go to new places together. That's the life I thought I would be having.

But then I learned I was gonna have a baby.

That definitely wasn't the way I saw my life unfolding. Zanny either. But we agreed that the only thing to do was to get married right away. It all happened so quickly. I didn't have time to think about a wedding dress. Neither one of us had any money. So I wore my one nice outfit, a brown business suit. Not very romantic.

He had two good suits, a plaid one and a light brown one. So he wore the brown one because it looked more formal, even though he said it wasn't as comfortable as the plaid.

And then suddenly we were married. In those days, it's what you did. We didn't have much time to really get to know each other under such circumstances. We'd only been dating a few months. I was working at the G. Ardoin's Department Store, doing the books and sometimes working at the register. Zanny came into the store one day and started talking to me. I was so shy, but he was good-looking, and I was flattered. Next thing you know, we're married with a baby on the way.

And the time flew by.

After Cassie, Andy, and the twins were born, we moved to Eunice. Zanny used his savings from his army pay and the work he did with the merchant marine and at Standard Oil. He had saved up eleven thousand dollars, and with that money he bought us a car, a three-bedroom house on Vine Street, and a little Esso station on Laurel Avenue. Can you imagine buying all that with eleven thousand dollars these days?

In Eunice I could take care of the kids and do the books at that station, and I was glad to be away from Ville Platte. Even if it was only twenty miles away, it was nice to be out of there.

So, to move things along, I'll tell you: I had a couple more babies: after the twins Gilda and Glenda, I had Morris and Dicky. I went to beauty school somewhere in between all that mothering and baby-having, and after I finished, we bought the little house next door to us. And that became this shop.

I had the shop all set up and was in business for about a year when I got pregnant with my seventh child, Thomas. That pregnancy was like every child that came after Cassie. I was filled with happiness. With Cassie, my circumstances made me so anxious I wasn't able to show my excitement before the birth like I did with the others. By the time I had Thomas, I knew what to expect. I had organized baby clothes, set up the crib again, and crocheted some new booties and a matching blanket for him.

When I woke up in the hospital room after the delivery, my focus was all blurry as usual, but as I was coming around, I saw Zanny's face first. It didn't look good. You know your husband's face better than your own. He was shaking his head. Before I could say anything, Dr. DeRouen says, "Eliza, I have some news."

He had encephalitis. That's when the brain is swollen, and the head is deformed. The rest of him was okay, but encephalitis in those days was nearly always fatal. The hospital wasn't advanced enough to help him properly. He wasn't going to make it past a day or two.

I was numb.

I never got to hold him. He was under a breathing machine the whole time and had tubes in his little arms. I only got to see him briefly a couple of times, and I touched his little chest. But I never got to hold him in my arms. That was for the best, they said. How do they know what's *for the best*? It wasn't for *my* best.

Looking back, I know now that I should have insisted on holding him at least once. I don't care what they think. I don't care what he looked like. But Zanny agreed with them, and so we went home the next day.

Without our little boy.

At the funeral I was so weak. We buried him at the St. Paul's cemetery on the other side of town. He was all alone there. I hated that. It's a good thing, of course, that no one in our family had died up until then, but still he was there in that cemetery all alone. We had a closed casket for him. I had given the people at the funeral home the little booties and the blanket I had crocheted for him, so he would have something from his momma with him. Looking down at that little gravesite by itself in a row of adult-sized graves is probably the saddest thing I've ever seen in my life. I wanted to be there with him. I didn't want him to be alone like that.

• • •

I tried my best to get past it. To move on. But nothing around you, not your husband, not your children, not your work, nothing really helps get you through the loss of a baby. Even several months later, I kept thinking I should be rocking my baby. Six months, a year passes. He should be crawling around now. I was so empty. It was the most horrible time in my life. I don't remember how long it was before I started getting back to my life, but I can tell you, losing a child changes you forever. I wish that on no one.

Time passes, of course, and you do move on. You have to.

• • •

One afternoon in 1967, out of the blue, Zanny came home and said he wanted to sell the Esso station and put a down payment on a motel just outside of town. His brother John had told him about it. John had a hotel in Baton Rouge and was getting tired of the city, so he was interested in it for himself. But the idea of running a place like that, especially if we had all the kids helping out, made a lot of sense to Zanny, too.

So we went have a look at the place. The people were nice. They had two grown daughters who had left for college, and they were ready to retire. The business had given them a good life. The possibility that the place could provide for our family, and that Zanny and I could work together and still be at home, helped convince me to say yes. It wasn't the big house, or all the space on the property. It was that I could see the potential for us to make a good life for all of us there. So I said yes when he asked me if I would do it with him.

What I couldn't see then was how hard it was gonna be. In hindsight, it did turn out to be a good place to provide for the family, and it was a great home for us all. We had room for all the kids in that big house. But it took *everything* we had to make it work. For the first few years we were in the motel, I kept the beauty shop going. Tuesdays through Saturdays I was right here in the shop all day, then I'd go home to the motel at night.

But the motel was a lot of work all by itself. Three hundred and sixty-five days, morning, noon, and night. A motel's gotta stay open. Round the clock. You can't just close when you feel like it, or get sick. Even on Christmas, you have to stay open. It never stops. People always coming and going, twenty-four hours a day. And so we had no time off, really. In fact, the weekends, when everybody else was having some time off, would be the busiest part of our week.

By the time we bought it, that motel needed a lot of work and improvement. The rooms all needed new carpets; they were all old and threadbare and musty. I had to order new towels and sheets right away and had to do that the whole time we were there. They wear out so fast with all that washing, and people would steal them, so that was a never-ending process.

Some of the rooms needed new air conditioners. The new ones they make these days don't last any more. In those days, you could get away with offering only black-and-white TVs in the rooms, but there's no such thing as a Louisiana motel room without air conditioning. And by the mid-seventies, color TV also became a necessity, too. Nobody wanted to rent a room with black-and-white TV any more, so we eventually had to phase those out and put a new color TV in each room. It was expensive. We could never catch up. Always something that needed doing.

So the kids were growing up, each one a very different person.

After Thomas, I had Scotty and, finally, Alisa. And thank God for them because without them I'da really gone crazy. I'd have to have strangled Zanny a long time ago.

Scotty became Zanny's favorite son, and Alisa his favorite daughter. After seven kids before them, Zanny had finally calmed down enough to look upon his children as gifts that so enrich your life, and not as he'd seen the others, as obstacles.

Cassie was my first musical one. At a very early age, she was singing and wanted a guitar, like her cousin Darwin's. For many kids, a musical instrument is a passing phase, but ever since we gave her her first guitar, she was hooked for life.

She was a sneaky girl, though. I once found a piece of chewed gum in my hamburger. I was so disgusted I got in the car and drove back to the burger place to complain. They apologized and offered me a new one after I raised hell. I didn't want another one. I was so disgusted. That's something you never forget.

Years later, Cassie tells me that *she* had put the gum in my burger. I wanted to hit her. All the same, I was always so proud of her. She was going to have the life that I couldn't, and I admired that determination in her.

Andy? Andy beat the odds. He had childhood epilepsy, which can really stunt a little person. But he punched his way out of it by the time he was six, and even with Zanny's terrible treatment of him, he grew up and made a good life for himself. He was never comfortable at school, but despite his self-doubts, he learned a lot of other things on his own. He loved the outdoors. Nature. Animals. Hunting. And made those things priorities in his adult life.

Gilda and Glenda, my twins, are easy to lump together, because they are so much alike. But at the same time, they are very different people.

There was always a kind of competitiveness that each of them had. Not necessarily with each other, but they were always competitive. I actually think it started when they were in my womb, where apparently Gilda had gotten most of the food for herself, because she came out a little bigger than Glenda, enough so that you could tell the difference. Gilda had a fuller face. So right after they were born, they both got lots of attention because they were so adorable and because everybody loves twins, but Glenda got a bit more attention, because everybody wanted her to fatten up and catch up with her sister. I think it was that early imbalance that started the competitive streak in each of them. I had no idea that little difference would affect them like that. But I really think it did, whether they know it or not.

Morris would ultimately be my middle child. I knew right away when he was the baby in the family that he was going to have to learn to be strong. A mother always knows when one of her children is not like the others. Growing up, *he didn't know how to be a boy.* Zanny picked up on this, and if you ask me, it was the reason he was so hard on him. I think Zanny thought he could toughen him up and make him change.

As he got older, Morris was a lot like Cassie in his relationship with me. He always sought my advice. My other kids didn't seem to care what I thought, but he did. I saw him leaving the house one January day without a hat on his head. He was so self-conscious about his looks. I told him, "You need something on your head." When he objected, I said, "There's no hat ugly as vanity."

Years later, he asked me for my advice on meeting the right man. I know he was joking, so I went along with it. I told him, "Dress like the man you want to go home with." You know, I think that's actually pretty good advice.

Then there was Dicky. I had to hide my purse from Dicky, because he was always going through it looking for gum. Dicky was like Morris in that he was not a typical boy, and we saw that right away. As a toddler, he loved getting into my makeup and jewelry box, and hiding. One Sunday we panicked because he was missing, so we looked all over the house for him, and I finally found him asleep in my closet. I asked him why he was in there, and he said he liked the smell. He would have a tough life ahead of him. Never really able to make a good living, unlucky in love, and always just out of reach of the things that came natural to most people. But of all my kids, I think he has the most tender soul.

Those four, Gilda, Glenda, Morris, and Dicky, were the closest group for several years. They mostly grew up together. They played together, did their motel work, then played some more around that dining room table. And they stuck together pretty much until one by one they became teenagers and began going their separate ways. I know for children the years pass very slowly, but then their teen years start and everything starts moving so fast. Of course none of them or the rest of the family, including me, could have possibly known that I'd be gone so soon, in just a few years.

• • •

So for twenty years in that motel, we *all* grew up a bit. We all became different people. It was a hard but rewarding life, and I was feeling toward the end that it was definitely time for a new phase.

In the last few years, I often told Zanny, "I can't wait till we can sell this place one day." I don't know how many times I said it, but I said it a lot and meant it. The kids were all gone except Alisa, who was about to graduate from high school and head to college. But Zanny always had an excuse about why it wasn't a good time to sell. It turns out it was never a good time to sell. But I was really, really tired, and the idea that I'd be trapped in that life forever with just him in that big house tired me out even more.

So my last two years on this earth were really hard for me.

I didn't feel like talking to anybody except my momma in Ville Platte. She was lonesome and I was depressed. But those trips to see her each week, sometimes twice a week if I could get up the energy to go, were what I lived for. Without those trips to see my momma, I might as well have been dead. I had no desire whatsoever to be at home alone with Zanny. He didn't wash regularly, so I couldn't even stand to sleep next to him in bed. It had been like that for years, come to think of it. In fact, I spent most of my nights and days those last coupla years lying on the sofa in the living room, with my face hidden from the world.

So one rare day I was feeling good enough to go run some errands in town. I get to St. Landry Bank, and the teller, a new girl who didn't know me, even though I'd been banking with them for thirty years, asked me for some ID to make a deposit. I searched around in my purse for my driver's license and couldn't find it. Maryanne Latiolais, who knows me, was working at the next window, and she vouched for me. Anyway, when I got home, I emptied out my purse and couldn't find my license at all. Then I searched all over the house for it.

I needed that license. The only thing keeping me even a little sane and happy those days was my weekly drive to Ville Platte to see my momma.

I had to have my license.

So the next morning I head to town to get my license replaced. I waited in line for a while, and when it was my turn, the girl at the window said I needed my old license to renew my license. She wasn't listening to me.

"But I can't find it. That's why I'm here."

"Sorry, ma'am," she says. "If it was stolen, then there'd be no problem, but since you say you only misplaced it, you're going to have to do a better job of looking for it, now aren't you?"

That didn't make any sense to me. Was she being difficult just to annoy me? Surely you can get a new license if you've lost it. But she insisted I go back home and look some more. I was so mad I couldn't think straight. I left and drove home, burning up inside.

She can't talk to me like that! She doesn't even know me. Who's her momma?

Somebody musta been mean to her for her to be so mean to me, a perfect stranger.

This is a small town, so I should know her. "Alva Bergeron" is what her badge said. Is that Shelly Bergeron's girl? Couldn't be. Shelly Bergeron would be too old by now to have a daughter that young.

Anyway, I couldn't believe how rude she was. I got home and got Zanny to help me look all over the place again. We went through the drawers in the office, in the kitchen, all through the bookcase in the living room, all of the pockets in my clothes in the closet. We turned everything upside down. It was nowhere to be found.

I was so frustrated; I really just wanted to lie down on my sofa again and forget the whole thing. Or better yet, if I could have, it would have been such a help to come *here* in my shop again, where I could figure it all out. And calm down. And get ahold of myself. But the shop, and all my kids, were gone, except the last one, Alisa, who would be graduating in a week.

And soon she'd be gone, too.

I was tired. I was so tired. But I got in that truck, determined to get to the license place and get back in that line and get to the window and insist that that girl give me a new license. Then and there, dammit. It was the only thing I had left. For me.

And so, all of that—*that's* what was in my head when I went through that intersection that day.

It wasn't suicide, you know.

I didn't kill myself.

I know people I left behind would like to know the truth about that, but that's not why I'm saying it now. Not for their comfort, although I'm happy to comfort them with this information.

I really didn't do it deliberately. When I stopped at that intersection and looked around, I wasn't capable of seeing that truck driver or *anybody* coming. So I stopped, and then just drove straight ahead. Like it was all clear. Because in my mind, it *was*.

40 | Zanny: Just Gone

I remember that Saturday like it was this morning. I had finally got up the nerve to ask Eliza out on a date. I had first met her a few years earlier at a party, right before leaving for the war. We talked a little that night, and that was that. Then I left and was gone for two long years.

So not long after I get back to Ville Platte, I walk into G. Ardoin's for something, and there she is, at a counter all the way in the back of the store. I see her from the front, the moment I walk in.

Beautiful girl. Redhead. I walk right up to her and reintroduce myself. When I had met her before that war, I was clumsy, didn't know what to say to her, hardly had the nerve to approach her. I could approach a horse, yes. But a girl like that? That wasn't so easy for me.

So this time I say, "How you doing?" or something like that. She goes all red in the face and is so shy I thought that would be that. But she looks up. Looks me right in the eye and says, "I'm just fine, thank you. What can I do for you?" I didn't think she remembered me at all.

And I was hooked right then and there. I ask her out, but she says no. Says her parents won't allow that. So I ask her where she lives and tell her I'll go and ask them for permission first. Which is exactly what I did.

Old man Thompson looks at me with one eye cocked. But I had put on my army uniform, and I think that helped make my case for me.

I'll never forget it. He says, "You can take her out, but you gotta make sure you take care of her. You gonna get her back home at a respectable hour, or you won't be seeing her again."

I said, "Yes, sir!"

And that's how we started. That's how I got to marry the most beautiful girl in Ville Platte. Hell, the whole state of Louisiana.

• • •

Eliza and I, we had us a lot of good years together. All those kids. All that hard work. All those ups and downs like everybody has. And all the way to the end, when the cops pulled up in front to come tell me she's out there on that road, dead, killed in a crash not half a mile from here, I was *faithful* to her.

I know in the end, during those last coupla years when she was saying how tired she was all the time, how she wasn't sure how to handle each day, and how she thought we should sell the motel, she didn't believe me about being faithful. She even told me so, that she didn't trust that I had been faithful to her. But I was. I *was*. And I regret that. So hard. That she thought I mighta been unfaithful to her. She took that thought to her grave.

But I loved her.

I never knew anything else but love for her.

I *loved* her.

• • •

Each one of us took Eliza's death a different way. Like me, I know for damned sure all the kids each suffered through it something fierce. But each in his own way. I guess that's to be expected. I have to do my best to put on a brave face. I gotta say it isn't at all easy to do. The memories of what we'd been through together, and the resentment that she was taken away from me, and all of us, so damned early. She was sixty-three. That's a cruel joke from God if you ask me.

Those kids had been tight growing up together like they did. They had spent several summers and falls and winters and springs together. And I'm proud to say that, up until Eliza's death, they matured, mostly intact as adults. They've been through a lot. There was that never-ending motel work they each had a part of. And that crazy summer heat that we all endured year after year. They'd be together talking for hours and telling stories, playing cards in the dining room, singing along to the radio. And, while I'm at it—and I'm embarrassed and sorry to admit it—but they endured all the hell I put them through because of my damned temper.

Eliza's crash marked the beginning of a new phase in each of our lives. "We are not guaranteed any tomorrows," she had said more than a few times. Boy, did she have that correct. That wreck revealed this blunt reality to us like nothing in our lives had until that point. Until then I thought the motel fire would have been the hardest thing we'd have to get through, but that was a piece of cake, compared to this.

Little Alisa was just seventeen when Eliza died. To kids, that seems grown-up, but that's really young to lose your momma. I was about her age when my own momma died. Alisa sometimes won't make a sound, but the tears will be coming down her face. She'll sit on that sofa at the front office and stare out one of the picture windows, silent. Whenever I check in on her, she says she's focusing on getting through it. That she is trying her best to think of the good things. When it hurts the most, she says she puts her mind someplace else, where it doesn't hurt.

It takes everything I have not to break down again right then and there. Sometimes, I have to admit; I feel that I am losing my mind. More than a few times I let myself go to those dark places I had just been learning to avoid after years of not being able to control myself.

• • •

Those years after Eliza's death—that was the time, right around the middle 1980s, that everything started changing around us so fast. That damned TV had exploded when the cable thing came along a few years earlier. Used to be three channels. Nowadays it's endless. Same thing happened to our food. We used to eat some good solid, Louisiana food pretty much every day. Now it's that damned McDonald's and those burger joints all over the place. The only one-a them fast-food joints I can stand is the Popeye's.

I would give anything to put it all back the way it was before, but I know that ain't about to happen. I wonder sometimes if we humans will ever be able to stop ourselves long enough to live life in the very best possible way if we could just understand and accept how quickly all our most wonderful days will be gone. Just gone.

41 | Mémère: Long as I Can, Me

My dog, Kitty. Cassie give me Kitty. Such a pretty little white dog just like her dog. Cassie know how good it is to have a dog with you. I love Cassie's dog and ask her to get me one just like that, so she got me one just like hers. Kitty takes care of me now. Kitty makes me some company, so I talk with him like he one of the kid. I'm so lonesome, he help me pass the time. I have to keep my doors locked at night, but Kitty bark and bark and bark, even when nobody knock my door. So thank God for Kitty.

I'm gonna stay on my house as long as I can, me. Long as I can, *cher*.

• • •

I wish it would be like when Billie Joe and me first got married and we went to live with Mae-Mae and Zanny and all those kids at that motel. We stayed on the little *apartment* in the back. And it was small, but we stay there for three month one time when Billy Joe was helping Zanny to work outside. Billy Joe was good then. He not drink too much at first. He work with Zanny on the buildings and in the yard. Zanny was good to give him something to do to keep him busy. That time was good for us both.

But that don't last. Billy Joe started to drink again, and that was not good for his work. We come back to Ville Platte, and there's nothing for Billy Joe to do no more, so he drank. It was like that for ten years.

So I have ten years with Billy Joe before he got too *couillon* to be with me. Florence take him to the City Hall and they find him a place to live, not too far from here. I can go visit him, but he can't come here no more.

After the City Hall put him on his own little place, he got worse off, because I wasn't there all the time to help him. Then, when he got the cancer, he was *finis*. He fight hard for three more months, and then he die, *pauvre bête*.

Even though he not with me no more on that time, I'm sad when that happen, because, no matter where he stay, he was still *something* in my life. I miss him like I miss DeJean.

• • •

Thank God for all my grandkids. I know Mae-Mae was a good momma to all them kid.

When Cassie was born I was so happy with her. She was so pretty. Mae-Mae put her in a pretty little dress and made her hair really pretty. Cassie like that. She like to look pretty. She always made herself pretty. I knew that when she grow up, she gonna be a real *belle*, that girl. And she like that music. That's so good when a kid likes the music. It help them make a happy life. Cassie never stop liking that music. I think, *peut-être* that's why I'm more close with her than anybody else, because I like that music, too, me.

Andy was a good boy, him. Andy help his daddy work all around the house and that motel. He like to hunt with his daddy, too, and I think his daddy like him the best. That's what I think. But Andy don't like school, him. He's not good with school, but he's good with his hands, *que même*, so that's fine. A man who know how to work hard can make a good life for himself.

Gilda and Glenda was hard on their momma. To have two babies at the same time, always hollering and fighting, it was hard. Mae-Mae would dress them up just alike. They were pretty little girls, them. They look like two li'l *catins*. *Catin* for an old person means a fast lady with the makeup and the short dress. But when I'm say *catin* for little girl, it mean like little fancy dolls. Two little fancy dolls.

But they were *brigand! Brigand*. I'm tell you, they make some *tracas* no matter where they go. And you know, when they grow up, they still *brigand*. Their poor old momma.

Then Mae-Mae had little Morris. And she leave him with me and Pépère when she was taking that beauty school. So he got more close with me than with her. All the time he wanna sit in my lap for me to rock him. I can rock him all day, and he still want more, him. I tell myself, "That's just little Morris. He just like that."

He say, "Mémère, hold me." *Cher bébé.* I know he was a smart one, him. He always bring a book with him. He liked pictures and wanted to read before anybody else. I felt bad because neither me or DeJean know how to read, us. That was hard for me. I wanted to read with him, *cher*, but I couldn't.

Now, Dicky—Dicky was a good boy, too, him. Him and Morris like to come and pass a big week with me and DeJean. Dicky was never *brigand* like Gilda and Glenda. Dicky was always sweet. He had some trouble in school because he was too sweet to ask for help. Everything was go too fast for him. He don't know what to do, so he keep quiet. I worry about him now. It's okay to be sweet when you little, but when you grow up you have to be more hard. I don't know if he can be like that. *Pauvre t' bête.*

· · ·

Now. Let me play you something. How 'bout "Jolie Blonde"?

My momma play violin. She play good violin, her. She teach me this one, "La Danse de Mardi Gras":

Les Mardi Gras sont su' un grand voyage
Tout l'tour autour du moyeu
Ça passe une fois par ans
Demander la charité
Quand même si c'est une poule maigre
Et trois, quatre coton d'maïs . . .

I believe when I play accordion, it make me feel good. Everybody on this street play something. Everybody in Ville Platte play something. Violin, accordion, gee-tar, something. We pass us a good time.

Now this one, they play at the Evangeline Club. That's called "Allons Danser Colinda":

Allons danser Colinda
Danser collé Colinda
Pendant ta mère est pas là
Pour faire fâché les vieilles femmes
C'est pas tout le monde qui peut danser
Tous les vieilles valses des vieux temps

Pendant ta mère est pas là
Allons danser Colinda . . .

Yeah, my momma play good violin. Her name was Eliza, too. I name my *bébé* girl after her. My momma Eliza had some long hair. Every morning she wake up and put it high on her head, then at night she take it down.

I have one brother, Felix. No sisters. Momma died at thirty-seven, when I was twelve or thirteen. Pneumonia. That "old flu." It was very easy to take that flu. They didn't have no good medicine then.

DeJean, him, he had two sisters, Tante T'tell and Tante Eva. T'tell took care of me and Felix after my momma die. When my daddy die—his name was Mayon—he died with the heart disease. He had that *arid-me-ah.* So at first my Pépère Joe took care-a me. One time on the porch on the house my Pépère Joe wanna sit and rock on the rocking chair. *Peut-être* it's true, *peut-être* it's not true, but what they tell me, he sit down on that chair, and the other one start to rock and rock all by itself. His hair stand up just like that. He never sat there again.

There's a lotta drôle things that happen like that around here all the time. All the time. My brother Felix die at thirty-seven too, just like my momma. Right before he die, Felix tell me, "I see my momma. Momma pull my feet and say, 'You have to come with me.'"

In those days when the people died, they died in the house. There wasn't no *ahs-pittal.* So all those old memories stay on the house, and don't have no other place to go.

• • •

Okay. Enough of that. Those old times is *finis, cher. C'est finis.*

Now I have to say something I never told Morris. Maybe he know. Maybe he don't know. I'm gonna tell y'all anyway.

Morris was too small to be in school. He came pass *la vie* with me and DeJean in Ville Platte. To pass a big week with us. I used to always say, "Come pass *la vie* with Mémère and Pépère." And he always said, "Yes, Mémère!" Morris *always* want to come stay with us.

So, anyhow, *que même,* we go to the city pool here in Ville Platte. And Morris was playing on that water with the other kid, not too deep. There was lots of kid that day, because it was so hot. And he was okay. I had my eye on him. But then this little fat boy grab Morris's head and push him under that water. *Bon dieu!*

I holler at him, *"Arrête-toi! Arrête-toi!"*

But nobody stop him. He hold Morris head under that water and nobody hearing me holler. *"Arrête-toi! Arrête-toi!"* Too much noise. Nobody can hear me holler. I was so scare, my whole body was shaking *comme-ça.*

And then I can't move, me. I'm so scare it was like I was froze. *Bon dieu!* I thought he was gonna die. That little fat boy was gonna drown him for sure right there. *Bon dieu!*

It still makes me *nerveuse* just to think about it, even after all these years. Morris was so small, and that little fat boy was so much bigger than him. I see his arms pushing and trying to get away and he can't. He was too big for him.

And me. I can't do nothing. Nothing. I just can't move. I don't know why. I'm standing there by that pool, and I can't move. It was like somebody was holding *me* down too.

And I couldn't protect him.

• • •

Madame Hadley has a needlepoint on her wall that say in English: "The kid. When they small, they step on you feet. When they grow up, they step on you heart."

That's so true, *cher.*

It's so hard to look at the kid and not worry about everything. They so small. You think they so helpless, even when they grow up. That's how I always feel about Mae-Mae. She was all those kid's momma, but *I* was *her* momma. That's something that never changes, no matter how old we get.

When Mae-Mae marry Zanny, I try to be happy with that. But no matter if he a good man or not, I'm worry all the time, all the time. I'm worry because she change when she marry him. Mae-Mae was a beautiful, happy girl. She have a good heart, like nobody else. Her brothers Paillasse and Florence was not like her. They *mean.* But she have a good heart. She remind me more like her daddy, the kids' *pépère,* than my boys. Pépère was quiet. He love strong. But he was quiet. When Mae-Mae was a little girl, Pépère take her and hold her, his *petite fille,* just like I did. She was my *petite fille,* too.

So when she marry Zanny, she have to grow up *au plus vite.* Real fast. And start to have her *bébés* right away. All those years and all those *bébés.* Everybody grow up in that big house. And everybody work. And I know their daddy hard on all them kid. He need that help to make that motel go, *cher*.

And he can be so mean, him. He tell Cassie she worthless. She not gonna be anybody. You know those words hit her hard. Like fists. More hard than fists. And then he hit Andy *with* his fists, like he was a man, not a boy. *Cher, pitié.*

And I know, I know, that he beat Morris real hard. Even more hard than the others. He kick him, he whip him with some wire and Mae-Mae have to jump on him to pull him off Morris. I don't know why he pick Morris out the bunch to beat, *que même* more than the others. When Mae-Mae tell me about that, it make me so sad. I want to take him to come live with me.

I don't know what's wrong with his daddy. I know he had a hard life himself, but everybody have a hard life. So I don't know why he pick Morris out the bunch. *Peut-être* is because he was like his momma and his *pépère*. He's quiet inside. He have a good heart. I know he has to be strong. He can make it. Just hold himself. He can make it through all that. I know he can.

• • •

I've been here for all my days.

The worst day for me in all those days, was when Florence come bang the door and tell me she's gone. "Eliza Mae is dead," he tell me. "Mae-Mae is dead. She was on a car crash by that motel. She's dead, Momma. She's *dead.*" He was crying hard.

That's all I remember from that morning. I think I fall on the floor, and Florence pick me up.

Then the next thing, I'm sitting with everybody at the funeral home in Eunice. And everybody is there. And all around me. Zanny is cry. Cassie is cry. Andy is cry. Little Alisa is cry. Everybody is cry.

I don't wanna get up and go see her on that coffin. Gilda come to me and ask me to come with her to see her momma on that coffin. She take my arm and take me there, in front of all those people. And I look at her and I see her. White. They put some rouge on her, but mostly, she white. I see her there and I can't take it. She have sixty-three year when she die, but to me she was still my little girl, *ma petite fille.*

Ma petite fille!
Ma petite fille!
Ma petite fille.

I know now what make Mae-Mae so sad before she die. She come to see me every week, sometime twice a week. She tell me she want to leave that motel. "One day, when we can sell that place," she tell me. "One day it won't be so hard." *Pauvre bête*. She tell me how Zanny is hard on her, *que même*, because in her mind it's just that big house, and all that motel to run. And he makes her *nerveuse*. She tell me that when she come see me it's the best time of the week for her. For me too. She needs to have a break from him.

She was lonesome like me. Even though she had people around, she feel lonesome anyway. All by herself in her mind. I know how hard that is. I can take it for me, 'cuz I'm old and I've had a long time with that Lonesome. But it was hard for me to see *her* like that.

I'm come so old now that I can't make for myself no more. Sometime I can't hardly move. I say all the time, all the time, I'm gonna stay on my house long as I can, *cher*. As long as I can.

Now Mae-Mae is gone for six year. DeJean is gone. Billy Joe is gone. Now Kitty is gone too. Cassie tell me I have to let him go stay at another place because I can't take him with me. I'm come too old to take care of him and myself, *que même*. I'm so old, me. Poor old me. But I know it's right. Somebody else gonna take care of him *peut-être*.

I miss my Kitty now.

• • •

I'm lonesome like hell.

• • •

Allo?

Okay. Okay.

Florence and that lady from that nursing home are coming now. You know I don't wanna go.

I have all my things in just three box. All my life in these three box.

I don't wanna go there. Nobody come outta that nursing home alive.

I'm scare, me. I'm gone be so lonesome.

Please don't forget me.

They can say what they want about me, but one thing is true. I stayed on my house long as I can, *cher*.

42 | *Nous Sommes Ensemble*

"Let's see: Hmm. Madame Ortense? Oh, yeah, *cher*. Room 11. Go through those doors right there, *cher* and all the way down that long hall," the lady at the desk said. "Then you need to make a left at that other hall that you'll run into all the way down there, and then it's the third door. Okay?"

"Yes, ma'am," I told her. "Thank you."

"Lemme know if you can't find it, *cher*."

"Okay. Thank you."

David looked lost, his sweet boyish face scrunched in confusion. "You understood, huh?" he whispered.

"Oh, sure. It's English."

"Maybe a *forrrm* of English," he asserted. "But not one I've ever heard."

David, a Glaswegian I met in New York three winters before, had an accent so strong I had to ask him to repeat himself throughout our first year together.

"You can talk," I said. "Listen to yourself—now *that's* not a form of English I've heard much ever, either. At least not before that wink of yours lured me over to you in that dark corner at The Monster."

"Right."

There was a tease of cool in the November air that would come and go from then through at least April, before the Louisiana summertime furnace reignited. But despite this bit of cool, the air in the nursing home was flat, and still overly warm, its smell a blend of subtle decay, an occasional note of sour sick, of mildew, that faintly sweet musk of perspiration unique to the elderly, and of chemicals intended to make sterile what was no longer fresh. An open window, or better yet, a whoosh of this November air sucked through the building by an attic fan like the one at Mémère's little house on East Jackson Street, would do the place a world of good.

We walked through the long corridor, then to the left as instructed, then over to the third door. My knock went unanswered, but I had heard she was no longer able to speak. I had come to say goodbye, although not actually "Goodbye" to her face, but goodbye for me. I knew it would be the last time I would get to see her alive, and that I probably would not be able to fly back for her funeral, which everyone said was imminent.

The door was open. After a quick peek to assure we had the right room, we walked in. She was awake. She had a feeding tube in her wrist; her shrunken body hardly made a lump under the covers. There wouldn't be many more days for her. But her bright eyes were very much alive. In the very first instant, those eyes said she's happy to see me, but then they puzzled into a squint as she saw this strange man I'd brought with me.

"This is David," I said to her. "He came with me. We are together." Her look didn't change. There was still puzzlement in those bright eyes.

"*Nous sommes ensemble*," I said, clasping my hands and nodding my head to underscore this fact. I needed her to understand. I needed her to know that I had someone in my life. Someone I loved. Someone I could be with so I was not alone. And not *lonesome*, the word that still haunted me from the last time I saw her in her house. Before the nursing home.

"I'm lonesome like hell, me," she had said to me then, not long before she would leave for this nursing home and wait here, for the most part alone, to die.

"That Lonesome? *Il est un monstre.*"

• • •

Since that rainy Saturday more than thirty years before when she buried her husband, my *pépère*, DeJean Thompson, I've known that being alone was Mémère's greatest fear in life.

Until his death, I only knew "Mémère *and* Pépère" collectively. I pictured them only *together*, because until then, I had no examples of them ever apart. In my mind they were still the couple standing close in their 1920 wedding portrait: he was nineteen, she was sixteen; he wore a borrowed, dark tweed suit and his own brown fedora, she wore clothes she designed and sewed; a dark green velvet dress with a tassel at the neck, and matching hat, also featuring a tassel, dangling below the wide brim that had been adorned with strips of silver silk ribbon.

Then they were older, yes, but always, *always* together in my mind; at their home on East Jackson Street, driving around Ville Platte in their big Bel Air, dressed in summer clothes barbequing at Chicot State Park, at family weddings, christenings, and funerals. I had a faint memory from very early in my childhood of walking in on them—sitting *together*—in the bathtub at the beach house we all shared in Biloxi one summer.

After Pépère's funeral we sat in the living room with Mémère for a couple of hours until she said, "I'm so tired, *cher*. I'm gonna have to go lie down." Uncle Florence and Tante Versie, whose back yard connected to hers, said they'd walk home, take a break, and then return to stay with her for the night.

In this slow-moving, but vivid memory, Daddy inched the Dodge away from the little house our grandparents had lived in since their wedding day. Momma's eyes were red from crying, the skin on her cheeks raw. Cassie, with Dicky in her lap, sat between Momma and Daddy; Andy, Gilda, Glenda, and me in the back seat. The silence was broken by a little cough from Andy, like in a quiet Mass.

We were waving goodbye. Mémère was standing at the screen door on the front porch, alone for the first time in forty-five years. Her face in that moment remains the saddest I've seen on any human.

• • •

"*Nous sommes ensemble*," I repeated. At this, the squint in her eyes finally softened. I decided that this acknowledgment was indeed her approval, of her being happy for me. Though her body was definitely soon leaving this earth, I sensed that her mind was still very much right there in the room with David and me.

I imagined she fully absorbed that I was now an adult, moving securely along with a grown-up life of my own, despite the obstacles I'd faced; obstacles she, more than anyone else in my world, assured were surmountable. That I was no longer that fey little waif with the big head, who once dusted his face, his arms, and his legs with her pink old-lady face powder, and then danced, unselfconsciously, around her kitchen to Nathan Abshire's crackly "Choupique Two Step" spinning on her phonograph at seventy-eight revolutions per minute. I was no longer that same flush-faced child lulled to sleep on a mat on the floor in front of her aqua "swamp cooler," a boxy portable appliance that extracted humidity to help erase a few degrees from the soupy August air.

And I certainly was not that vulnerable little five-year-old who became the unwitting focus of a nervous breakdown that rendered her bedridden for a month.

Abutting a patchwork town park that features a baseball diamond with a viewing stand, and a few brick barbeque pits and picnic tables, is Ville Platte's municipal pool. It is the end of June, and Mémère has taken me in her black, round-fendered 1952 Bel Air to cool off with the other thirty-five kids in the pool that day. On the drive over, even with the windows down to provide some relief from the summer heat, my legs stick to the stiff vinyl seats of the big car. I am not yet school-aged and stand just about the height of a yardstick. I will splash for a while in the two feet of chlorine and urine that make up the shallow end. Mémère sits in a folding lawn chair as close as she can to the edge of the pool without actually being in the water, with both of her unblinking eyes trained on me.

Within about three minutes of entering the pool, the little round boy next to me wearing blue trunks that he's outgrown, so much so that his sides and belly hang over the edges, nudges me in greeting. I don't know him or any of the other children playing there; they are all strangers to me. I am shy and not so keen to play with him or anyone, actually. I just want to stand there in the water and bob up and down until Mémère says it is time to go. Besides, the little round boy doesn't look to be nice like some of the other kids. In fact, he looks mean, but I am closest to him, and there isn't much room in this crowded pool, so I acknowledge him with a forced smile.

Then he grabs me, and I am underwater.

I struggle to get away from the boy. He has put all of his weight into holding me under. I am not big enough to push him off of me. He is now practically sitting on my head. I choke down several gulps of pool water. Water in my nose, burning, burning, burning.

But I emerge, spit and gasp. I see Mémère has jumped up from her lawn chair and knocked it over. She screams something I can't understand. She flails. She stomps.

Once more the boy is on me, doing his best to push me under again, but like a threatened animal, I am now pushing back.

Mémère screams at the boy:

"*Arrête-toi!*"

"*Arrête-toi!*"

"*Arrête-toi!*"

So many people, so much noise. Children splashing, parents talking, the lifeguard at the opposite end of the pool, not looking in our direction and unable to hear her over the din.

"*Aidez-moi!*"

"*Aidez-moi, s'il vous plaît!*"

"Help me, *cher!*"

"Help!" she continues, stomping and pointing to the boy, who still has me in his grip. My head goes under, then emerges for a moment, long enough for me to gasp. I am choking and spitting up water.

Mémère, unable to get anyone to help, or even to notice, has become paralyzed with fear. Her screams stop. The stomping and flailing stop. She simply stands, looking out, her hands at her sides, her face fixed; the blood has gone out of it. I know it must have occurred to her to get into the water and get me out. But for some reason, she can't. She looks frozen in panic.

The boy pushes me under again, and again I push myself up, gasping and spitting.

Lying on a lounge chair several spaces away from Mémère, a young woman who has been preoccupied with a paperback raises her head long enough to notice her son, the little round boy, doing his best to get me back underwater.

"Philippe! What are you doing?!" she yells.

"Get off that boy right this minute!"

He pushes me underwater again and is bearing all of his weight on me to keep me there. In the next few moments, things go blurry for me, then black.

I don't know how much time has passed, but when I regain consciousness, I see I have been removed from the pool and am now lying on a towel on the concrete, exhausted, chest heaving, still panting, nostrils and throat burning, eyes bloodshot, but otherwise not drowned. The lifeguard kneels next to me. Better late than never.

The boy and his mom are gone.

Mémère is now sitting, still silent, in her righted lawn chair; three women stand over her saying things to calm her.

"*C'est* okay, *cher,*" one lady says. "*C'est finis.*"

. . .

I intended to stay with Mémère in the nursing home for a good, long, *last* while. Although she was unable to speak with her voice, my conversation with her bright eyes continued for a few more minutes before I saw that she was getting sleepy. Those eyes drooped and drooped, and then drooped to a close.

I wanted to be there with her when she awoke, but when would that be? I looked over at David, sitting quietly in a chair in the corner. He was being a saint to do this with me. He was unable to meet Momma before she died, and he knew how much Mémère meant to me. And I knew he'd rather be anywhere else in the world right then. I understood that completely.

"I guess we can leave now," I whispered to him. "She's asleep." I looked back down at her lying in that strange nursing home bed, a bed belonging to no one for very long.

I kissed her forehead.

"Goodbye sweet, sweet Mémère. *Nous sommes ensemble.*"

. . .

Ortense Thompson, my Mémère, a remarkable woman who had in many ways become both parents for me because Momma was overburdened and Daddy was troubled and violent. She happily played this role very seriously. She rocked me to sleep; helped me grow up; helped me endure; then helped me overcome.

43 | Zanny: Broken

The day they came and got me to take me away from my motel, well, that was something else. I realized pretty quick that they weren't gonna back down. This time, they were the boss. I had to give up and do what they said I had to do.

Nobody needed no whip.

Boy, that sure was a day I'll take to my grave.

And they barged in and hauled me away without letting me have my dinner. I had gone all the way to town and back to get me some chicken, and then, when I got home, I got distracted by a customer, so I put the bag in the oven and went to take care of him. Not five minutes later, after my customer is gone, Andy and Glenda come through the front door with some guy from the sheriff's department. I got so turned around I forgot all about my chicken. And I was hungry.

Sure, they had good reason to haul me outta there. To tell you the truth, I think I was losing my mind. *You* try running a place round the clock all by yourself.

The last coupla years after Eliza died, I ran that place by myself. Overall, it was a good thirty-year haul. In that thirty years, me and Eliza fed eight kids, got them all through high school, and got them on their way. It was hard for me to leave all that behind. That motel was my life. I sure didn't set out to run no roadside motel, but in the end, it was my *life*.

By the time that sheriff came to haul me away, everybody had disappeared, one by one, by one. The kids all grown, then Eliza gone and buried. Anybody in my shoes woulda sold it all a long time ago. But I couldn't. I couldn't. I just couldn't. It's not like me to give up.

"Mister Ardoin," the sheriff guy says to me. "You okay?"

"Hell yeah, I'm okay. What's on your mind?"

"Well, Mister Ardoin, your children think you need some help. We need to take you to get you some help."

Andy and Glenda chiming in, saying, "Yeah, Daddy, it's time to get you outta here and get you some help."

And that was pretty much that. I knew they were right.

• • •

So, after Andy and Glenda and that sheriff come and hauled me away from my motel, they had me checked out by a doctor, and then I spent my last days in a room at what I thought at first was a nursing home. It was nicer than that, though. They call that an "assisted living" place. It's for people like me who didn't need to be in bed all day. They allow you some freedom to move around and be a little independent.

At that assisted living place, I had a lot of time to think about everything in my life. That's better I guess, than to be put in a nursing home, where they pretty much let you rot. At least the food there was good. They made gumbo, fricassee, jambalaya, *sauce piquant*, fried chicken, and the best catfish court bouillon I ever tasted outside of my own home. I looked forward to the mealtimes. Breakfast, lunch, and dinner. I even liked the little stroll down the hall to the lunchroom they had at the other end of the building there.

• • •

So one Saturday, Morris was in from New York and came to visit right before lunchtime and asked me if I wanted to go to Popeye's, which I thought was odd. I have all my meals right here, I told him. But he come back with the idea that I might want to get out a little. He said they had found my chicken in the stove a couple days after they hauled me outta my motel. I hadn't really thought about that chicken till he mentioned it. So I said, yes, let's go, even though I woulda preferred to stay right there and have my lunch in the cafeteria.

You know, it's funny how quickly you get used to the things around you in your life. No matter what your circumstances. For me, that food in the lunchroom was better than anything outside, but I couldn't tell him no.

I think he wanted to put it right, the fact that they hauled me outta my home and nobody bothered to ask if I had eaten that day. I was so thrown off by the whole damned thing it didn't faze me. It wasn't the first time in my life that I didn't get to eat.

• • •

So old Morris and me are sitting at that Popeye's, and he asks me point-blank: "Are you happy these days? You been through a lot."

"That's for damned sure," I tell him.

So he says, "You know it's hard for me to not to think about all those times growing up that I had to keep my eye out for you. All of us, every day, had to watch out that we didn't do something to piss you off."

"I know that," I tell him. "I know."

• • •

That damned phone. Let me get that.
Stone Motel.
Babe. It's Morris on the phone. He wants to talk to you.

• • •

Nobody ever wants to talk to me.

• • •

Them last few years, I had been thinking a lot about why I was so hard on my family. A good twenty years before all that, I had a bit of a nervous breakdown before I bought that motel. I was at my Esso station. This old nigger from Coontown came by for a car battery. He said he didn't have the money, but he needed a battery for his car to get to work so he could earn some money. "As soon as I can I'm gonna pay you back, before the month is out," he tells me. He looked okay to me, so I let him have one-a them Interstate batteries and off he went.

I shoulda known better, 'cuz a month came and went and no money. So I find out from Mildred, that maid Eliza had helping out at the house, that the man lives right by her in Coontown. I get in my truck and drive out there to his house and knock on his door.

"Well," I tell him when he come to the door. "What you got to say for yourself? Where's my money for that battery?"

And don't you know that nigga laughed in my face and said, "I ain't got no money, and you ain't gonna get no money off-a me."

That's what I get for trusting a damned negro.

That was it. I got home and I stewed all night. The next day at the Esso station, my mind wouldn't let it go. I got so mad I started chewing out a customer right there in front of the gas pumps. I could feel my head burning. I was sweating from head to toe. Next thing I know, I'm so wound up I'm feeling like I'm gonna pass out, and sure enough, my legs give out.

When I wake up on that concrete, that customer's gone and there's a lady wiping my head with a cold rag.

"Mister Ardoin? Mister Ardoin?! You okay?"

"I don't know," I remember telling her. I didn't even know who she was. Turns out she was a regular customer. Next thing, I'm in an ambulance headed for the hospital. Eliza gets to the hospital out there, and Doctor DeRouen says we ought-a go right away to the veterans hospital, so they put us in a car to Alexandria.

I was there in that VA hospital for three days. Them doctors sat with me and asked me all kinds of questions.

I had been having some nightmares about the war. Two, three times a week. I couldn't get some of the things I saw over there outta my head. Hell, there was bodies piled up in trenches. Living people walking around in rags. They were so skinny I couldn't believe they were alive.

• • •

I was getting more and more jittery around people.

People made me anxious.

I couldn't control my temper, and any little thing at that Esso station would set me off.

I didn't trust nobody.

In my mind, they were all stealing from me.

At night I would get home from that station and it was the same at home.

I couldn't stand being around *anybody*.

There was no place where I could just think without somebody around me.

That kind of thing.

• • •

Them doctors gave me some pills to help me control my nerves, help me sleep at night. They told me all kinds of things I could do when I was feeling myself get anxious.

Try to focus on what is important in your life.

Take a big, deep breath any time somebody upsets you.

Walk away from any situation where you feel yourself getting heated up.

When you have thoughts about that war, try to shake them off.

Pick something good to think about instead.

Camping, making a big bar-b-que, whatnot.

• • •

Of course I wasn't always like that. Before that war, I was working hard on old Ortego's farm, but I didn't have no nightmares. I wasn't anxious all the time.

That all started to happen not long after I come back from that war.

When I got back from Europe, I signed up with the merchant marines and spent a few months up there in New Jersey training and working as a mechanical engineer. That's where I first became involved with that Standard Oil Company. Up there in New Jersey. I decided I was gonna settle down and get myself my own Esso station. Best place to start was small, so I headed home to Louisiana and went right to work at a little station in Ville Platte to learn the ropes.

• • •

So in no time, Eliza and I got married, and after a coupla years in Ville Platte we moved to Eunice, and with some savings I had from the merchant marines and that GI Bill, I got that Esso station right there on Laurel Avenue. And just when you'd think that my life was going to finally smooth out and calm down, I'll be damned if *that's* when my troubles started, really. When I no longer had the distractions of getting settled. Once I was finally feeling some security, when most people would have begun to live their lives, was when things started going off with me. That's when the nightmares started coming. I can't explain it, but that's what happened.

All in all, after I saw them doctors out there at that VA in Alexandria, and began to focus on the present, and not the past, I gradually came out of it. Mostly. Not totally. I sure don't know what I'da done, what my life woulda been like, if I hadn't collapsed at my Esso. But that's all water under the bridge now, as they say.

44 | Popeye's in the Oven

Three decades had passed since Daddy and Momma drove us all, in a newly acquired baby-yellow Cadillac, to meet the C. H. Melancons at the Stone Motel. Over that time our family expanded by two, Scotty and Alisa, both of whom grew up there, and like the rest of us, left to start lives in places of their own. Momma, having for years dreaded seeing the house empty of her children, sank into a deep and prolonged sadness as Alisa, the last to be leaving, planned for college.

Momma's depression choked her spirit for at least two full years and rendered her pretty much catatonic. On most days she managed to summon up some moments, maybe even a few hours, of lucidity. It was in those fleeting moments of mental clarity that she clung to the surest way to break through her sadness by visiting Mémère in Ville Platte. A short drive there, an hour-or-so visit, and a short drive back. As long as she could drive, she was convinced those brief escapes to see her momma were her best therapy, and that they kept her from sinking further into complete helplessness.

Daddy, unable to fully grasp what was troubling her, never quite accepted that what scared Momma most was being left alone with *him*. It was in that deep state of depression that had gripped her for so long, that Momma was driving in Daddy's pickup on an errand to renew her driver's license on what would be her last day on earth.

• • •

Our family's time at the Stone Motel, which all those years ago was impossible to imagine properly functioning without a large family like ours keeping all the moving parts moving, did finally come to an end after nearly a decade of Daddy's own slow decline, brought on by Momma's sudden, incomprehensible death. All of us were gone: off to college, to marriage, to families of our own.

Everyone but Daddy. He struggled a few years after Momma died, having hired a string of housekeepers to keep the place running. But no one stayed more than a few months. He often found himself cleaning rooms and doing laundry, because he could not imagine leaving the place. But there was no one watching over him to make sure the work was done right, no one saying, "Towels. Soap. Sheet. Toilet paper," to make sure he'd not forgotten anything he might need for a room.

He'd forget to put clean towels in the bathrooms or, worse, leave them completely uncleaned. He missed ashtrays filled with cigarette butts and had on at least one occasion forgotten to replace a soiled bedspread he had removed, leaving the bed covered with only sheets, until the customer who rented that room let him know.

In the yard, the thick summer grass flourished for a couple of weeks before he thought to ask Andy or Glenda to come help with the mowing. In the laundry room, the fifty-pound sack of industrial washing powder was depleted completely before he realized he had to order more—something Gilda or Momma used to take care of. He had to make a special trip into town to buy a big box of Tide to tide him over until the commercial detergent arrived.

In the big empty house, he had focused only on the rooms he needed: the front office, the kitchen, his bedroom, and the big bathroom. All the other rooms—the living room, the back office, the other bedrooms and bathrooms, the TV room—remained fixed in place. Dust and stillness thickened the air in those rooms. The dining room, where we kids played our games all those summers ago, was largely unused as well, serving merely as a passageway between the front office and the kitchen.

Left alone, all the hours in the day and night become longer for him. He had increased the frequency of his drinking. The beer or occasional highball he had enjoyed throughout his life had become a nightly comfort. His age, the weight of sadness that smothered him daily, and the toll of his increased consumption of alcohol quickly revealed his stark vulnerabilities.

"We have to do something," Glenda finally insisted to Gilda and Andy, who, as she had, had each witnessed different parts of Daddy's decline. "It's time."

···

Around eleven in the morning of what would be his last day at the motel, Daddy latched the two front office doors, exited through the kitchen in the back of the house, drove the three miles to Eunice, then another mile or so down Laurel Avenue to the Popeye's Fried Chicken at the far end of town. It took forty-five minutes to make a round trip to pick up a three-piece meal with a biscuit, park the truck, the red Chevy that had replaced the black one in which Momma died, and that had itself replaced the 1959 Apache five years before it.

By the time he went around the house and through that back door again, any number of customers might have driven up to rent a room, only to find the motel office abandoned. Apparently, this kind of thing had become common and, had anyone of us been paying attention, presented a big red flag. Something was definitely not right. If you're in the motel business, you never, ever close.

Indeed, a regular customer was buzzing the door as he drove up. "Hang on. I'll be right there shortly," he said to the man as he walked past. When he got around to the kitchen, he hurriedly put the bag of chicken in the oven and tended to his customer.

"Sorry about that," he said to the man. "I'm by myself here these days. I had an *envie* for some Popeye's fried chicken, and dammit if you can't get that kinda thing off your mind until you just get up and go get it."

The man laughed.

"I don't eat much of that fast food crap, to tell the truth. But that Popeye's knows how to make some good chicken," Daddy said.

"Yeah, you are so right," the man said.

Just as the man was walking back to his car, a St. Landry Parish sheriff's car pulled in, followed by Glenda's green sedan and Andy's silver pickup.

"Hello, Mr. Ardoin," the sheriff said, getting out of his car to shake Daddy's hand. "How you doing today, Mr. Ardoin?"

"I'm just fine, thank you," Daddy said. "What brings you here?"

"We need to make sure you are being taken care of," the man said, "so we're going to need for you to come with us."

Glenda and Andy had parked and were standing behind the sheriff. "Your children want what's best for you," the sheriff continued.

"Glenda? Andy? What's goin' on here?" Daddy asked, obviously startled. "I'm okay. I'm all right. I don't need to go nowhere," he protested.

"It won't take too long," the sheriff continued. "We just need to take you to somewhere where you can get some help."

"You need help, Daddy," Glenda interjected. "You can't run this place all by yourself. It's too dangerous, and you're getting too old."

"Andy?" Daddy said, plaintively. "You think this is what we need to do, too?"

"I think so," Andy said quietly, his head bowed, doing his best not to betray deep discomfort and overwhelming sadness.

Within a few minutes, Daddy was sitting with Andy in his truck, and they followed the sheriff as he drove off the property. Glenda stayed behind to lock up the place and put a sign on the front door to the office that said "CLOSED" in all capital letters she had drawn with a Marks-A-Lot.

The next day, after Daddy had been taken to a hospital in Lafayette for evaluation and observation, before he was to be placed in an assisted-living facility, Glenda went back to the motel to make sure she hadn't forgotten to take care of anything, and to have a final look around the property. She found everything eerily ordinary, but there were no cars in front of the motel rooms. She walked through the back yard, had a look inside the laundry, and checked to make sure Apartment 21 was locked. The tractor shed door was open, so she closed that.

She walked back to the house, unlocked the back door, and walked quickly through the kitchen and dining room, to the front office. There stood Daddy's still rocker; it had left grooves in the carpet where it had rocked back and forth since 1967. Next to it was the brown vinyl sofa that had traveled from the house in town to this spot where it had, like the rocker, stood undisturbed for thirty years. The registration desk with its shiny hotel-desk bell, the Seth Thomas clock on the wall behind it; to the right of that, the board of motel room keys stamped in gold-colored letters that read, "Drop in any Mailbox," and the big picture windows letting in the brilliant yellow sunlight from a beautiful, warm May day.

In the rest of the house, as in the office, it seemed as if everything was just as it had been forever. An overwhelming sense of sadness. Memories flooded through her. She was crying, and she felt an almost panicked need to leave. She found herself disoriented, standing in the doorway between the living room and dining room, thought she might have to sit down. She shook her head quickly and started toward the back door again, when she noticed a smell, not the stale musty smells of old carpet, wood panels, dead air that she'd noticed upon entering, but the faint scent of something definitely in early decay. A mouse? A dead cat?

She sniffed her way through the dining room, with its wagon-wheel chandelier hanging over the brown dining table where all those summers ago she, Gilda, Dicky, and I had spent our days playing canasta or *bataille* or solitaire or *bourré* or Monopoly or a number of other board games. She followed the smell to the yellow-brown latticework vinyl-wallpapered kitchen. The green-laminated breakfast nook was still jammed with condiments. The smell was stronger then, and obviously coming from the stove. She opened the oven. In it was the cheerfully designed red and white paper bag that held Daddy's three-piece chicken dinner with a biscuit.

THE END

EPILOGUE

Momma wasn't supposed to die first. Of the three adults who most shaped my life, I had imagined Mémère would be first to go, and then Daddy; both before Momma. In fact, that night at the Purple Peacock, she and I had her future all planned out: As she entered her mid-sixties, she would have a life-course correction: after her nest was finally empty, she would leave Daddy in time to reclaim some life for herself. We kids would rally around her, help her set up a new life, help take care of *her* needs for a change. She could live with me as long as she wanted, or for just a few years, then with Cassie, or one of the twins, or with Alisa and her new family when she had one. Or we would set her up in her own house where she could just *be*.

Away from the cloak of Daddy's negative energy and that all-absorbing, round-the-clock motel, she would smile again. She would be eager to embrace each new day, instead of dreading waking up. Her sad days behind her, she would enjoy the world's gifts. She'd travel to the places depicted in her beauty shop magazines and take her momma with her, so they could see it all together. She would take time to appreciate nature, fill her heart and feed her soul with the giggles of grandchildren and great-grandchildren, nurture old friendships, go out to eat whatever she wanted as frequently as she wanted, have a glass or two, or a whole bottle, of wine. And a big piece of cake. All without guilt. And have someone else do all the dishes. She more than deserved this fate.

When she instead died at a cruelly young sixty-three, alone and violently in that crash not a quarter-mile from home, of course she left behind shock and profound, enduring sadness in us all. But there was also an overwhelming sense in me that she had just been *cheated* out of what was duly hers: a good, full, happy, and *long* life.

· · ·

Mémère, who feared being alone more than anything else, was supposed to have had Momma by her side in that nursing home on *her* last days on earth. Instead, she died in a bed that was not her own, surrounded by naked walls in a soulless room. The last people to see her alive were not family, but strangers doing their jobs. As sad as that is, I suppose it's not as bad as the way many other people die every day: from painful, protracted illnesses; gory gunshot wounds; abject starvation; and worse. Momma's horrible, preventable death in a car crash six years before Mémère's was a perfect example of how life just does to us whatever the hell it wants.

I was at peace with Mémère's death as it approached, because I was able to say goodbye to her just a few weeks before she passed. I would like to have been in the room when it happened. I understand that in those final days she wouldn't have known I was there, but my being there would have been for my benefit, not hers. For me, her passing at ninety-two was as natural as a backyard magnolia leaf cooling from brilliant green, to warm ochre, to sallow brown before a November breeze sends it falling to the ground.

I know from the experiences I was lucky enough to have had with her, especially when it was so critical to have someone who could see the me no one else could see, that I am who I am because she was who she was: a selfless guardian, generous and genuine with her unconditional love, and wise beyond ordinary human capacity. And I am grateful for that more than anything else.

· · ·

It was with more than just a sense of sonly duty that I attended Daddy's funeral four years after we buried Mémère and ten years after Momma died in that crash.

Daddy was hard to mourn. Back when he was regularly attacking me I didn't yet fully appreciate the trauma he had suffered in his own life. I would learn about that later, in conversations with Andy and the twins, and by connecting some of the pieces of information he himself had told me over the years: the early death of his mother, and then his father, and the dispersal of his big family in an effort to survive the leanest years of the Great Depression; the almost daily bloodshed he witnessed in World War II; and the paranoia and nightmares he endured for years after returning home.

Two months before his death, I visited him in the assisted living facility that would be his last home.

I knocked on his door. He greeted me clinically:

"Hello," he said as if I were a delivery boy. He didn't even say my name. I didn't know if this was because he was medicated or if this was the only way he knew how to greet me after all we'd been through.

"Hi, Daddy. Are you okay for a visit?" I asked.

"I guess so," he replied.

Standing there in his doorway, dressed in the same type of gray coveralls he had worn pretty much every day for three decades, he was now just a harmless, elderly man to me. His frame had shrunken a bit, his hair was completely white, his voice still deep, but softer. I was crushed with pity for him, a pity I had begun feeling years before when I called home and overheard him saying to Momma, "Nobody ever wants to talk to me," as he handed her the phone.

A quick peek into his room revealed not much to see of his final world. Pale terra-cotta colored walls. I suspected he did not like being surrounded by such a color all day and would have chosen something else had he been given a choice. There was a bed, a small desk with a chair, a wall-mounted TV, and a round side table with another chair. Besides the bed, he had only two places to sit, as if there would never be a need for more than two visitors.

He'd already had his lunch, and it was too early for dinner, so we sat on the bed and chatted briefly, with me doing most of the talking. Health, weather, the quality of the food in the cafeteria, how I liked my job. His yawns after about half an hour revealed his sleepiness and that he'd probably prefer to be having a nap, although he didn't say that. His afternoon nap was often the best part of his day all those years at the motel, especially on weekends, when he routinely stayed up till two or three in the morning.

I wanted to tell him about the difficulty I have trusting people, and about never being able to feel truly safe in any situation. I wanted him to know about the recurring nightmare I had for years involving electrical wires stinging me, and a big black work shoe crushing into my ankle. And I really wanted to finally let him know about the cracked rib he gave me with one of those same work shoes just months before I was to graduate from LSU, because I had the temerity to disagree with him on how best to help Dicky choose a profession. That it was hard to keep all these things to myself because for years I couldn't explain any of it, to anyone.

I had gone there planning to get so much off my chest. But seeing him then, in that strange place, living alone, and quickly approaching the end of his life, I realized that saying anything about any of that was perfectly pointless. After all, I had for years convinced myself that getting through tough situations in life merely took creative transference. A person's gotta just keep going, or at least that's what Mémère's message to me was. So I was gonna be just fine without any real closure with my father.

"I'm going to come again soon, and we'll go for a drive if you want," I offered.

"That's okay. I'm fine right here. I don't like being in cars so much any more."

I got up to leave. He stood as well. I went in for a big goodbye hug—he was never a hugger—fully expecting to get in return a perfunctory, awkward embrace as clinical as his greeting. Instead he hugged me with what seemed to be all his might, and then some, and held on longer than I've been hugged by anyone, ever.

Driving away from the facility, my heart was racing; my mind was suffocating in confusion. I opened the windows of my rental car to try to shake off the sensation that I was drowning. The fresh air cleared my head somewhat, but I couldn't stop the tears that were filling my eyes. They came freely. I pulled over into a shopping center parking lot and let them fall for a good ten minutes before they subsided. Deep breaths. Then back on the road. My gut said this was the last time I would see him alive.

On the morning at the funeral parlor several weeks later, I approached his casket as if the act of inspecting his corpse were an everyday occurrence. I did not cry that day.

And the Canasta Team Turns Out Okay. *Ish.*

During and after college Glenda had a short list of boyfriends and finally married a man very much like her daddy: he was headstrong and ambitious, and had a temper. They built a house and had two daughters to help occupy it. A few years down the road, they divorced when their girls were still preteens. She kept the house in the settlement and worked hard to stay distracted from the emotional toll of the divorce by participating in area tennis and golf tournaments. Later, she remarried, and then happily assumed the role of the doting grandmother to the children of her daughters.

Four years out of high school Gilda was putting her respiratory therapy training to use at the hospital in town. She married a low-key hardworking man with whom she would celebrate many anniversaries. They wouldn't have a child for a number of years, fifteen after Glenda's first child was born, in fact. In the years before the baby came, Gilda's veneer became somewhat hardened. She was more cautious and reserved than her younger self. The appearance of this child in her life helped crack that veneer, and re-exposed a funny, joyful soul who once chased us around the living room with the paper witches she'd made from the Montgomery Ward catalogue; drew immaculate caricatures of people who caught her eternal artist's eye; strummed Joan Baez and Peter Paul and Mary songs about fighting for justice and freedom. This was the Gilda we all grew up with, admired, and envied for her wit, compassion, and boundless talent. It was a welcome reemergence.

Dicky, who clawed his way through school easily flummoxed by all around him, decided that leaving home was his best strategy for success in life. As soon as he could put together the money and courage to do so, he moved to Seattle, where he managed to find work, eke out a living, and attract a boyfriend or two. He became one of America's HIV-AIDS statistics in the plague's first decade. The diagnosis shattered him, but he still managed to forge his way. He would get life-sustaining treatment from Washington State's exemplary health care system. And he is a miracle man: he would live more than thirty difficult, often harrowing years after his initial diagnosis. He would fight successfully through the epidemic's experimental and ravaging early drug cocktails, through medical procedures that replumbed the organs in his disintegrating body, and through the relentless indignities hurled upon him by a paranoid, ill-informed, and self-absorbed society.

As for me, those long-ago days spent playing cards and other games around the dining room table shaped my life far more profoundly than I could have imagined at the time. Face-to-face game-playing with my siblings gave me a sense of security in an environment where that was not always a reliable commodity; taught me the art of patience and strategic thinking; and helped me develop my storytelling skills, which I continue to use in my career.

When I left Cajun Country behind for good to take a job in New Orleans, I was reticent about living there because I had known it only as a tourist, and in that capacity was convinced it was best left to the tourists. But I soon learned that the hand that the famous/infamous city displayed for the busloads of sightseers and frat boys was nothing compared to the world carefully concealed and then shown only for those of us who stayed behind when the buses left.

New Orleans in fact proved to be enchanting and magical, terms rightfully overused to describe it. Its seductions and mysterious wiles are fully, joyfully intoxicating, worthy of the complete and utter abandonment of its citizenry. I spent five intense and unforgettable years there before landing in New York, the only place on earth that has ever matched the rhythm of my soul's metronome. The old lyric "If I can make it there, I'll make it anywhere" reads backward to me: what I quickly came to love about my home of the past quarter-century is that it absorbs and genuinely embraces anyone and everyone, especially if they've already proven themselves *elsewhere* first. I have difficulty imagining living anywhere else.

Happiness

I wonder sometimes if we are all guilty of finding happiness only in hindsight. I believe there is a short list of precise memories spread through the course of every life to which we each can point as unquestionably happy ones. Those are easy to chronicle. They protrude readily, seem more visually stunning, more fragrant, more titillating and thrilling, more delightful and delicious than all those on that other, infinite list of mundane moments that absorb the vast expanses in between. But it is precisely in those ordinary, in-between moments where, if we are really seeing, it is impossible to deny the fullness of true happiness.

• • •

Pépère has driven us all in his big black Bel Air to the fairgrounds out on the highway approaching the city of Ville Platte. Mémère sits in the middle between him and Momma up front. In the back, Andy, Gilda, Glenda, and Cassie, holding me in her lap. It is the first time in anyone's memory that the annual Cotton Festival includes a full circus.

The fairgrounds aren't really fairgrounds at all; they are merely a five-acre plot cut into cotton fields that stretch as far as the eye can see and straddle both sides of the road. The plot provides just enough space for a big tent, a few food wagons, the circus trucks, and an area for visitors to park. The ground surrounding the tent and wagons is covered by hay.

As we stand just outside the big tent in the ticket line, all eyes are now on a tall man in a fancy red, white, and black uniform pointing a white-gloved finger at me. He says something about me not being tall enough to enter, by authority of the big letters I can't yet read painted plainly right there on a sandwich board. Just a few feet inside the entrance, the clowns, the acrobats, the elephants, and the other animals are about to start their show.

"But we came all this way," Momma says plaintively to the uniformed man.

"I'm sorry, Ma'am," he says. "That's the rules."

Pépère, who had said in the car that he was eager to see a real elephant for the first time in his life, crouches down, takes my little shoulders in his hands, and looks right into my eyes. "It's all gonna be okay, *cher*," he says to me. "Y'all go in," he says to everyone else. "We'll be right here when y'all come out. Go on in. We'll be fine."

I am sad for him; he isn't going to get to see a real elephant, and it is my fault.

"Now, don't you worry," he says when they've gone in and he sees that my bottom lip is trembling. "You and me are gonna have us a nice long walk around this big old tent," he continues, taking my soft little hand into his big calloused, blacksmith's hand. That morning before dressing in his clean khaki trousers and a crisply starched, short-sleeved, sky-blue cotton shirt, which he only ever wears for church or family gatherings, he had scrubbed his big hands and made a special effort to scrape the black from under his nails.

"We don't need to go in there to know what's inside, *cher*," he says, smiling.

Indeed, on our walk around the perimeter of the big tent, he tells me all about the animals he imagines are inside: *"les elephants, les lions, les chevaux, et les tigres. Les oiseaux exotiques, et les macaques brigands."*

"Are they okay in there, Pépère? I ask.

"Well, yeah, *cher*," he replies. With a puzzled look on his face, he asks, "What makes you say that?"

"Maybe they don't want to be in that tent. Maybe they want to be outside."

"Well, you know, little Morris, I think you might be right. You have a good heart, *cher*. That's gonna help you all your life. Don't let anybody take that from you. *Comprends*? Understand?"

"Um, okay," I say, even though I have no idea what he means.

Dramatic music issues from a pipe organ, the ringleader barks his rehearsed lines. A pungent bouquet of animal scents and hay thickens the air all around us.

When our slow walk around the tent is done, Pépère leads me over to the edge of the fairgrounds, where the cotton fields create a tidy border boxing us, the circus trucks, the tent, the wagons, and the visitors' cars, all in. He plucks a cotton blossom from the first plant we encounter and puts it into my hand. He tells me how the hard boll of the plant bursts to reveal the fluffy cotton inside; and how the cloth in his blue shirt and khaki pants, and for my shirt and red shorts, was all made from it. He lifts me up so I can see that all around us in all directions are acres and acres of flatland, perfect for growing cotton. And indeed it is just cotton fields and more cotton fields, all separated by the long road leading west to Opelousas, and beyond.

We head back towards the entrance, to one of the food wagons. A display of beautiful little cakes like the ones I've only ever seen in the glass case at the back of Teet's Fruit Stand on Main Street, catches my eye. Pépère pulls his black rubber oval coin purse from a pocket in his khakis, puckers it open, and takes two dimes to buy us each a little gingerbread cake. Mine is decorated with leaves in green icing; his is done in white polka-dots. We eat our cakes sitting on a hay bale behind the wagon.

A few minutes pass and the performance ends. Momma and Mémère, and Andy and the twins stream with all the other people out of the big tent, and we head back to town in the Bel Air.

• • •

In that country circus, surrounded by cotton fields, Pépère and I did not get to see the somersaults performed by the fearless acrobats, or the shenanigans of the wide-eyed clowns. We didn't witness the unflinching lion tamer cracking his whip, or the mischievous monkeys playing on stage. And the closest we got to the elephants was the smell of their dung near the back of the tent. But those sweet moments with my grandfather that day and others like them over the years have been a comforting companion throughout my life. Because of them my heart is full.

• • •

Acknowledgments

Stone Motel is dedicated to Moby, the loving pooch who sat quietly and endured being read to as he occasionally scratched and yawned, nonetheless attentive, waiting for me to take him out for his pee walks. His sweet, departed soul dances with mine, every day.

Merci beaucoup to my siblings for their varied recollections, wildly differing opinions, and/or genuine, big-hearted encouragement: Cassandra Ardoin, Andy Ardoin, Gilda Bellard, Glenda Tucker, Dickson Ardoin, Scott Ardoin, and Alisa Gothreaux.

To those in my big family who have passed on: my parents, Eliza Mae and Zanny Ardoin, my grandparents, Ortense and DeJean Thompson, and my little brother Thomas Ardoin. I hope when we meet again in the wherever, you'll all be happy to see me.

To my husband, Aubyn Gwinn, who provided positive energy throughout the writing process, even though there were many times I am certain he was wishing that I'd just shut the hell up about it.

To my early readers for their insightful feedback: Andrew Amelinckx, Valerie Andrews, Margaret Barry, Annick de Bellefeuille, Jay Blotcher, Cathé Charlier, Esther Cohen, Niva Dorell, Kimberly Elliott, Ginger Gannaway, David Meechie, Karen Miller, Ginger Portnoy, Fabian Thibodeaux, Kara Thurmond, and Nannette Toups.

• • •

To my publishing industry advisor Kathy VerEecke; and my Ville Platte detail-corroborator Philippe Vidrine.

And finally to the editorial, design, and promotion teams at the University Press of Mississippi for adding this book to their renowned collection. I am profoundly grateful for their confidence in my work, and humbled to have my book in such good company.

ABOUT THE AUTHOR

Morris Ardoin lives in Manhattan, and Cornwallville, New York, with his husband, Aubyn, and their dog, Hugo. He has spent his career working with nonprofit organizations focusing on health care, global migration, family poverty, and education. Cooking, writing, reading, painting, and travel keep him amused and excited to be alive.

Printed in the USA
CPSIA information can be obtained
at www.ICGtesting.com
BVHW041136200823
668692BV00004B/11